Chinese Theories of Theater and Performance
from Confucius to the Present

Chinese Theories of Theater and Performance from Confucius to the Present

Edited and translated by Faye Chunfang Fei

Foreword by Richard Schechner

Ann Arbor

THE UNIVERSITY OF MICHIGAN PRESS

Copyright © by the University of Michigan 1999
All rights reserved
Published in the United States of America by
The University of Michigan Press
Manufactured in the United States of America
♾ Printed on acid-free paper

2002   2001   2000   1999   4   3   2   1

A CIP catalog record for this book is available from the British Library.

Library of Congress Cataloging-in-Publication Data

Chinese theories of theater and performance from Confucius to the
   present / edited and translated by Faye Chunfang Fei.
      p.   cm.
   Includes bibliographical references and index.
   ISBN 0-472-10974-X (cloth : alk. paper)
      1. Theater—China—History.   I. Fei, Faye Chunfang, 1957–   .
   PN2871.C535   1999
   792'.0951—dc21   99-17404
                                                                CIP

Contents

Part 3. Qing Dynasty (1644–1911)

Part 4. The Twentieth Century

RICHARD SCHECHNER

Foreword

Faye C. Fei's collection will open new vistas for most persons who do not read Chinese; it may even open a few windows for Chinese readers. In considering the selection Fei has made, three related themes are evident. First, those familiar with Indian, Japanese, or Western performance theory will be surprised that so many of the Chinese selections— especially those prior to the modern period—are very short and, on the surface at least, "untheoretical." Second, the writings collected here reveal an emphasis on reception, and consequently close attention is paid to the social functions of performance. Third, for the last 100 years, the core concern is the relationship between indigenous Chinese theater and ideas coming from the West. These three themes are closely intertwined, but let me take them up in turn.

There is no Chinese writing or set of writings by a single author comparable to Bharatamuni's *Natyasastra,* Aristotle's *Poetics,* or Zeami's *Fushikaden* and other treatises.[1] Thus there is no preeminent Chinese text around which a planetary system of commentaries and reactions revolve. Take this as a difference, not a disadvantage. Rather than explanations of and debates concerning *mimesis* or *rasa* or *hana,* Fei's collection offers readers a panoply of diverse observations and opinions regarding what constitutes performance, what its functions may be, the nature of aesthetic pleasure, and various practices of acting and playwriting. Out of this diversity, certain key debates emerge, but no dominant opinion, no orthodoxy of theory against which all other opinions must strive.

Taking the writings in this book as representative, one can say that Chinese theater theory emerges from the conviction that theater is a regular and necessary part of *social life.* Many of the writings are descriptive, not about theater, dance, and music "in themselves" but, instead, locating performance as part of social life, state and religious ritual, and

---

1. The *Natyasastra* was composed in Sanskrit and dates from between the second century B.C.E. and the second century C.E. Several English translations are extant, most recently the one by Adya Rangacharya (New Delhi: Munshiram Manoharlal, 1996). Zeami's dates are 1363–1443. His major treatises have been translated by J. Thomas Rimer and Yamazaki Masakazu in *On the Art of the No Drama* (Princeton: Princeton University Press, 1984).

popular entertainment. Theater is not seen as a stepchild of religion,[2] as it is in the West; or of divine origin, as the opening chapter of the *Natyasastra* relates. Instead, most of the writers in this book welcome theater as an important participant in and contributor to a well-ordered society. When writers condemn theater, they do so not on the basis of an ontology that sets the arts at a double remove from true reality (as Plato does), but because theater can be immoral and disruptive. In 1904 Chen Duxiu disagreed with a strain in Chinese thought, namely that theater is "vulgar, bawdy, licentious, wasteful, and useless."

The antidote to such goings-on is to make theater useful, as Mao Zedong insisted it ought to be. In his 1942 "Talks at the Yan'an Forum on Literature and Art," Mao ordered theater workers to use theater as a weapon against the Japanese invaders and as a tool to advance the class struggle. The roots of Mao's attitude—that theater is an excellent educator and that rulers ought to use it as such—go deep in Chinese history. From an early date, theater was seen as a way of reaching ordinary people who could not read. And at various times, theater served Confucian or Taoist thought, disseminated imperial edicts regarding proper behavior, helped people understand their place in the social hierarchy, or sewed revolutionary ideas. All along, theater also entertained, brought pleasure, and showed beauty its own proper shape. This leads to the second main point.

Earlier Chinese writing about theater, up until the Yuan Dynasty (1271–1368), is almost entirely concerned with reception. And throughout, reception is a key operator. This sets Chinese performance theory apart from other Asian writings and from Western theories. Both Indian and the Japanese theories are addressed to practitioners and are therefore mostly concerned with ways of performing (acting, music, dance) and, to a lesser degree, ways of playwriting. Western theater theory after Aristotle, and until relatively recently, concentrated on drama. The Chinese writings place the spectator at the center of the performance experience. What does the spectator see and hear? Is the experience pleasurable, and, if so, on what is the pleasure based? What are the functions of theater?

As noted, many of the writings in Fei's book are short and descrip-

---

2. Writings about ritual theater and ritual-folk theater as such, about *nays* and the *dixi*, as they are called, are mostly recent theatrical and anthropological studies. These theaters and the writings about them is not the purview of Fei's collection. It is enough to note here that religious practices as performance, from shamanism to temple rituals, from harvest and New Year's festival performances to exorcistic ceremonies, comprise a very rich part of Chinese performance. What Fei has concentrated on, because this is what the Chinese themselves until recently have written mostly about, are performances that comprise or feed into the dominant genres of sung and spoken theater.

tive rather than analytical. A sizable number are excerpts from longer works that do not concern the theater only. This is because theater was for a long time not considered separate from other aspects of social life. The theory inherent in these earlier writings is implicit rather than explicit. The subjects of these writings range from simple observation and description to answering questions about why and how theater moves people, what are the functions of theater, and what is the beauty of performance. In the earlier periods, written drama does not figure. The early theater is almost entirely music, dance, and physical actions. But from very early times, writers were concerned with how performance affects people. Themes enunciated in the fourth century B.C.E. by Xun Kuang are still central to Chinese performance theory: "Music is joy, which is humanly and emotionally indispensable. . . . Listening to music . . . we aspire to greater things. . . . Music is the unifying center of the world, the key to peace and harmony." Fei is clear that by "music" (*yue*), Xun and others mean a wide variety of aesthetic performances as well as state ceremonies and ritual performance. Nor are "peace and harmony" solely or even primarily personal matters. Xun is talking about how performance contributes to a well-ordered society. The details are different, but the regard for what performance does suits Marxist Mao as well as Confucian Xun.

From the start of the Yuan dynasty (1271) onward, more is written that deals with how theater is made. A balance is struck between reception and production. This is due to the increasing interdependence of literature and theater. Theories are written by playwrights concerning the internal structure of performance and the relationship between plays and performance. Perhaps the single-most important theoretical writing from this period is Tang Xianzu's (1550–1616) "Epigraph for the Theater God Master Qingyuan." Addressing questions about how theater ought to accomplish its goals led to the development of the codified performance styles that continue to be practiced today as various Chinese sung dramas, or "operas," as they are often called in the West. These "*-ju*" forms—*kunju* and *jingju* are but two of the better known among a set of dozens, if not scores or more, of classical and folk sung dramas—demand extremely well-trained performers skilled in singing, dancing, acrobatics, poetic recitation, and emotional acting. The "*-ju*" forms also demand a sophisticated audience, able to read the symbolic languages of the stage. For unlike the representational forms in the West—or even the Elizabethan theater where a great deal of information about time, place, and situation is contained in the dialogue—the

Chinese theaters depend on a fully semiotized stage, where flags represent whole armies, where a circular movement around the stage indicates a long journey, where a single table and chair can be anything from an inn to a royal palace to a courtroom to . . . whatever, where female performers play both woman and man roles, and where male performers play both man and woman roles. Gender, like everything else on "-*ju*" stages, is a formalization based on a combination of traditional gestures and the observation of everyday life. Troupes of performers may be all-male, all-female, or mixed; but in every case the roles include men, women, children, aristocrats, commoners, clowns, gods, ladies, scoundrels, scholars, warriors, and many more.

But this resilience and sophistication of theater semiosis in Chinese "-*ju*" forms precipitates the great crisis in modern Chinese performance, a crisis not yet resolved. This is the third theme in Fei's collection that I referred to at the outset. This theme may be summarized as a question: What is the relationship between older, traditional forms that have encoded in them not only a definite aesthetic, but an equally determined socio-political-ethical outlook and the "new China"? This has troubled reformers in China since the turn of the twentieth century and cannot be treated in isolation. It must be considered in the context of how the Chinese deal with influences coming to China from the outside.

An Orientalist cliché says that this populous, vast, ethnically and geographically diverse country is isolationist. From the outside, China has appeared both self-sufficient and unified. But in fact Chinese unity has always been a struggle, and Chinese culture has long been affected by new ideas coming from outside of China. These "foreign" ideas—brought by travelers, missionaries, conquerors, and more recently by newspapers, radio, television, and computers—have often totally shaken up Chinese culture and society, for example, Buddhism from India, the Manchus from the interior of Asia, and Marxism from the West. But the cliché also has some foundation in practice. What the Chinese tend to do is take, or accept, and then assimilate. For example, Buddhism and Marxism as *Chinese systems* are different in China than they are elsewhere. The process of assimilation is not smooth or peaceful but full of intellectual disagreements and social turbulence.

At present, in theater and performance (as well as other modes of thought not the purview of this foreword or this book), China is in the midst of taking and assimilating ideas and practices introduced from the turn of the twentieth century onward. The question confronting Chinese performance theorists, writers, directors, and performers is what is the "real" Chinese theater? For 100 years now, *huaju,* "spoken theater," has taken its place next to, and to some degree upstaged, the various traditional "*-ju*" forms of sung theater, not to mention the extreme pressure put on live performance by film and television. *Huaju* may have begun as an imitation of the West, but it has long since become its own Chinese kind of theater. And throughout the twentieth century, attempts have been made to integrate the traditional "*-ju*" forms and the new *huaju.* Jiang Qing's "model operas" during the Cultural Revolution (1966–76) were a radical attempt to "update" traditional forms. As Huang Zuolin writes in this collection, many Chinese sought to reconcile the theater teachings of Mei Lanfang, Konstantin Stanislavsky, and Bertolt Brecht.

The book in your hands ranges across an enormous span of time and cultural practices. It is an "unfinished book" in the best sense. Not only is it a selection from an extremely large field, but new materials are being conceived and written. Down the line, new editions of this book will be necessary. The Chinese presence on the world stage is strong and continuing to increase. A book like Fei's will help people who do not read Chinese to understand a key aspect of Chinese culture. And for those who are primarily interested in theater/performance, this book will give Chinese theater theory its proper place at the table.

Preface

In 1988 Richard Schechner started teaching a course on Asian Performance Theories at New York University. William Sun and I gave him a rough translation of three pieces of Chinese theoretical writings on theater, which have remained on his text list ever since as the only discourse representing classical Chinese conceptions of the theater. Having learned of these translated writings, Daniel Gerould of the City University of New York asked to include one of them in a book he was editing, *Theater Theory, Theory Theater*. Encouraging as all this may be, the fact remains that very little is known in the West about how the Chinese theater, both traditional and modern, is conceptualized by artists, scholars, philosophers, and political leaders in China. The enigma around the Chinese theater exists partly because no systematic English translation of Chinese theories on theater and performance exists.

It was while I was writing my doctoral dissertation, "Huang Zuolin: China's Man of the Theater," that I realized further how important it is to have Chinese theatrical theories known in the West today. Huang, a leading modern Chinese theater director, was a strong advocate of integrating traditional Chinese aesthetics with modern dramaturgy, but a basic concept he took from ancient Chinese aesthetics, *xieyi,* was so difficult to understand without certain theoretical contexts that he puzzled many Western scholars and artists, including Arthur Miller. Only after a comprehensive study of Chinese theories of the theater was I able to clarify this concept in my own dissertation. While doing research and teaching over the years, I gradually and consciously compiled a list of Chinese theories for an anthology that I would edit and translate.

The need for such an anthology of annotated translations is even more urgent if one takes a look at the other two major Asian theatrical cultures of India and Japan. The English translations of the Indian classic *Natyasastra* and Zeami's treatises such as *Teachings on Style and the Flower* (both have been compared to Aristotle's *Poetics*) shed invaluable lights on Indian and Japanese theaters. The reason for the lack of any equivalent translation of Chinese theories so far is mainly that there is not a single treatise or an individual's body of theoretical work that fits the Aristotelian model or those of its Asian counterparts. In Chinese history, however, there are numerous shorter, but no less important, theoretical writings on theater and other related performing arts that are keys to understanding not only Chinese theater but also theater and culture in general.

To provide a historical overview, the writings in this anthology of annotated translations are arranged in chronological order, falling into four major periods: antiquity to the Song Dynasty (Fourth century B.C.E.–1279 C.E.; the Yuan Dynasty (1271–1368) and Ming Dynasty (1368–1644); the Qing Dynasty (1644–1911); and the rest of the twentieth century. All the translations, except one, are new, and the majority of them are available in English for the first time. The writings that I have chosen to include in the book are by noted Chinese thinkers, scholars, writers, directors, and performers. These writings deal with such issues as origins, aesthetic principles, and functions of theater. Some are virtually manuals on playwriting and performance techniques. Some describe the practices, conditions, and government policies concerning theatrical performance. Some writings will forcefully dispute the myth that Chinese theater is only valuable in performance but lacking in literature. The fact is that there is an equal, if not more prominent, emphasis on theme and content. What emerges from the writings is a highly evolved and sophisticated aesthetics.

The task here is more difficult than translating a single book or person's writings. It may, however, also be more significant in terms of its contribution to the humanities because it will present a broader picture of a country's complex and little-known theatrical culture. For me, personally, this project has proven both challenging and tremendously rewarding. I often feel very frustrated by what I have had to leave out, after having gone through piles of material, more than half of which are in the form of archaic classical Chinese. Mostly, it is because the material is too specialized or simply untranslatable. I regret that writings by such fine minds as Wu Mei, Yao Hua, Liu Shipei, just to name a few, cannot be included in this book.

A note on a technical matter: throughout this book I have consistently used the *pinyin* system of romanization, which the Chinese introduced in the 1950s and which most books and journals in the West have adopted since the 1980s.

I would like to express my gratitude to the National Endowment for the Humanities, the Minnesota Humanities Commission, and the Pacific Cultural Foundation for their grants in support of this project.

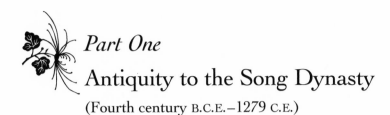

Part One
Antiquity to the Song Dynasty
(Fourth century B.C.E.–1279 C.E.)

From the Book of History

Shu (*Book of History*), also called *Shang Shu* or *Shujing,* one of the Chinese Five Classics, is China's earliest collection of historical documents of the court. In part it records the words and deeds of the rulers of the Shang Dynasty (1760– 1066 B.C.E.) and the Zhou Dynasty (1066–256 B.C.E.). It contains, however, mainly the historical records from the time of the legendary King Yu Shun (2300–2205 B.C.E.) to the Xia Dynasty (2200–1760 B.C.E.) as compiled by Confucian scholars of the East Zhou Dynasty (770–256 B.C.E., Confucius 551– 479 B.C.E.) and Warring States period (475–221 B.C.E.). Strictly speaking, *Shu* is more a book of ethics than a work of history. Its account of actual historical events is usually set up for relevant moral discussion. The following selections from *Shu* represent the earliest recorded Chinese writings about the arts. "Yao Ceremony" indicates the intimate relationship between poetry, music, and dance as these forms first emerged and considers them as integral parts of a whole. It also presents an aesthetic of harmony. "Benefit Ritual" describes a performance in the sixteenth century B.C.E. Part of "Yi's Lecture" records the earliest opposition against the arts, or their excesses.

Book of Yu: Yao Ceremony

King Yu Shun said to Kui: "I want you to be in charge of music (*yue*).[1] Teach our children and help them to grow. Teach them to be upright and gentle, generous and respectful, resolute but not abusive, succinct but not arrogant. Poetry expresses one's hope and desire. Lyrical singing conveys the poetic emotions through musical rhythm. Sound, pitch, and rhythm adjust to one another accordingly. The musical instruments

Excerpts translated from *Shang shu xuanlu,* in *Zhongguo lidai julun xuanzhu,* ed. Chen Duo and Ye Changhai (Changsha: Hunan wenyi chubanshe, 1987), 1–2.
1. The word *yue* means music and much more in ancient Chinese. According to Guo Moruo (1892–1978), a renowned Chinese poet, dramatist, historian, archaeologist, politician, and classical scholar, *yue* not only refers to the trinity of music, poetry, and dance but also includes painting, engraving, and architecture and sometimes even encompasses rituals, hunting expeditions, feasts, and so on. Some ancients believed that *yue* in itself stood for something moral and proper. Also the character for *yue* is the same character as for *le* (happy) in Chinese. Because of the complicated nature of the word, one may find that *yue* changes its precise meaning quite often. When *yue* means more than music, it is capitalized in translation.

made of eight different materials should strive for harmony among themselves, not discord.[2] Then gods and men will live in peaceful harmony."

Kui exclaimed: "let's play the instruments, and get the dance of a hundred animals started!"

Book of Yu: Benefit Ritual

[Music director] Kui proclaimed: Let's play the percussion and string instruments to accompany lyrical singing." Ancestral spirits had all arrived, so did the guest of honor, Prince Yu Bin, who, along with the other members of royalty, showed polite modesty to one another. The ritual performance began with the beating of the *zhu* and concluded with the sounding of the *yu;* in between the *sheng* and the *yong* were played alternately.[3] The musicians played the music piece *xiaoshao* nine times to the energetic and graceful dances modeled after the movements of birds and beasts.

Kui said: "Let's sound the instruments and get the dance of a hundred animals started." Without exception everyone present immersed in joy and harmony.

Book of Shang: Yi's Lecture

In the twelfth month of the first year of King Taijia,[4] Chief Minister Yi Yin administered a memorial service in the temple for the former king. The young King Taijia came to pay respect to his own grandfather. And the princes from the provinces were also present. Officials of all ranks came to hear the chief minister. Yi Yin cited the former king's achievements and virtues as shining examples for everyone. . . . He said: "The establishment of the new special penal codes is meant for people in official positions. These codes are intended to warn those who dare to indulge in shamanism, in other words, to be obsessed with dancing and singing in the palaces and in private quarters. They are to warn those who dare to indulge in material gains and sexual favors, and to warn those who dare to indulge in excessive game playing and animal hunting.

---

2. The eight materials include metal, rock, silk, bamboo, reed, clay, hide, and wood.
3. *Zhu* and the rest are names of ancient musical instruments.
4. King Taijia was the first grandson of King Shang Tang, the founder of the Shang Dynasty (1760–1066 B.C.E.).

They are also to warn those who dare to insult the sacred teachings, abuse the honest, distance the virtuous, and keep company with the ignorant. If an officer is afflicted by one of these ten evils, his family will be ruined; if a ruler is afflicted by one of these ten evils, the country is doomed. Those who do not mend their ways shall have their foreheads tattooed in black ink. All this is to be thoroughly drilled into the minds of those beginning to learn the ways of the world."

From the *Book of Rites*

The *Book of Rites* (*Liji*), another of the Chinese Five Classics, compiled again by Confucian scholars, came into existence around the same time as *Shu*. It is a collection of miscellaneous essays dealing with issues of ceremony and general propriety. Its chapter on *yue* is the foundational work of Chinese classical aesthetics and critical theories of arts and literature. It assimilated aesthetic views expressed in *Shu*, inherited and developed the *li yue* ideals of Confucius, and presented a quite comprehensive picture of highly developed theory and practice of musical performances before the Qin Dynasty came into being in 221 B.C.E.

The Origin of Music (*Yuebeng pian*)

All melody originates from the heart.[1] The external, material world affects one's heart, which then expresses itself through sound. Sounds in turn are organized into a melody, which becomes *yue,* music, when played on instruments and accompanied by dance.

Music comes from the melody originated in the heart that feels the impact of external matters. That is why when the heart feels sadness the music it makes sounds anxious, woeful, and rapid. When the heart feels joy the music sounds relaxed and leisurely. When the heart feels pleasure the music sounds buoyant and smooth. When the heart feels rage the music sounds violent and harsh. When the heart feels respect the music sounds upright and pious. When the heart feels love the music sounds gentle and tender. These six feelings named are not innate in human nature but come from the heart's response to external stimuli.

That's why the great rulers in the past were careful about the things that affect people. They used *li,* the rites or etiquette, to guide people's desires. They used *yue,* music, to harmonize people's nature. They used *zheng,* government, to moderate people's behavior. They used *xing,*

Excerpts translated from *Yueji xuanlu,* from *Liji,* in *Zhongguo lidai julun xuanzhu,* ed. Chen Duo and Ye Changhai (Changsha: Hunan wenyi chubanshe, 1987), 4, 8, 25.
1. In ancient China it was believed that a person's heart controls his thoughts and emotions. As a concept, "heart" refers to men's spiritual world.

penal codes, to guard against people's base inclinations. *Li, yue, zheng,* and *xing* share the same ultimate purpose, that is, to pull people's hearts together in creating a peaceful, safe, and stable world.

All melody comes from the heart. Emotions externalize themselves in the form of sounds, which then cooperate into melodic tunes. Melody in a peaceful land is tranquil, expressing contentment with the orderly and amiable nature of government policies. Melody in a chaotic world is full of grievances, manifesting resentment toward unpopular political measures. Melody of a conquered nation is full of sorrow, lamenting human suffering. The sounds and melody from the heart are closely related to the way of the world.

Wei Wenhou

[King] Wei Wenhou asked Zixia:[2] "When I listen to the ancient *yue* during a sacrificial ritual I am really worried about falling asleep. But when I listen to the popular melodies from the states of Zheng and Wei,[3] I don't feel the least bit tired. I'd like to know why I react to the ancient *yue* and the new *yue* so differently."

Zixia replied: "I'll first talk about the ancient *yue.* In a performance of the ancient *yue,* every movement is precisely regulated and unified, and music is moderate, well centered, and expansive. The *xuan, pao, sheng, huang,* and other musical instruments all remain quiet until the *fu* drum is sounded. When the music starts the singers perform songs of civic themes, followed by dance and martial arts. The dance is paced by drum beat. If the dancers are moving too fast or out of step, the *ya* is played to control the pace. When the whole performance is over, the master of ceremony delivers his speech. He exalts the greatness of the past and encourages everyone to better himself and his family and help maintain a fair and balanced world order. All this is what the ancient *yue* promotes.

Now let's look at the so-called new *yue.* It is decadent, indulgent, and excessive. Midgets, men and women all dance together like monkeys in a disorderly fashion. You can't tell the fathers from the sons. In

---

2. Wei Wenhou was the founder of the state of Wei during the Warring States period. He was in power between 445 and 396 B.C.E. Zixia was a student of Confucius.
3. The songs of the region of Zheng and Wei are famous in early literature for their licentious nature.

the end there is nothing to be said in respect to the forefathers. That's what the so-called new *yue* is.

What your Majesty asked about is *yue,* but what you like are some musical tunes. *Yue* and music are similar but not the same."

Wenhou asked: "Why so?"

Zixia replied: "In the ancient time the heaven, the earth, and the four seasons were in perfect order and harmony. The people were virtuous. Food crops were abundant. There were no plagues or disasters. This is *dadang;* things were just right. [To maintain this state of affairs] the wise men put forth the ethical hierarchy to ensure proper relationships between the monarch and his subjects, between a father and his sons.[4] When everyone knew his proper place, the world was at peace. Thereafter, six proper forms and five scales were established for musical instruments, songs, poetry, and eulogy. Proper music is considered moral and is termed *yue.* *Shi* (*Book of Odes*)[5] says: 'With peaceful, quiet and harmonious music we eulogize our former king [Wang Ji], whose nobility is our guiding light. It guides one to tell right from wrong and good from evil. It guides one to be a wise teacher or a good ruler. It guides us to build a great kingdom with a benevolent monarch and loyal and obedient subjects. [King Wang Ji's] nobility has passed on to our King [Zhou] Wen Wang, whose moral character is beyond reproach. This godly blessing will go down to posterity.' My Majesty, now do you still tell me you like the self-indulgent new music?"

Wenhou asked: "Where does this type of new music come from?"

Zixia said: "From the state of Zheng come the disorderly tunes that turn a person dissolute. From the state of Song come the licentious tunes that make a person despondent. From the state of Wei come the reckless tunes that turn a person petulant. And from the state of Qi come the haughty tunes that make a person contemptuous. Since all these four are sensually excessive and morally detrimental, they cannot be used for sacrificial rituals. *Shi* says: 'The music our ancestors listened to manifests veneration and harmony.' You can accomplish anything when you have veneration and harmony. As a ruler, one should be careful about what one likes and dislikes. Subjects do what the monarch likes; people follow

---

4. The ethical code consists of the three cardinal guides (ruler guides his subjects, father guides his sons, and husband guides his wife) and the five constant virtues (benevolence, righteousness, propriety, wisdom, and fidelity).

5. *Shi* (Book of Odes), also called *Shijing,* one of the Chinese Five Classics, is a collection of ancient Chinese classical poetry. Consisting of 305 poems, it was probably compiled about 600 B.C.E. Except for a few verses found on archaeological objects, it represents the only known Chinese poetry from pre-Confucian times.

their leaders. *Shi* also says: 'The people are very easily led.' This is exactly what it means."

From *Zaji:* Miscellanies

Zigong [a disciple of Confucius] was watching a [new year's eve] *la* ritual.

Confucius asked: "Are you enjoying all this?"

Zigong replied: "The whole country has gone wild, but I don't see what the fuss is all about."

Confucius said: "That's because you haven't understood [the significance of] having one day's festivity after a whole year's hard work. All work and no play will not do, just as all play and no work will not do. The proper way of King Zhou Wen and King Wu is to play after work."

MO ZI

From "Condemnation of Music"

Mo Di (480–420 B.C.E.), more commonly known as Mo Zi, or Master Mo, was born the year before Confucius' death in present-day Shangdong province, like the former great thinker. His father was a handicraftsman. Mo Zi himself was once a carpenter. It is said that he studied with followers of Confucius and subsequently broke away to found his own school, the Mo-ist school of thought (*Mojia*). Like Confucius, Mo Zi traveled a good deal, visiting one after another of the feudal rulers of the time in an attempt to gain hearing for his ideas, and for a while he served as a high-ranking minister in the state of Song. He was particularly anxious to spread his teachings of universal love, nonviolence, and utilitarianism. Mo Zi was also the first ancient philosopher to make effective use of polemic prose. For several centuries Mo Zi's fame was no less than that of Confucius himself.

The following essay, "Condemnation of Music" ("Fei yue"), is taken from *Mo Zi,* a book of Mo Zi's most important ideas and thoughts. The book was probably written either partially by Mo Zi himself or recorded and developed by his immediate followers, and it is the earliest surviving work of Chinese literature that contains complete essays and dialogues of some length. This essay on music—musical rituals and such—can be seen as one of the earliest full-force attacks on theatrical entertainment. It challenges Confucians, who favored rituals and rites, as the rest of the book does on many other points. The Mo-ist school, which represented the interest and desire of the working poor—farmers, craftsmen, and soldiers—was in direct opposition to Confucian school, which was speaking for conservative landed gentry, scholars, and officials.

The term *music* (*yue*) in ancient China customarily represented more than music itself, as is made clear in this text. Here Mo Zi seems to be using the term even more broadly to include the lavish banquets and sumptuous surroundings that in his mind were associated with the musical entertainments of the aristocracy. When *yue* means more than music, it is capitalized, as Music, in the translation (see also p. 13, n. 1.)

The benevolent should seek to promote what is beneficial to the world and to eliminate what is harmful to the world. This should be an un-

Excerpts translated from "Fei yue," from *Mo Zi,* in *Zhongguo meixueshi ziliao xuanbian* (Beijing: Zhonghua shuju, 1980), 17–19.

equivocal law: do what is good for the people, and stop what is not. The benevolent should think of the world, not of the pleasures for his own eyes, ears, mouth, and body. The benevolent would not take food, clothing, or property from the people to satisfy his own sensual desires. The reason that I, Mo Zi, object to Music is not because the sound of the great bells and rolling drums, zithers and pipes, is not delightful; nor because the sight of delicate engravings and ornaments is not beautiful; nor because the taste of expertly fried and broiled meats is not delicious; nor because the comfort of lofty towers, grand pavilions, or secluded mansions is not enjoyable. All these things gratify the senses, but, if we examine the matter, we will find that such things are not in accordance with the Way of the sage kings; and, if we consider the welfare of the world, we will find that they bring no benefit to the common people. That is why Mo Zi says: It is wrong to perform Music!

Now, if the rulers and nobles need musical instruments to use in their government rituals, they cannot extract them from the water or dig them out of the ground. For this they must place heavy taxes on the common people before they can enjoy the sound of great bells, rolling drums, zithers, and pipes. The sage kings in ancient times had also taxed the people heavily, but it was in order to build boats and wagons. When finished, the sage kings ordered the boats be used on water and wagons on land, so that not only the nobles could rest their feet but the common people could also relieve the burden on their backs and shoulders. The people all contributed and nobody dared to complain. Why? Because they knew the taxes would be used for their benefit. If building musical instruments were good for the people, I would not object. If they could be as useful as the sage kings' boats and wagons, I would not object either. There are three things the people worry about most: that when hungry they will have no food, when cold they will have no clothing, and when weary they will have no rest. These are the three great worries of the people. Now let us try sounding the great bells, striking the rolling drums, strumming the zithers, blowing the pipes, and waving swords and spears like in the war dance. Does this do anything to provide food and clothing for the people? I hardly think so. But let us leave that point for the moment.

Today big states are attacking small states, big families are assaulting small families, the strong are taking from the weak, the majorities are ganging up on the minorities, the cunning are cheating the slow-witted, the privileged are lording over the humble, and bandits and thieves are rising from all sides. And there is nothing to stop them. Now let us try by sounding the great bells, striking the rolling drums, strumming the zithers, blowing the pipes, and waving the swords and spears like in the war dance. Does this do anything to rescue the world from chaos and restore it to order? I hardly think so. Therefore, Mo Zi says: If you try to promote what is beneficial to the world and eliminate what is harmful by placing heavy taxes on the people in order to make bells, drums, zithers, and pipes, you will get nowhere. That is why Mo Zi says: It is wrong to make Music!

Now the rulers and nobles, seated in their lofty towers and grand pavilions, look about them, and there are the bells, hanging like huge cooking vessels. But unless the bells are struck, how can one get any delight out of them? Obviously, bell strikers must be found. But we cannot employ old people or young juveniles, since their eyes and ears are not keen and their arms are not strong, and they cannot create harmony with the sounds or see to strike the bells front and back. Therefore, we must have young people in their prime, whose eyes and ears are keen and whose arms are so strong that they can create harmony with the sounds and see to strike the bells front and back. If we employ young husbands, we will be taking them away from their plowing and planting; and, if we employ young women, we will be taking them away from their weaving and spinning. Yet the rulers and nobles will have their Music, though their enjoyment interferes so much with the people's efforts to produce food and clothing. That is why Mo Zi says: It is wrong to make Music!

Now that the great bells, rolling drums, zithers, and pipes have all been provided. Still, if the rulers and nobles sit quietly all alone and listen to the performance, how can they get any enjoyment out of it? Obviously, they must listen in company of others, humble men or gentlemen. If they listen in the company of gentlemen, they will be keeping them from attending the affairs of the state; if they listen in the company of humble men, they will be keeping them from fulfilling their responsibilities. Yet the rulers and nobles will have their Music, though their enjoyment interferes so much with the people's efforts to produce food and clothing! That is why Mo Zi says: It is wrong to make Music!

In former times the Duke Kang of Qi loved the musical ritual of *wan* dance. The *wan* dancers could not wear robes of cheap cloth or eat coarse food, for it was said that, unless they had the finest food and drink, their faces and complexions would not be fit to look at, and, unless they had beautiful clothing, their figures and movements would not be worth watching. Therefore, the *wan* dancers ate only millet and meat and wore only robes of patterned and embroidered silk. They did nothing to help produce food or clothing but lived entirely off the efforts of others. Yet the rulers and nobles will have their Music, though their enjoyment interferes so much with the people's efforts to produce food and clothing! That is why Mo Zi says: It is wrong to make Music!

We humans are surely different from birds, beasts, and insects. The birds, beasts, and insects have feathers and fur as their robes and coats, hoofs and claws as their leggings and shoes, and grass and water as food and drink. The male need not plow or plant and the female need not spin or weave because their food and clothing are always available. But the humans are different from such creatures! Hard work is a matter of survival. If the gentlemen do not work hard at attending to the affairs of the state, chaos will erupt. If the common people do not work hard [at producing], shortage will arise. If the scholars and officials today do not take my words seriously, I'll show them the harms of Music by looking at how it interfered with each person's given duties. It is the duty of the rulers and nobles to appear at court early and retire late, hearing lawsuits and attending to affairs of government. It is the duty of the officials and scholars to fill the granary and state treasury by devoting physically and mentally to managing the court, the border, towns, hills, forests, rivers, and crops. It is the duty of the farmers to produce more grains, beans, and fruits by toiling in the fields from morning till night. It is the duty of the women to produce more linen, silk, cotton, thread, and so on by getting up early and going to bed late. If everybody loves and indulges in Music, neither the ruler and the nobles, nor the officials and scholars, nor the farmers and their wives, would be able to fulfil their duties.[1] What is interfering with the affairs of the state? Music, of course! That is why Mo Zi says: It is wrong to make Music!

---

1. In this translation some lines have been condensed to avoid the repetitiveness in Mo Zi's rhetoric.

XUN KUANG

From "A Discussion of Music"

Xun Kuang (c. 313–238 B.C.E.), also known as Xun Zi or Master Xun, ranks with Confucius and Mencius as one of the three great thinkers of classical Confucianism. He lived at the very end of the era of the Warring States, an age of political instability and ferment, of incessant intrigue and strife. Xun was a native of Zhao state (in present-day Hebei and Shanxi region)—an area considerably west of the main centers of Chinese culture. He studied and taught in the state of Qi (in present-day eastern Shangdong), whose ruler was at that time the most generous patron of learning in China; he held high official posts in the larger southern state of Chu. His experience of the world was thus broader than that of either Confucius or Mencius. His personal experience of a variety of cultural environments led him to observe that not all peoples conform to a single standard of conduct, which is quite probably the basis for his opinion that human beings in their natural state are basically immoral and that they can be made good and wise only as a result of culture and training. Xun did not trust individuals to evolve their own standards of behavior, and he placed great emphasis on the importance of social ceremonies and ritual forms. The following essay "A Discussion of Music" (*Yue lun*) was written as a direct opposition to Mo Zi's indictment of musical rituals. It is quite clear that Xun wished to maintain traditional rituals as a measure of social control. For this reason he defended the musical rites in honor of spirits and ancestors and justified them on rational and pragmatic grounds, which is a Xun trademark.

Music (*yue*) is joy (*le*),[1] which is humanly and emotionally indispensable. Since humans cannot help but feel joy, they must find an outlet in voice and an expression in movement. Sounds and movements are all connected with the ways of the human world and various personalities and emotions. Humans cannot live without joy, and joy has to have a form to show itself, but, if the form does not follow the proper Way

---

This essay originally appeared in the book *Xun Zi*, some of which Xun Zi probably wrote himself, though other parts apparently were composed by his students. The text on which this translation is based is from *Zhongguo lidai julun xuanzhu*, ed. Chen Duo and Ye Changhai (Changsha: Hunan wenyi chubanshe, 1987), 12–14.
1. In Chinese the same character represents both the word *yue* (music) and the word *le* (joy).

(*dao*),[2] there will certainly be chaos. Our ancestral kings detested chaos; that is why they created musical forms such as "Odes" (*ya*) and "Hymns" (*song*)[3] to guide the way. In this way they made certain that the voice would fully express the emotions of joy without being overindulgent, that the lyrics would be well ordered without being unduly restrictive, that the directness and subtlety, complexity and simplicity, and rhythm and tempo would be just right to bring out the best in human nature and prevent all that is evil and base. It was on this basis that our ancestral kings created their Music. And yet Mo Zi objects to it. Why?

When Music is performed in the ancestral temple of the ruler and enjoyed by the ruler together with his ministers, superiors, and inferiors, there is a shared harmony of peace and reverence. When it is enjoyed at home by the father together with his sons, elder brothers and younger brothers, there is a shared harmony of peace and affection. When it is enjoyed in the village by the elders together with the young, there is a shared harmony of peace and obedience. Hence, Music is melodic harmony achieved through temperament, it is rhythmic variations created by different instruments, it is musical compositions brought into being by unifying sounds. Music is the Way, the way to deal with all changes. It was our ancestral kings who fostered the art of Music. And yet Mo Zi objects to it. Why?

Listening to Music like the "Odes" and the "Hymns," we aspire to greater things. Holding the spears and learning the proper movements and postures of war dance, we appear more dignified. Abiding by the choreography and moving to the rhythms, we move correctly in ranks and advance and retreat in good order. Music can teach us how to march abroad to punish offenders as well as how to behave with civility at home, because they are based on the same principle: submission to order. Music is the unifying center of the world, the key to peace and harmony, and an indispensable need of human emotions. This is the manner in which our ancestral kings created the art of Music. And yet Mo Zi objects to it. Why?

Furthermore, our ancestral kings used Music to show joy and used military forces to show anger. They were expressed in such perfect ways that joy created peace on earth and anger stopped chaos. The proper rituals and music are the highest expressions of our ancestral kings' ways. And yet Mo Zi objects to it. He does not know what he is talking about. He is like a

---

2. The Chinese word *dao* is spelled as *tao* in some translations.
3. "Odes" (*ya*)— also divided into "Greater Odes" (*da ya*) and "Lesser Odes" (*xiao ya*)—and "Hymns" (*song*) are sections in the ancient classic *Book of Odes* (*Shijing*).

blind man attempting to distinguish black from white, a deaf man attempting to tell a clear tone from a muddy one, and a misguided journeyman attempting to get to the state of Chu [in the south] by going North.

Because Music impresses people deeply and transforms them swiftly, the ancestral kings were very cautious about its form and content. When Music is moderate and tranquil, people will be harmonious and shun excess. When Music is stern and majestic, people will behave properly and shun disorder. When the people are peaceful and united, the military will be strong, the state fortress will be indestructible, and the enemy states will not dare to invade. Thus, the common people will live in safety, take delight in their community, and look up to their ruler with complete satisfaction. Then the good name of the state will get around, and its glory will shine forth brightly, and the people from all four seas will all wish to be under the same ruler. Then it will be the new beginning of a true great king.

[On the other hand,] if Music is frivolous and immoral, people will become dissolute and mean-spirited. If people are dissolute and mean-spirited, chaos and disputes will follow. Chaos and disputes will weaken the military and render the state fortress vulnerable to enemy attacks. If this happens, the common people will not find safety in their homes and no delight in their community and certainly will feel dissatisfaction toward their ruler. Replacing the proper music and rites with heretical musical entertainments is the cause for ruin and shame. That is why our ancestral kings favored the proper rituals and music and despised heretical musical entertainments. As I once proposed in another essay, "let us set the things right by revising the [current] ordinance, examining the [current] poems, songs and writings, and prohibiting lewd tunes. It is the duty of the chief director of Music to prevent the elegant Music from being subverted by heretical foreign or folk music entertainments."

Mo Zi claims that the sages were against Music, so it is wrong for the Confucian scholars to encourage it. But a gentleman will see that this is not so.

The sages were [in fact] in favor of Music. Because it cultivates the good in people. It moves people deeply, and it helps shape and change the prevailing habits and customs. Therefore, our ancestral kings guided their people into peaceful harmony through the proper rituals and music.

People have emotions of likes and dislikes. If they have no way to express their joy or anger, there will be chaos. Our ancestral kings abhorred chaos, so they improved people's behaviors and provided them with the proper Music, and as a result the world became obedient. Funeral attire and mourning tears make one's heart grieve. Wearing armor and helmet and singing in the marching ranks make one's heart brave. Flirtatious beauties and music from the states of Zheng and Wei fill one's heart with excessive lust. [Dressed in elegant] aristocratic costumes and doing *Shao* dance and singing *Wu* songs make one's heart filled with stately dignity. [Since what one sees or hears or says matter a great deal,] gentlemen do not listen to lewd tunes, or look at seductive women, or utter foul words. These three things gentlemen are careful about.

Music embodies the unchanging harmony, while rituals epitomize unalterable reason. Music unites, while rituals differentiate; and through the union of rituals and music the human heart is reined!

To understand origins and changes is the nature of music; to illuminate the truth and eliminate falsehood is the essence of ritual. Because he was opposed to Music, Mo Zi almost committed a criminal offense. And yet in his time the enlightened kings had all passed away, so his errors went uncorrected. Today imprudent men continue to study his doctrines and bring peril to themselves. Learned gentlemen understand the nature of Music and virtuously offer the world their wisdom. But an age of lawlessness despises goodness and will not listen to their teachings, which are, alas, alas, left unfulfilled. Study the teachings well, my students, and do not let yourselves be misled.

Music is symbolic: the drums represent a vast pervasiveness; the bells represent fullness; the sounding stones represent restraint and order; the pipes (*yu, sheng*) represent austere harmony; the flutes (*guan, yue*) represent zestful outburst; the ocarina (*xun*) and bamboo whistle (*chi*) represent broad sweep; the zither represents gentleness; the lute represents gracefulness; the songs represent purity and fulfillment; and the dances represent merging with the Way of Heaven. The drum is surely the king of Music, is it not? Hence, it is like Heaven, while the bells are like earth; the sounding stones are like water; the flutes and pipes and whistles and so on are like the sun, the moon, and the stars; and the rest of the scrapers (*tao, chu, fu, ge, qiang, qia*) are like all the creatures of the world.

How does one understand the spirit of dance? The eyes cannot see it; the ears cannot hear it. And yet, when all the postures and movements, all the steps and changes of pace, are in perfect order, when every muscle and every bone are fully energized, when all is matched exactly to the cadence of the drums and bells, and when there is not the slightest hint of discord, there is the spirit of the dance in all its profundity and sensitivity!

From *Huainanzi*

The following excerpt is selected from *Huainanzi,* a collection of writings by courtiers under Liu An, prince of Huainan (179–122 B.C.E.). While the main philosophical thrust of the book is Taoist, it also brings together the Legalist, Confucian, and Yin-Yang schools of thought. *Huainanzi* contains a rich variety of classical Chinese ideas on aesthetics.

A grief-stricken person will weep even when he hears a song playing; a deliriously happy person will laugh even when he sees somebody crying. It is one's own inner state that causes a person to be saddened by something delightful and to laugh at something pitiful. Real feelings of delight, anger, sorrow, and joy are all natural. Cries coming out of one's mouth or tears streaming out of one's eyes are outer forms of inner disaffection. Just like water flowing downward and smoke floating upward, there is no altering their courses. No matter how hard one tries, forced sad tears carry no sorrow, and faked happy intimacy brings no harmony, because real emotions inside are heard outside.

Excerpt translated from *Huainanzi xuanlu,* in *Zhongguo lidai julun xuanzhu,* ed. Chen Duo and Ye Changhai (Changsha: Hunan wenyi chubanshe, 1987), 27.

SIMA QIAN

From "Anecdotes of Comedians"

Sima Qian (145–90 B.C.E.) was the great historian and literary man of the West Han Dynasty. He held the post of great historian under Emperor Wu. His voluminous *Records of the Great Historian* (*Shiji*) is his account of the history of China from earliest antiquity down to his own time. The book has 130 chapters. One of them, "Anecdotes of Comedians" ("Huaji Liezhuan"), is the first record of actors and their lives in China. The following excerpts are the opening and closing paragraphs of the chapter and a well-known anecdote Sima Qian related about a court jester who entertained with wit, satire, and perfect mimicry.

Confucius says: The six great books together contribute to establishing the perfect world order. *Li* (*Book of Rites*) provides standards for lifestyles. *Yue* (*Book of Music*) brings about harmony and unity. *Shu* (*Book of History*) records the past. *Shi* (*Book of Odes*) expresses feelings and aspirations. *Yi* (*Book of Changes*) explains the changes going on around us in a supernatural light. *Chun Qiu* (*Spring and Autumn Annals*) shows right and wrong through justice. The great historian of the court ventures to add: The great Heavenly Way is all-encompassing and interconnecting. Laughter and wit [being the best medicine], are also part of the solution to the problems of the world.

    [. . .]

    Jester Meng was from the state of Chu. He was an eight-foot-tall man with a silver tongue. Through fun and laughter he often mocked and criticized his superiors. . . . Prime Minister Sun Shuao considered him a worthy man and treated him well. On his deathbed the dying prime minister said to his son: "You will fall into hard times after my death. You should go to see Jester Meng and tell him you are my son." In a few years the son was poverty stricken. While carrying firewood on his back one day, he ran into Jester Meng and said: "I'm Sun Shuao's son. Before he passed away, my father asked me to look for you if I am in trouble." Jester Meng said to him: "You shall have what you deserve before long." He

Excerpts translated from *Huaji liezhuan jielu,* in *Zhongguo lidai julun xuanzhu,* ed. Chen Duo and Ye Changhai (Changsha: Hunan wenyi chubanshe, 1987), 30.

promptly put on the robe and hat, such as Sun Shuao used to wear, and started mimicking the way the late prime minister gestured and talked. He was so like Sun Shuao that the king of Chu and his courtiers could not tell the difference. King Zhuang was holding a banquet; Jester Meng came to wish him longevity. Zhuang was so surprised that he thought Sun Shuao had come back to life, and he wanted to reappoint him prime minister. Meng said: "Please allow me to go home and discuss this with my wife. I will be back in three days with the decision." When Jester Meng came back three days later, the king asked: "What did your wife say?" Meng replied: "My wife cautioned me not to take the job because it's not worth it to be the prime minister of Chu. Take Sun Shuao, the former prime minister of Chu, for example. His dedication, loyalty, and honesty helped the king of Chu to reign the land as its supreme ruler. But now, after his death, his son doesn't own an inch of land, and he is so poor that he has to carry firewood himself to cook his food. It's better to commit suicide than to be like Sun Shuao." Jester Meng proceeded to singing: "Living in the hills and toiling in the fields do not bring one enough to eat, so one pulls himself up to become a court official. If shameless and greedy, one grabs for fortunes so that his family will still be rich when he passes on. But one worries if he is caught taking bribes, obstructing justice, or committing treason that he will be sentenced to death and ruin both himself and his family. How can one rest at ease if one is a corrupt official? So one reminds himself to be an honest and clean official, following the rules of law, doing his duties, and never taking a false step. But how can one rest at ease being an honest official? Prime Minister Sun Shuao was honest and clean till death, but today his wife and children are so poor that they have to carry firewood in order to have food. It's just not worth it!" King Zhuang first thanked Jester Meng. Then he summoned Sun Shuao's son to court and, in honor of the dead, awarded him land together with four hundred families of tenant peasants. The arrangement lasted at least ten generations. From this we learn that acting can affect state affairs.

The great historian of the court notes: Chunyu Kun's sardonic laughter steered King Wei of Qi to a new course of action.[1] Jester Meng's song of

---

1. This refers to an anecdote about Chunyu Kun, a comic known for his erudition, wit, and eloquence, during the time of the Warring States (475–221 B.C.E.). When the Qi state was attacked by the Chu state, the king sent Chunyu with a skimpy amount of gifts to the Zhao state asking for assistance. Chunyu performed a comic routine in which he laughed and joked about "a small gift for a big favor." The king took his cue by sending a greater gift and got the relief he wanted.

irony earned the firewood carrier his just reward. Jester Zhan's jocular reenactment of the attendants' discomfort [in front of the king] helped cut those men's long shift by half.[2] These performances have real worthy impact too!

---

2. Zhan was a jester in the court of Emperor Qin (221–6 B.C.E.).

Preface to *Mao's Poetry with Notes and Commentaries*

During the time of the West Han Dynasty (206–8 B.C.E) there were four major schools of interpreting and teaching the *Shi* (*Book of Odes*). While the works of the three other schools are missing or incomplete, *Mao's Poetry with Notes and Commentaries,* compiled by Mao Heng and Mao Chang, survived. The following excerpt is from the preface to the poem *Guanju.* The preface is considered to have synthesized the previously scattered records of Confucian poetics into a more systematic and comprehensive one.

Poetry comes from desires and dreams. Poetry expresses one's heartfelt desires with words. When inner impulses are compelling, one finds words; when [written] words alone are not enough, one recites them with an expressive cadence; when this is not enough, one sings with all his heart; when singing is not enough, one finds his hands and feet dancing by themselves.

Emotions voice themselves through sounds, and sounds fall in line to become melodic tunes. The melody in a peaceful land is serene, expressing satisfaction with the fair and amiable nature of the government. The melody in a chaotic world is full of grievances, demonstrating resentment toward the unpopular political measures. The melody of a conquered nation is woeful, lamenting the human suffering. To show right from wrong, to shake heaven and earth, to move gods and ghosts, there is nothing more up to the mark than poetry. Our ancestral kings used it to enhance people's marital harmony and filial love, to improve civility, and to change customs.[1]

Translated from *Mao shi xu,* in *Zhongguo meixueshi ziliao xuanbian* (Beijing: Zhonghua shuju, 1980), 130–31.
1. The rest of the preface describes the categories and styles of classical poetry. The three categories are namely *feng, ya,* and *song. Feng* is popular and folksy, which, according to the author of this preface, is the genre of satire. *Ya* is the realm of political and historical epics. *Song* is the domain of odes performed at ancestral worship rituals. The three styles of writing are namely *fu, bi,* and *xing. Fu* uses a straightforward narrative. *Bi* employs allegory. *Xing* relies on metaphorical inspiration.

FU YI (?–90 C.E.)

Preface to On Dance

Fu Yi was a literary writer during the early part of the East Han Dynasty. Here, by describing a dialogue that allegedly took place between King Xiangwang (r. 298–63 B.C.E.) of Chu state and his senior literary adviser Song Yu, Fu Yi disputed the two notions that favored the aural over the visual and preferred moral instruction to sheer entertainment.

There was a story about Song Yu composing a *fu* rhyme-prose for King Xiangwang of Chu when they visited the Lake Yunmeng and Gaotang Temple. The king was about to throw a feast. He asked Song Yu: "I'm going to wine and dine my officials; what entertainment should I offer them?"

Yu said: "I've heard that singing gives voice to words and that dancing completes the meaning. So I feel talking about poetry is less desirable than listening to it, yet listening to it is less desirable than seeing it in motion. Ancient musical dance pieces such as *Ji Chu, Jie Feng, Yang A*, are absolutely superb. Could we offer these?"

The king asked: "How do they compare to the [popular] musical entertainment from the state of Zheng?"

Yu replied: "The popular Zheng entertainment and the elegant classical musical rites are each suited for different occasions. The wise and learned should know how to balance playfulness and seriousness. *Yue Ji* [in *Book of Rites*] recorded the solemn spear dance, yet *Ya* [in *Book of Odes*] praised the joyous dancing scene. *Li Ji* [in *Book of Rites*] stipulated that the nobles should retain dignity when taking drinks offered by the kings, yet *Song* [in *Book of Odes*] described drunken revelry. [The elegant rites like] *Xian Chi* and *Liu Ying* are used by the emperor and nobles in honor of the ancestors. [The popular] Zheng or Wei entertainments are used just for fun and amusement in people's spare time, not for moral instruction. There is no harm in that!"

The king said: "Please write this down in the [straight forward rhyme-prose form] *fu* for me."

Yu said: "Sure."

Translated from *Wu fu xu*, in *Zhongguo lidai julun xuanzhu*, ed. Chen Duo and Ye Changhai (Changsha: Hunan wenyi chubanshe, 1987), 35.

ZHANG HENG (78–139)

From *Xijïng Fu*

Zhang Heng was an important man of letters as well as a great astronomer of the East Han Dynasty. *Xijing Fu,* one of a few literary works of his still extant, is a succinct yet vivid eyewitness account of the great popularity, variety, scope, and technical know-how of theatrical performances at the time.

The imperial carriages have arrived in Pingle,[1] and feather-decorated tents are set up. Treasures and luxuries are gathered all around for the pleasure [of the imperial entourage]. On an enormous square the wonderful *jiaodi*[2] variety entertainments are being presented.

[First there are opening pieces.] Like the legendary Wuhuo, a man of incredible strength lifts up a heavy cooking vessel. Like the tree-swinging folks from Dulu, performers climb up high poles. Some leap through wreathes spiked with knives. Some perform swallow dives in big water tanks. Hard chest muscles meet the challenge of sharp daggers. Jugglers, fencers, and tightrope walkers all show off their skills.

[In the staging of a gathering of deities and beasts, there is scenery showing] the high peaks of Mount Hua, rolling hills and valleys, enchanted forest and meadows, and trees heavy with ripe fruits. The performers impersonate supernatural beings and animals, such as a playful leopard, a dancing bear, a drum-beating white tiger, and a flute-playing green dragon. The legendary princess Nu-e sits to sing a long aria, her voice clear, smooth, and winding. The celestial Hongya stands to command his followers, his feather cloak light and elegant. Before the beautiful music ends, [special effects of] gathering clouds and falling snow appear—first just a few flakes then coming down really heavy. In the space above the stage stones are rolled to create the sound of thunder—

Excerpt translated from *Xijing fu,* in *Zhongguo lidai julun xuanzhu,* ed. Chen Duo and Ye Changhai (Changsha: Hunan wenyi chubanshe, 1987), 37.

1. Pingle was an imperial resort during the Han Dynasty.
2. *Jiaodi* originally refers to a type of primitive entertainment in which men wearing horns charged at one another like bulls. Later the term was used interchangeably with *baixi* (literally "a hundred shows") to encompass all popular music-dance performances during the Han Dynasty.

getting louder and louder imitating the mighty wrath of heaven. A beast over eight hundred feet long roams around. In the background suddenly arises a magnificent high mountain. A bear and a tiger get in a fight, while apes and monkeys swing high. Strange-looking beasts stroll calmly, as big sparrows skip around merrily. With her trunk hanging, the white mother elephant walks as she nurses her young. A big fish transforms into a slithering dragon. The puffing mythical beast *hanli* turns into a flower-covered fairy carriage pulled by four deer. A toad plays with a turtle, while a snake charmer mesmerizes a snake. How fantastic are all the changes in appearance and shape.

[There is also an enactment of the story of the great sorcerer] Huang Gong of the East Sea, who in his prime could swallow knives, spit flames, control the forces of nature, or draw a line on the ground to make a flowing river. [Old age and heavy drinking took their tolls.][3] Now, hoping to kill a deadly white tiger, he brings along his proverbial pure gold sword and casts his once legendary spell, but, instead, he himself gets killed. None of his tricks of sorcery could save him.

[Last but not least,] as performance wagons are set up and long red banners raised, little children cartwheel their way onstage to display talents. Some kid climbs to the top of a high pole and jumps off, and, just as one's hairs rise in fear of him hitting the ground, he saves himself by wrapping his ankle around the pole. There is no limit to what they can do on the high poles: one person reins a hundred galloping horses, while others shoot arrows. After all this fun and excitement is over one feels spent and a little melancholy, too.

---

3. The story about Huang Gong of the East Sea was so popular that the author left out some well-known details here.

WANG YI

Preface to *Nine Songs*

Wang Yi (d. 158 C.E.) was a man of letters who worked in the East Hang Dynasty court between the years 106 and 144. He edited the anthology of poetry known as *Elegies of Chu* (*Chuci*), which included poems dating back as early as 330 B.C.E. In his preface to *Jiuge* (*Nine Songs*) by Qu Yuan (c. 340–278 B.C.E.), he mentioned that people in ancient times used song-dance-music rituals to appease the spirits. This is often cited as evidence that shamanism is one of the early origins of Chinese theater.

Nine Songs is the work of Qu Yuan. In the old days, in the capital of Chu, Nanying, and in the area between the Yuan and Xiang Rivers, people believed in spirits and frequently offered sacrifices. Whenever they held a sacrificial ritual they always sang, danced, and played music to entertain the spirits. Qu Yuan, deeply depressed, was in exile in that region. When he saw the common people's song-and-dance rituals, he found the lyrics so poorly written that he decided to write *Nine Songs*. In doing this, he showed respect for the spirits, relieved his own unhappiness, and also expressed his criticism of the authorities. This is the reason why his poems have different intentions, varied forms, and ultimately broad meanings.

Translated from "Jiuge xu," from *Chuci*, in *Zhongguo lidai julun xuanzhu*, ed. Chen Duo and Ye Changhai (Changsha: Hunan wenyi chubanshe, 1987), 41.

LIU YU

Prohibit Popular Entertainment

Liu Yu was a court historian during the reign of Emperor Wendi (581–604 C.E.) of the Sui Dynasty. The following piece is a letter he sent to the emperor, proposing the prohibition of popular entertainment. This is one of the earliest attempts in Chinese history to prohibit theatrical activities, but it also inadvertently reflects the popularity of the entertainment forms of the time.

Your humble servant has learned that the great wise kings in the past instructed their people and ruled their lands in accordance with the law and proper rituals and ceremonies. Unlawful or improper ways were prohibited. There were various specific ways of behavior for men and women, preventing them from going astray.

But nowadays, around the capital and also in the provinces, streets at night are crowded with all sorts of people watching theatrical performances on every first full moon of the lunar calendar. Amid deafening drums and burning torches, humans don animal masks, men wear women's clothes, actors and acrobats assume the most outlandish and bizarre expressions and postures. Obscenity and vulgarity are taken as entertainment and amusement. Tall canopies bridge high across the streets. Huge banners flutter above the clouds. [You also see everywhere:] dazzling garments, beautiful ornaments, delicious foods, crafts of silk and bamboo, and carriages and horses that cause traffic. People spend all they have as if there were no time left. Whole households show up, and there is no distinction between the noble and the lowly, between men and women, or between monks and laymen. In such an environment indecent acts, theft, and robbery all get started. And before anyone knows it they become prevalent. [These theatrical activities] do not teach good morals but only bring harm to the people. Please officially prohibit all of them immediately.

This letter is selected from *Jin Shu: Liu Yu Zhuan*, in *Zhongguo lidai julun xuanzhu*, ed. Chen Duo and Ye Changhai (Changsha: Hunan wenyi chubanshe, 1987), 45. The title is added by the editor/translator.

CUI LINGQIN

From *The Conservatory Records*

While very little is known about Cui Lingqin (fl. c. 749 C.E.), who once was a Tang Dynasty literary official, his book *The Conservatory Records* (*Jiaofang ji*) is one of the most important books about the theater from the Tang Dynasty (618–907). Jiaofang (the conservatory) was established in the year 714 to train talented individuals in popular music, dance, and theater. Cui's book contained information about the school's history, management, repertoire, actors' lives, as well as many valuable historical documents about the performing arts (such as costuming, makeup, musical instruments, and teaching techniques). The following excerpts are brief descriptions of two plays in the conservatory repertoire, *Damian* (*Big Mask*) and *Ta Yao Niang* (*The Stepping-and-Singing Woman*). Theater historians in China consider the two plays to be the earliest pieces of pure musical theater as differentiated from rites and rituals.

Damian

The story took place in the state of Northern Qi [550–77]. The brave and courageous Prince Lanling Changgong had a feminine appearance. He believed this made him less feared by his enemies, so he carved a big wooden mask to wear on the battlefield. From this came a play, with song and music.

Ta Yao Niang

In the state of North Qi lived a brandy-nosed man named Su. He held no official position, but he called himself "langzhong" [a ranking official's title]. He indulged in excessive drinking and beat up his wife when he was drunk. The wife told her misfortune to the neighbors. Some acted out the story. A man dressed as a woman sang a ballad as (s)he slowly stepped onto the stage. After each stanza the chorus sang the

Excerpts translated from "Damian," from *Jiaofang ji*, in *Zhongguo gudian xiqu lunzhu jicheng* (Beijing: Zhongguo xiju chubanshe, 1959), 17; "Ta yao niang," from *Jiaofang ji*, in *Zhongguo gudian xiqu lunzhu jicheng* (Beijing: Zhongguo xiju chubanshe, 1959), 18.

refrain: "Ta-yao, helai! Ta-yao-niang ku, helai!" ("Step and sing, come on! Poor and unfortunate step-and-sing woman, come on!") It was called *ta yao* because (s)he stepped as (s)he sang the ballad. She was considered *ku* because she sang about her misfortune. Then [the actor played] her drunken husband came on and pretended to beat and fight with her, making everyone laugh. Nowadays women play the woman's part. The husband doesn't call himself *langzhong* anymore but simply a *shuzi* (uncle). "Pawning for money," a new plot, is added to the piece. It is quite different from the original. Sometimes the piece is called *Tan Rong Niang,* again different from the original.

SU SHI

From "On Capturing the True Spirit"

Su Shi (1037–1101), also known as Su Dongpo, was a famous man of letters of the Northern Song Dynasty. Still extant are his over twenty-seven hundred poems, over three hundred *ci*,[1] and a great number of prose pieces. The following excerpt of his essay argues that the great artists, painters, and actors always capture the distinctive spirit rather than the appearance of their subjects. This argument is often cited as one of the first to point out the fundamental characteristic of Chinese theater.

According to the famous Jin Dynasty painter Gu Hutou,[2] the key to capturing the spirit of one's subject lies in the difficult task of drawing the eyes. But different people have different places for their uniqueness or idiosyncrasy to reside, some in the area of the brows and eyes, some in the nose and mouth zone. When Hutou added three hairs to the cheek of [Pei Shukai's] portrait, he captured his extraordinariness; because this person's spirit was centered on the cheek and sideburn region. The famous Jester Meng impersonated [the late] Sun Shuao so vividly that people thought the dead man had come back to life.[3] It was not because the actor was an exact copy of the man but because the actor had captured the essential spirit of the man.

Excerpt translated from "Chuanshen ji" from *Su Dongpo ji* (*Collected Works of Su Dongpo*), in *Zhongguo lidai julun xuanzhu,* ed. Chen Duo and Ye Changhai (Changsha: Hunan wenyi chubanshe, 1987), 54.
1. *Ci* refers to a special type of poetry that follows a strict metric scheme related to a standard repertory of musical tunes.
2. Hutou (Tiger Head) was the nickname of the famous painter Gu Kaizhi (346–407).
3. See Sima Qian's "Anecdotes of Comedians" in this book.

CHEN CHUN

An Indictment of Immoral Theater

Chen Chun (1153–1217) was a student of Zhu Xi, founder of the neo-Confucian school, Lixue (Rationalist School). The following memo he submitted to the imperial minister Fu Sicheng is only one example of many attempts made by the conservatives to stop the theatrical activities that thrived during the Song Dynasty (960–1279).

I consider it an unsavory custom of this land that when the autumn harvest is over the actors collude with the heads of several villages to put on indecent shows. And they call this "begging winter for mercy." Teenage hooligans gang up to promote the events. They go from door to door demanding money or other valuables to help pay for the performers who put on plays or stage puppet shows. They set up stages in densely populated and easily accessible areas to attract more spectators. They fight over one another for sites near shopping districts and city gates. This fall, since the lunar seventh and eighth months, many villages in the country are swept up by this type of activities. They are called plays and entertainments, but in fact they are extremely harmful. First, people are being wantonly fleeced. Second, working people are turned into idle spectators. Third, young men are tempted to become playboys without proper ambitions. Fourth, young women are lured out of their boudoirs and instilled with improper ideas. Fifth, envious husbands begin to desire other men's wives. Sixth, young people are encouraged to resort to violence. Seventh, scandals are created in which unmarried people elope after casual meetings. Eighth, the county and provincial courts are inundated by lawsuits; some even wantonly commit murder because of some personal grudge.

These plays and entertainments give birth to so many social evils that, if not outlawed, they can easily sway the people and make trouble for the righteous ones running the government. I cautiously present to you my opinions, hoping that you establish strict rules and have them posted in

Translated from "Shang fu sicheng lun yinxishu," in *Zhongguo lidai julun xuanzhu*, ed. Chen Duo and Ye Changhai (Changsha: Hunan wenyi chubanshe, 1987), 56.

public places, in the counties, in the villages, and make sure the village heads carry out the prohibition. If this is done, the people's minds will be stable, their property safe, their behavior proper, and their lawsuits fewer. The whole land will then have the great fortune of enjoying the peace and quiet bestowed by your Highness.

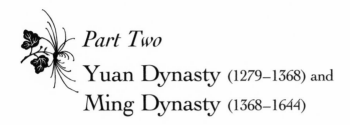

Part Two

Yuan Dynasty (1279–1368) and
Ming Dynasty (1368–1644)

HU ZHIYU

Foreword to Huang's Poetry Collection

Hu Zhiyu (1227–92) was a Yuan Dynasty scholar who held important positions in both the central and local governments. Because he loved the theater and had some close relationships with performers, especially female performers, he developed a true interest and understanding of the art of acting. In the following preface Hu expounded his theory of acting by enumerating his famous "jiu mei" (nine beauties), the nine essential qualities for a good performer. Both his theory and the way it was presented had resonances in the discussions of acting in the Ming and Qing Dynasties.

Singing and speaking are the most important in an actress's array of skills. If one possesses the [following] nine essential qualities, she will stand out among her peers.

1. Master body movements to such a high level of perfection and brilliance that the audience is dazzled.

2. Cultivate a graceful and demure disposition, and stay away from the vulgar and the commonplace.

3. Use intelligence and sensitivity to observe the affairs of the world.

4. Speak with eloquence, make every sentence and every word ring true and clear.

5. Sing with a voice as clear and round as dropping pearls.

6. Employ expressive gestures and expressions to help the audience's understanding.

7. Maintain appropriate volume and tempo even when singing or speaking old familiar lines; keep it fresh and do not sound like old monks reciting scriptures.

8. Revitalize classical plays and characters, making their emotions, words, and deeds so immediate and vivid that the audience hangs onto every word and has no time to feel tired.

Translated from *Huangshi shijuan xu*, in *Zhongguo lidai julun xuanzhu*, ed. Chen Duo and Ye Changhai (Changsha: Hunan wenyi chubanshe, 1987), 63.

9. Gain new insights when working on old materials; create novel terms and expressions; in short, make it unpredictable.

In the near past several actresses excelled in all these areas, such as Lei Xinxin, Zhao Zheng, and Qin Yulian. I'm so pleased that today Huang is trying to emulate them. So when she presented me with her volume of poetry and asked me to write something I readily consented.

ZHONG SICHENG

Preface to *The Register of Ghosts*

The Yuan Dynasty witnessed the various theatrical elements developed in the preceding centuries come together to create the first full-fledged Chinese literary dramas. Under the Mongol rulers the native *han* Chinese intellectuals were excluded from government posts, the traditional outlet for their talents. Inadvertently, this brought about a golden age of Chinese literature, especially music-drama, into which the native intellectuals poured their creativity. Zhong Sicheng (c. 1279–1360) was one such man, who wrote good plays and songs. But Zhong's greatest contribution was his *The Register of Ghosts* (*Lu gui bu*), a little book about the playwrights and plays of his time. It contained brief biographical notes of 152 writers and listed over 400 plays. In the preface to the book Zhong proclaimed that his intention was to give playwrights, who were usually neglected and belittled, their rightful place in history. Because, like the sagacious, the virtuous, the faithful, and the filial in the past, who had their deeds written in books and thus lived on eternally, writers should also be remembered and be the ghosts who never die. Zhong's book was the sole contemporary source of information on Yuan Dynasty playwrights, first written in 1330 and revised twice by himself. Later Jia Zhongming (1343–1422) wrote a sequel to the book. In the same spirit Xia Tingzhi (1316–70) wrote *The Green Bower Collection* (*Qinglou ji*) in 1355 to immortalize outstanding actresses of his time.

It's decided by fate if one is capable or not, lives a long life or not, dies or not, suffers misfortune or not, but it does not stop the wise and worthy from talking about these matters. The changes in *yang* and *yin* correspond to the life and death of men and ghosts. If men can figure out the Way of life and death and follow it accordingly, there will be no unfortunate deaths in jail shackles. The living live on earth. But it is wrong to think only those already dead are ghosts, because some not yet dead are ghosts too. What's the difference between the dead ghosts and those who are mere drunken or semiconscious receptacles of wine and food. I have no time to talk about these mud blocks. There is, however, another group of people. They know something about duties and reasons, and

Translated from *Lu gui bu,* in *Zhongguo gudian xiqu lunzhu jicheng* (Beijing: Zhongguo xiju chubanshe, 1959), 2:101.

they speak well, yet they pay no attention to scholarship. They are completely forgotten after death, and they are worse off than those mud block ghosts. I have seen the not-yet-dead ghosts mourning those who are dead; they feel almost dead. Don't they know that since the creation of the world and the beginning of time there have always been ghosts who remain deathless? The sagacious, the virtuous, the faithful, and the filial have their deeds written in books. No matter how the world and time change, they live eternally. They are the ghosts who do not die.

On a leisurely day I was remembering some deceased friends. They were from humble backgrounds and unlucky in officialdom, but they were all highly talented, learned, and worthy of being remembered. Unfortunately, as time went on they became unknown. In their memory I would like to record their lives and works in verse composition. For those [playwrights] before my time, I will cite their names and relate their works. I hope all this will have the happy result of encouraging the new writers to be dedicated to their writing and do even better. I call this book *The Register of Ghosts*. My heavens, I am a ghost, too! What good does it do me to try to turn the dead and not-yet-dead ghosts into the ones who do not die? If the high and respectable feel offended, just ignore them. What do they know?

This preface is written on 22 June 1330 by Zhong Sichen in Gubian.

DU RENJIE

An Ignorant Peasant Goes
to the Theater

The title of the following piece literally reads *A Peasant Doesn't Know about
Goulan*. *Goulan* here stands for the setting where popular entertainments were
held. This piece of *sanqu*, a popular song form, provides one of the best records
of theatrical conditions of the time, vividly describing elements such as the
building, audience, players, and plays. An excellent translation by William
Dolby of portions of this text can be found in the chapter on Yuan drama in
Chinese Theater from Its Origins to the Present Day, ed. Colin Mackerras (Honolulu; University of Hawaii Press, 1983).

Favorable wind and rain make people happy and content, and I'm the
happiest of them all. My harvest of silkworm and grains are heavy, but
my taxes are not. To show my gratitude for my blessings I've come to
town to buy ceremonial papers and candles, just like I told everyone in
the village. As I walk down the street, I see colorful posters and people
bustling about.

A man at the gate is shouting, "Please come in, please." "The house
is filling up and late-comers may not have seats." He also announces:
"First, you'll see the popular *Tiao Feng Yue* (*Playing with Wind and Moon*),
followed by the comic *zaju Liu Shuahe*." He again shouts: "It's easy to
catch a fair, but such a pair of good shows are hard to come by."

He takes two hundred [qian] from me and lets me in. I walk up a
slope lined with wooden seats and see rows and rows of people sitting in
the round. Looking up, I see something like a clock tower, and, looking
down, I see swirls of people. Several women are sitting on a side plat-
form. It's not like they are holding a sacrificial ritual or something, but
they keep beating the drums and gongs.

A girl comes on to make a few rounds, followed by a group. In the
middle is a clown, who has wrapped his head in a black cloth with a
writing brush sticking out on top and drawn black lines on his white-

Translated from Sui Shusen, *Quan Yuan sanqu* (Beijing: Zhonghua shuju, 1964), vol. 1.

washed face. What does he have on? Neck to toe he wears a flowery cotton gown.

He recites some verses and sings some songs, all flawlessly. When he starts to gab he sure has the gift, very witty, flowery, and audacious. Before he is finished [with his curtain-raiser] he even does some tricks with his feet.

Now one man comes on as old Squire Zhang, and the clown acts as his servant. They are taking a stroll through town. When they see a young maiden behind a screen, the old man wants to take her as his wife and asks the servant to be the matchmaker. [The young woman] asks for beans, millet, rice, and wheat and, of course, satin, silk, and yards of other weaving.

The servant has his awkward master twirled around his little finger, giving all sorts of whimsical orders. Finally, the old squire gets so vexed that he hits his hide drumstick very hard, and it breaks in two. I cry out, "Somebody's head is broken, and let's get a court order!" The people in there roar with laughter.

I've got such a full bladder that I'm dying from the pain. But, if it wasn't for those stupid donkeys laughing at me, I would have done anything to hold the urge and stay to see more.

GAO MING

Prologue to *The Lute Song*

Gao Ming (c. 1306–59), born and raised in Wenzhou, the birthplace of *nanxi* (southern drama), was a late Yuan *nanxi* dramatist himself. His play *The Lute Song* (*Pipa ji*) is a reworking of a well-known folk story in which a scholar named Cai left the care of his parents to his wife and went to attend the imperial civil service examination in the capital, where he stayed to enjoy his success and married the daughter of a high official. In the meantime his hometown was ravaged by famine. After burying her parents-in-laws, who died one after another, despite her valiant efforts to save them, the first wife sets out for the capital to look for her husband, along the way playing her lute and singing as she begs for alms. In the original story the distressed first wife ended up being trampled to death by a horse, and Cai himself was killed by lightning. In Gao Ming's play, however, Cai became a sympathetic character who suffered deeply because he was caught in the middle of some complex social and parental pressures. Instead of the two violent deaths in the original story, Cai and his two wives lived together in reconciliation. With *The Lute Song* Gao Ming developed to its full potential the multifaceted form of *chuanqi* (marvels or romances), writing with equal brilliance highly refined lyric songs, broadly colloquial comic speeches, intermingled with vivid poetry and ornate prose and forceful moral argument. In the following prologue the author put forth his intention to write plays that are moving and teach good morals. Both the play and the prologue had a far-reaching influence on the writers and critics of the Ming and Qing Dynasties.

An autumn lantern shines upon the blue curtains as I sit reading by the night table. Between the rue-scented volumes there are countless tales, ancient and present, about beautiful women and brilliant men, about magical fairies and blithe spirits. No matter how finely written some of them are, they are worthless stories if they do not promote good moral orders. As for plays, to amuse people is easy but to move them is hard. For those of you who deserve better, here is something that's different. Don't get sidetracked by the clowning and jokes or get caught up by the lyrical modes or musical tunes, but give your fill attention to the theme of filial piety and wifely virtue. Among the tens of thousands of plays this one is like the legendary steed Hualiu way ahead of the rest.

Translated from *Pipa Ji,* in *Zhongguo shida gudian beiju ji,* ed. Wang Jisi (Shanghai: Shanghai wenyi chubanshe, 1982), 99.

ZHU QUAN

From *Taihe Records of Music/Drama*

Zhu Quan (1378–1448) was the sixteenth son of the Ming Dynasty founding emperor, Zhu Yuanzhang. He read avidly and wrote extensively, his subjects ranging from classical schools of thoughts, poetry, and history to divination and alchemy. Among the over a dozen plays he wrote, only two have survived. He also wrote three books about theater, although *Taihe Records of Music/Drama* (*Taihe zhengyin pu*), which is excerpted here, is the only one extant. The first part of this best-known theater book of the Ming Dynasty contains theory and documents of classical theater, dealing with different schools, forms, styles, types, themes, and origins. He recorded and commented on more playwrights and plays than *The Register of Ghosts*. The second part of the book is a detailed recording and description of standard musical scores for northern *zaju* plays. Despite its various limitations and prejudices, Zhu Quan's book established critical models and standards for many to follow.

Styles of Great Dramatists Past and Present

Ma Dongli's lyrics[1] are like the phoenix singing in the rising sun.[2] Elegant and refined, they are comparable to [the famous ancient classical *fu* writings about the great halls of] *Lingguang* (spiritual light) and *Jingfu* (fortunate sight). They are like the great cries of the almighty stallion that silence the voices of ten thousand horses. They are also like the mythical phoenix singing way up on cloud nine, where no uttering of ordinary birds could ever reach. [Ma Dongli was] the most superior of the great dramatists.

Excerpts translated from "Gujin qunying yuefu geshi," from *Taihe zhengyo pu, Zhongguo gudian xiqu lunzhu jicheng* (Beijing: Zhongguo xiju chubanshe, 1959), 3:16–18. This section of the book offers stylistic appraisals of 187 Yuan dramatists and 16 Ming dramatists. The names of another 105 Yuan dramatists are also evoked. Excerpted here are the first 7 Yuan dramatists analyzed.
1. Ma Dongli (c. 1250–1323), also known as Ma Zhiyuan, was one of "Four Greats" of Yuan dramatists. Of his fifteen plays the best known today is *Autumn in the Han Palace* (*Hangong qiu*).
2. Phoenix singing in the morning sun is usually taken as a metaphor for a very good omen.

Bai Renfu's[3] lyrics are like the mythical bird *peng* soaring above the nine clouds. Righteous and magnificent, they are like the *peng* from the North Ocean soaring high and determined to cover the distance of ten thousand miles in one flight.[4] [Bai Renfu was] the leading dramatist.

Fei Tangchen's[5] lyrics are like the surging waves of the Three Gorges [on Yangzi River]. Majestic and spectacular in a way most natural and unrestrained, one moment they are stormy like waves hitting the sky, the next they are tranquil like a mirror reflecting the hills. [Fei Tangchen was] undoubtedly outstanding.

Gong Dayong's[6] lyrics are like swift eagles. Sharp, incisive, and imposing, when they lift up their wings and look down, foxes and rabbits tuck in their necks and scramble for cover.

Wang Shifu's[7] lyrics are like a beauty standing in the middle of a flower garden. The narrative is subtle, tactful, and so very tantalizing. One often comes upon lines so beautifully rendered that one seems to see Yuhuan after her bath in the Huaqing Pond and Liuzhu picking lotus flowers on Luopu Pond.[8]

Guan Hanqing's lyrics are like an intoxicated guest at a feast. There are ups and downs. I have chosen to name him as a top dramatist because with him the Yuan drama began.[9]

Zheng Dehui's lyrics[10] are like the pearls and jade jewels from the

---

3. Bai Renfu (c. 1226–1360), also known as Bai Pu, was another one of the Four Greats of Yuan dramatists. Of his sixteen plays the best known today are *Raindrops on the Parasol Tree* (*Wutong yu*) and *Qiangtou Mashang*.

4. This refers to the well-known fable related in *Zhuangzi,* a Taoist classic. Part of it reads: "In the North Ocean there is a fish whose name is the Kun; the Kun's girth measures who knows how many thousand miles. It changes into a bird whose name is the Peng; the Peng's back measures who knows how many thousand miles. When it puffs out its chest and flies off, its wings are like clouds hanging from the sky. This bird, when the seas are heaving, has a mind to travel to the South Ocean. (The South Ocean is the Lake of Heaven.) In the words of the *Tall Tales;* "When the Peng travels to the South Ocean, the wake it thrashes on the water is three thousand miles long; it mounts spiraling on the whirlwind ninety thousand miles high and is gone six months before it is out of breath."

5. Fei Tangchen (?) was a Yuan dramatist.

6. Gong Dayong (?) also known as Gong Tianting, was a Yuan dramatist.

7. Wang Shifu (?) was a Yuan dramatist. Of his fourteen plays the most famous was *The West Chamber Story* (*Xixiang ji*).

8. Yuhuan and Liuzhu were two imperial concubines known for their peerless beauty and charm. The former was the favorite of the Tang Dynasty emperor Tang Minghuang, who loved taking baths in Huaqing Pond. The latter was the favorite of the Jin Dynasty emperor Jin Shichong.

9. Guan Hanqing (c. 1245–c. 1322) was the most famous of the Yuan dramatists, often referred to as the Father of Chinese Drama.

10. Zheng Dehui (?), also known as Zheng Guangzhu, was one of the Four Greats of Yuan dramatists. The most famous of his eighteen plays is *The Beauty's Soul Leaves Her Body* (*Qianniu lihun*).

highest heaven. They are so unusual that it is as if they were pearls and jewels dropping from heaven. His were true masterpieces.

[. . .]

Twelve Types of *Zaju* Plays[11]

The first type concerns gods, fairies, and other supernatural beings.
The second type are about Taoist recluses (who chose to live near woods, springs, hills, and valleys).
The third type deals with the emperor in relation to his officials.
The fourth type presents loyal officials and martyrs.
The fifth type treats such issues as filial piety, righteousness, honesty, and moral integrity.
The sixth type rebukes treachery and slander.
The seventh type is about exiled officials and orphaned children.
The eighth type excels in scenes of combat and chase.
The ninth type is about love and romance.
The tenth type concerns life's vicissitudes: joys and sorrows, partings and reunions.
The eleventh type centers on colorful women's roles.
The twelfth type employs the masks of deity and ghosts.

Zaju plays, when acted by lowly entertainers, is termed *chang xi* (prostitute plays); that's why where the plays are performed is called *goulan* (another word for brothel). Mr. Zhao Ziang[12] said, "When *zaju* plays are performed by people of good families, they are regarded as 'superior accomplishments.' When actors and prostitutes perform them, they are deemed 'inferior tricks.' Since respectable and decent people are concerned about their reputations, fewer and fewer of them perform in plays. Their number is so small today that the lowly entertainers are considered 'superior.' That's such a disgrace." When asked why, he replied: "*Zaju* are written and composed by learned scholars and men of letters who are all respectable and decent people like myself. If we didn't create them in the first place, what could those actors act in? If we get to the roots of the matter, we can see the actors are still 'inferior.' " Guan

11. Translated from "Zaju shier ke," from *Taihe zhengyo pu*, in *Zhongguo gudian xiqu lunzhu jicheng* (Beijing: Zhongguo xiju chubanshe, 1959), 3:24–25.
12. Zhao Ziang (1254–1322), also known as Zhao Mengfu, was a famous Yuan Dynasty painter.

Hanqing once said: "Theater is not his (meaning the actor's) calling but mine. He is just doing a servant's chore by keeping us merry and entertained. It's my breeze and my moon that he is offering." I am quoting him because there is truth in what he said in jest.

Those young people of good families who are gifted in music and verse are very fortunate to live in a time of peace, harmony, and propriety. Throughout history there are many terms describing the act of making theater: *kang qu xi* (theater of the Avenue of Harmony) in the Sui Dynasty, *li yuan yue* (music of the Pear Garden) in the Tang Dynasty, *hua ling xi* (theater of the Magnificent Forest), and *sheng ping yue* (music of ascending peace). The talented young people today desire to return to the old tradition [of theater making] to celebrate the glory of the age they live in.

LI KAIXIAN

From *Ci Xue*

Li Kaixian (1502–68) was one of the "Eight Gifted Scholars of the Jiajing Period." He was greatly interested in popular arts and literature, particularly theater, of which he was both a connoisseur and a practitioner. In fact, he had under his own roof a theater troupe of twenty, thirty, or forty members, according to different sources. He wrote extensively, but only a handful of plays, a collection of poetry, and a collection of theatrical criticism, entitled *Ci Xue*, survive. Excerpted here are two anecdotes about famous performers in the section "Ci Yue" from *Ci Xue*, dealing with the art of acting and the art of teaching acting.

Zhou Quan from Xuzhou was very good at singing the arias from both the southern and northern plays. One day he was singing the piece "Appreciating Flowers" ("Shanghua shi") at a tavern. His voice was loud and clear, and his range was wide, from very high to very low. The old merchant next door, who had always prided himself as a real connoisseur of good singing and lamented about the shortage of good singers, had just gone to bed. But, when he heard [Zhou Quan's] singing, he quickly sat up in bed with his eyebrows knotted, worrying that the singer might not do the fifth line, since it was the most difficult. [To his great delight] the singer [not only sang the line] but modulated his tone so well that it reminded the old merchant of the ease he himself used to experience [when singing simple tunes]. He jumped out of bed, and, as he turned around, he saw on the night stand ten *liang* silver, a thousand or so coins, and two bolts of colored silk, all of which he placed in a tray. He carried the tray on his head and then proceeded in a kneeling position to where Zhou Quan was. He said [to Zhou Quan]: "Great master, it is the first time at my ripe old age that I have ever heard such great singing. Please accept this meager offering as my token of admiration." (The merchant was not a wealthy man.)

This incident made Quan famous all over the land. Two of the apprentices he trained, Xu Suo and Wang Ming, were both from Yan

---

Excerpts translated from "Ci yue," from *Ci Xue*, in *Zhongguo lidai julun xuanzhu*, ed. Chen Duo and Ye Changhai (Changsha: Hunan wenyi chubanshe, 1987), 105–6.

Zhou and were both able to pass on the art of their master. Whenever someone wanted to be an apprentice, [Quan] would first ask the person to sing one or two arias of his or her own choice, and then he would train the apprentice according to his or her natural ability to carry [the five notes of traditional Chinese music]. [He was very particular about the time of his lessons.] It had to be dark at night when the master, holding a lighted incense, sat face to face with the apprentice. As the hand holding the incense went up or down or came to a halt, so would the apprentice's voice. The key to singing is modulation—the proper control of rise and fall. [Just suppose] the master did not use the incense and used words, instead, to guide his apprentice, who then would have to listen carefully to the master and try to sing at the same time. As a result, his concentration would become divided. Following the incense with his eyes, on the other hand, enables him to concentrate on the singing.

When the noted scholar Wu Hui gave tutorials for the imperial exams, he first asked each of his students to write a couple of essays on some dull and slight subjects just to get a sense of the student's strength and weakness and then guide him accordingly. This method was the same as Quan's. In this way the superior ones don't get stagnant [because of too little challenge]; the lesser ones don't get choked [because of too much], which is very important. When teaching singing, Quan penned careful marks alongside the lyrics in a manner similar to [traditional Chinese] music notations. I saw such a lesson plan twenty years ago, but none could be found today.

Yan Ron, also known as Keguan, was from Dantu, in Zhengjiang, and was a contemporary of Quan. He came from a good family and loved theater. Every time he got onstage he used to behave and emote artificially, which was further amplified by his loud and clear voice. Once he presented in front of an audience [the tragedy] *The Orphan of the House of Zhao* (*Zhaoshi guer*), in which he played the part of Gong Sun Chujiu. After he saw no sad expression on the faces of the audience, upon returning home he grabbed his beard with his left hand and slapped his cheeks with his right hand until they turned red. Then holding a wooden doll representing the infant orphan, he stood in front of a dressing mirror. He took turns speaking, singing, and lamenting about all the loneliness and suffering, a truly pitiful and touching sight. The next time he performed the same play, thousands of people were moved to uncontrollable sobbing. Back home he came up to the mirror again, taking a deep bow, and smiled: "Yan Rong, really spectacular!"

Xu Wei on Theater

Xu Wei (1521–93) was an exceptionally gifted man in the history of Chinese literature and arts. Having been a child prodigy, he matured into an outstanding poet, writer, calligrapher, and painter, in addition to being an influential playwright and critic. His *Four Cries of an Ape* (*Sisheng yuan*), a collection of four plays, had a tremendous impact on the development of playwriting in the late part of the Ming Dynasty. His major theoretical work *On the Southern Drama* (*Nanci xulu*) deals with the history, literary and folk origins, stylistic characteristics, and various dialects of southern drama as well as criticism of some of its major playwrights and plays. Xu Wei advocated that plays should have the quality of being unembellished, natural, and unconventional. He stood in direct opposition to the conservative and pretentious tendencies of his time, serving as an inspiration to many. The following selections reflect Xu's belief in being natural.

Prologue to *Roar with Songs*

Let's not talk about correcting the times or improving morals,
Nor shall we hold onto the wise and virtuous of bygone days,
For there is no need to ask the blue sky for permission
Just to bend and stretch your limbs.
No point to grinding the sword of wisdom,
Let's go drinking the spring of freedom.
The world is full of defects from the start,
So is man sly and wicked deep in his heart.
What you see and hear every day
Are more than enough for many a new play.

Excerpts translated from *Ge dai xiao kaichang ci,* in *Zhongguo lidai julun xuanzhu,* ed. Chen Duo and Ye Changhai (Changsha: Hunan wenyi chubanshe, 1987), 125; and *Ti kunlun nu zaju hou,* in *Zhongguo lidai julun xuanzhu,* ed. Chen Duo and Ye Changhai (Changsha: Hunan wenyi chubanshe, 1987), 122.

    The authorship of *Roar with Songs* (*Ge dai xiao*) is undecided among scholars, but many believe Xu Wei wrote the farce, in which everything was contradictory, irrational, and absurd. *Kunlun Nu* is a play by Mei Dingzuo (1548–1615), in which the title hero, Kunlun Nu, a servant, helped his master to get the maid he wanted to marry by carrying her out of her master's house late at night.

It may be ridiculous and not right,
You give it straight, and so be it.

Comments on *Kunlun Nu*

Writers lacking in naturalness often have this weakness, that is, when coming upon a crucial moment in a play, they like to embellish their language with so-called richness and color. They feel that in this way they are making the moment more moving, but in fact the real force of the sadness or joy has been reduced. A writer with Mei's attainments should not be swayed by such fashion. [Those who write naturally] can point at iron and turn it into gold. The more common, the more elegant; the less spice, the more flavorful; the less affectation, the more fascination.

LI ZHI

Miscellaneous Commentaries:
Huagong versus *Huagong*

Li Zhi (1527–1602) was a prominent Ming Dynasty thinker and literary theorist. After resigning from his government post at age fifty-four, he lived as a
Buddhist and devoted himself to writing and giving lectures. Li was condemned
by the authorities as a "heretic," a label he proudly assumed because he was
openly against the traditional Confucian orthodoxy, especially the hypocrisy of
the neo-Confucian moralists who were running the country. His writings, both
philosophical and literary, were highly influential and eagerly embraced by the
progressive minded but got him into deeper and deeper trouble with the
authorities. He died in prison because he "dared to promote iconoclastic
views." Fearing the power of his unconventional ideas, the neo-Confucian
authorities never stopped attacking Li Zhi, even after his death, and his books
were banned. All this, however, could not stop the spread of his powerful
influence.

   In matter of arts and literature Li vehemently despised what he considered
artificial, superficial, and conventional and passionately championed what he
considered truthful, natural, and original. Li elevated the status of drama and the
novel by giving extensive critical attention to these relatively new genres. One
of the most influential of his theoretical concerns is *tongxin* (literally, "child's
heart," childlike innocence, unembellished honesty), a quality he regarded as
most essential to a true work of art. Another critical concern is the distinction
between the two key concepts, which he ingeniously turned into homonyms,
huagong (inspired art) and *huagong* (well-crafted art). The following essay is taken
from the third volume of his *Burning Books* (*Fen shu*).

The Moon-Worship Pavilion (*Baiyue ting*) and *The West Chamber Story*
(*Xixiang ji*) are works of inspiration. *The Lute Song,* on the other hand, is
a work of fine craftsmanship. Some believe that with perfect technical
skills they can recapture the art of creating heaven and earth, but don't
they know that heaven and earth are artless? In love with the marvelous
beauty that lives under heaven and grows on earth, people search for the

Translated from "Zashuo," from *Fen Shu,* in *Zhongguo lidai julun xuanzhu,* ed. Chen Duo
and Ye Changhai (Changsha: Hunan wenyi chubanshe, 1987), 137–38.

art that created it all, but to no avail, and it is not because of any lack in faculties. The Creator is artless. Even the sagacious and holy do not know where lies the inspiration—how can anyone else know? Thus, a work of pure craftsmanship, no matter how refined, has already fallen to be only second *yi,* or second rate.[1] Writing is tremendously important because it may impact generations to come, and the writer always knows in his heart the weakness and strength of his work. Quite tragic!

What determines if a horse possesses supernatural speed is neither its gender nor its color. True kindred spirits are not found among those who only know to recite classics by rote. Genuinely inspired writing does not spring from some well-turned words or lines. When talking about literature, one may contemplate such technical aspects as if the structure is tight, if the parallelism is apt, if the story is moral and reasonable, if the beginning works in concert with the ending, if non-realism fuses congenially with realism, but none of these apply to the kind of writing that is supreme.

Zaju classics such as *The West Chamber Story* and *The Moon-Worship Pavilion* are the best of plays, yet what artful techniques can they boast of? Especially when compared to the technically perfect *The Lute Song.* Gao [who wrote *The Lute Song*] obviously spared no efforts in crafting the work, thus leaving nothing more to be desired. Because the author did everything possible to ensure literary excellence, words and lines are too perfect to arouse further new meanings or feelings. I have tried to play[2] *The Lute Song.* The first time around I gasped in admiration; the second time around I cried with woe; the third time around I felt none of these emotions any longer. Why? It is because its truthfulness is only on the surface that it does not reach deeply into a person's heart? It is really not surprising that, in spite of its technical precision, its power of affecting people only goes skin deep. *The West Chamber Story* and *The Moon-Worship Pavilion* are not like that. Thank heaven for the truly inspired among us in this vast universe; like the creation of the world, their marvel is beyond reason.

The world's truly great writers as a rule do not start writing for its own sake. They feel many things that they cannot name; they are choked

---

1. Here Li Zhi is using some terminology from Buddhism. The Buddhists believe that their teachings pertain to spirituality and reveal the true essence of existence, so it is the first *yi,* the supreme truth. The worldly teachings, on the other hand, only reflect reality in some superficial and illusional manner, so it is inferior and second in *yi.*

2. The verb *tan,* meaning to play a string instrument, is used here to denote both the title of the play and the manner in which Li Zhi read the play, that is, reading aloud, chanting, or singing different parts as required by the script.

up by many emotions that they cannot or dare not utter. Over time these feelings keep building and building in intensity and power and are very hard to contain. A mere sight or mention of something can trigger a torrent of sentiments gushing from the writing brush. Like grabbing somebody else's wine cup to vent one's own pent-up feelings, they protest the injustices in their own lives by using as analogies the misfortunes of others through the ages. After spouting writings absolutely inspired, impassioned, and incredible, they are still not completely gratified. They cannot help but indulging themselves further in uncontrollable raving, shouting, crying, or wailing. They would rather directly inflame people into teeth-gnashing wrath or murderous rage than have their writings preserved in the ivory tower or fed to fire and water. When I read the play [*The West Chamber Story*] I could see the author in my mind's eye. He must have been a man feeling very alienated from the imperial court and his well-placed peers, and writing a play about courting and marital relationship was just his way to express his sense of alienation and disappointment. Thus, we have a play in which he celebrates a beautiful maiden with rare and laudable qualities, admires the young man Zhang Sheng for his romantic adventures, and at the same time exposes the inconstancy of human affection and deplores the unworthiness of his fellow men. What may strike some people as especially laughable is that a mere boy-meets-girl story seems to have been exaggerated out of proportion, as in the case in which [the young girl Yingying's calligraphy is deemed] even superior to the great masters like Zhang Xu, Zhang Dian, [Wang] Yizhi, and [Wang] Xianzhi. Yao Fu once wrote: "[There is much more to] Tang Yu declining three cups of wine, or Tang and Wu feuding over a chess game."[3] To feud and to decline are serious in state affairs, but, if you keep your eyes only on a wine cup or a chess game, they diminish in significance.

Alas! Past or present, the truly exceptional people all seem to have that ability, that is, to see the big in small and to see the small in big, or [as the Buddhist scripture puts it] "a grand temple on the tip of a hair, the cycle of karma in a speck of dust." This famous saying is absolutely true. You don't have to take my word for it; you can test it yourself. When

3. Yao Fu (1011–77), also known as Shao Yong, was a philosopher of the Northern Song Dynasty. For better understanding I have included in this note my translation of Yao Fu's original text, from which Li Zhi quoted only two lines. Yao Fu wrote: "It's not that Yao Fu loves to make poetry; poetry is what Yao Fu does when he is overwhelmed by despair. Dishonesty breeds distrust, and we have plenty of both. [There is much more to] Tang Yu's declining three cups of wine or Tang and Wu feuding over a chess game. Something big is intended in a small act. It is not that Yao Fu loves to make poetry."

the moon is perched over the courtyard, when the autumn leaves are falling to reveal the open sky, when all is quiet and still in the study, and you are alone and looking for something to do, you should try *The West Chamber Story*. Go over it again and again, and you will always be awed by its richness and power, which is infinite and beyond measure, unlike its literary facility, which is finite and measurable. Alas, only if I could be like the said author!

Tang Xianzu on Theater

Tang Xianzu (1550–1616) is sometimes called the Chinese Shakespeare, not just because the two were contemporaries and passed away in the same year. After serving at different positions in the government for fifteen years, Tang became increasingly disillusioned. At age forty-eight he quit office to devote himself to writing plays and became the best playwright and a force of liberation of his time. Tang left behind five plays: *The Purple Flute* (*Zixiao ji*), *The Purple Hairpin* (*Zichai ji*), *The Peony Pavilion* (*Mudan ting*), *The Dream of Nanke* (*Nanke ji*), and *The Dream of Handan* (*Handan ji*). These plays, collectively referred to as the "Four Dreams" (because the first two overlap), all develop the theme that life is but an illusion. *The Peony Pavilion* is the most admired of them all. In fifty-five scenes it tells a story of a young woman who pines her life away for a lover she has only seen in a dream; later, when he actually appears and falls in love with a portrait she painted of herself, she is resurrected. Her father, believing a deception is being practiced on him, has the lover arrested and beaten before harmony is restored. The play has great variety—a trial in Hades, combats, farcical episodes, suspense, and rescues—but is most noted for its love scenes and poetry. Personal letters and the prefaces to his plays make up a crucial part of Tang's theoretical writing. In addition to talking about the conception and intention of his plays, Tang revealed in these prefaces a great deal about his world outlook, his state of mind, and his linguistic styles. His preface to *The Peony Pavilion,* dated 1598, is considered a romantic manifesto. Also selected here is Tang's most important writing about theater, "Epigraph for the Theater God Qingyuan," in which he deals with a wide range of issues such as the origin and function of theater and the art of acting.

Preface to *The Peony Pavilion*

Has the world ever seen a woman's love to rival that of Du Liniang?

Dreaming of a lover she falls sick; once sick she becomes even worse; and, finally, after painting her own likeness as a legacy to the

Translated from *Mudan Ting,* ed. Xu Sufang and Yang Xiaomei (Shanghai: Gudian wenxue chubanshe, 1958), 1; "Yihuangxian xishen qinyuanshimiao ji," in *Zhongguo lidai julun xuanzhu,* ed. Chen Duo and Ye Changhai (Hunan: *Hunan wenyi chubanshe,* 1987), 148–49.

world, she dies. Having been dead for three years, still she is able to live again, when in the dark underworld her quest for the object of her dream is fulfilled. To be as Du Liniang is truly to have known love.

Love is of a source unknown, yet it grows ever deeper. The living may die of it; by its power the dead live again. Love is not love at its fullest if one who lives is unwilling to die for it, or if it cannot restore to life one who has so died. Why must the love that comes in dreams necessarily be unreal? There is no lack of dream lovers in this world. Only for those whose love must be fulfilled in bed, and for whom intimacy grows only after retirement from office, is it entirely a corporeal matter. . . .

Epigraph for the Theater God Master Qingyuan in the Yihuang County Temple

People are born with feelings. Melancholy, joy, anger, and anxiety, to name just a few, can all be aroused by small and subtle matters. Feelings can be expressed through chanting and singing and through body movements. Sometimes they are completely poured out, and sometimes they are pent up for such a long time that they make one restless. Since the phoenix, birds, beasts, and even those savages in southwestern China can all sing, dance, and revitalize themselves ingeniously, we human beings can certainly do so, too.

How great Master Qingyuan was! He performed the ancient sages' eight skills of acting and sang their thousand melodies.[1] He created the Tao (the Way) of theater. He started out as a comic actor doing satirical skits and then played various male and female stock characters in different plays—long ones of fifty acts as well as short ones of only four.

Theater creates heaven and earth, ghosts and deities. Theater can exhaust ten thousand possibilities of human characters and present a thousand changes in human history. Several actors on a stage, performing with all the ease, brilliance, rhythm, and grace, may show spectators the illusions of people a thousand years from now or scenes from any dream. They can make all people under the heaven happy or sad just by creating these illusions. The spectators react simultaneously and differently. Sometimes they like to comment or applaud; sometimes they become excited or feel exhausted. Sometimes they sit up straight to listen; sometimes they

---

1. In classical Chinese the number 8 as well as the numbers 1,000 and 10,000 indicate variety and/or plenty.

shake their heads in sneer. Sometimes they watch and chuckle quietly; sometimes they rush to the stage in a huge crowd. The rich and the privileged put aside their arrogance, even the poor and miserly vie to make charitable contributions. The blind hunger for sight, the deaf crave for sound, the mute want to shout, and the lame want to run. The impassive become passionate; the reticent speak with eloquence. The silent make noise; the noisy grow silent. The hungry feel sated; the drunk sober up. People walking stop; people sleeping wake up. The coarse become refined; the foolish become intelligent.

Theater reinforces the order between the emperor and his subjects, strengthens the tie between fathers and sons, improves the affection between the old and the young, and enriches the love between husbands and wives. Theater can express friendship, relieve conflict, soothe anxiety, and amuse the common people. A theatrical performance is usually requested by a devoted son to please his parents and elderly relatives and to entertain his ancestors. It is commissioned by a virtuous man to honor the emperor and to appease the spirits. Theater is there when the old pass away; theater is there as the young grow up. Wherever there is the Tao of theater, doors of the houses need not be locked, people's bad addictions can be reduced, plagues will not happen, and peace can be maintained. Theater pleasingly presents the supreme moral doctrine through rich human feelings, does it not?

I have heard that Master Qingyuan is a god from Guanko in Xichuan. He was an honorable man and obtained the Tao by performing among the people. Because there is not yet a temple erected for him, his disciples just have a few drinks and sing a little something in his honor before each performance. I always find it a disgrace. Scholars eulogize Confucius in his temples. The disciples of Buddha and Laozi[2] all have temples in which to worship their masters. Master Qingyuan is recognized to have obtained the Tao and his disciples reside everywhere under the sun. He is as great as the other masters aforementioned, but he does not have a temple! Would not this fact cause the nontheater music entertainers to ridicule his Tao as inferior?

The following is what I said to Master Qingyuan's disciples who are going to erect the temple for him: "Do you know how Master Qingyuan obtained his Tao? Concentration. Sit upright and clear the mind of random thoughts. Choose good teachers and companions; delve deeply into the written words and understand their rich meanings in the context of the

---

2. Laozi, sometimes spelled Lao Tzu, was the founder of Taoism.

entire play. Go out and observe closely the changes of heaven and earth, the changes of people, ghosts, and things. Then think calmly about them. Do not be tied down by obligations to parents and other family members. Do not indulge in sleeping and eating. If young, you should reserve your sperm and spirit so that your appearance can be improved. If older, you should eat plain food so that your voice can be preserved. If playing the female role, you should often imagine you were really a woman. If playing the male role, you should try to behave as if you were whom you play. In this way you will have total control of your voice; it could reach high above the clouds or be as subtle as the finest string. Its mellowness resembles pearls rolling, its continuity is like a spring gurgling. When a performance reaches the most exquisite point, one can hear the soundless and see the Tao as big as life. The performer/dancer does not know where his feelings come from, and the enraptured spectator does not know where his own mind has gone. The situation would be just like the famed performance in which a puppet's flirting with the royal ladies-in-waiting was so lifelike that the enraged emperor was ready to kill the master puppeteer. If your performance has entered such a realm, you are worthy to be called disciples of Master Qingyuan, for you too have obtained the Tao. Actors, really push yourselves so that the Great Master would not sigh in the yonder world saying that the Tao of theater vanished after his death."

I have written this epigraph for the temple of Master Qingyuan, the god of theater.

Pan Zhiheng on Acting

Pan Zhiheng (1556–1622), also known as Jingsheng, was a gifted poet, even though he was not successful during his lifetime. Pan pursued a carefree lifestyle as he traveled extensively up and down the Yangtze River, writing travelogues and forging friendships with writers and artists like Li Zhi, Tang Xianzu, Wu Yueshi, and many others. Pan was immersed in theater ever since childhood, as both his father and grandfather were connoisseurs of the theater. During his years of travel Pan saw a great deal of theater and put down his observations and comments in his book *Luanxiao Essays* (*Luanxiao xiaopin*), which has since become a classic of acting theory. In this book of essays Pan compared different schools of acting styles, critiqued individual performances and performers, talked about rehearsals, and discussed the nature of relationship between performers and characters and audiences.

Possessed by Emotions
(written to the two young performers after seeing them in
The Peony Pavilion)

If the court entertainers like Jester Meng and Shi could move the ancient kings deeply with their clever mimicries, how could not a play about true love performed with true passion touch our hearts profoundly?! My friend Tang Xianzu's play *The Peony Pavilion,* with its power of love that transcends life and death, has shaken up the world of arts and letters. My friend Wu Yueshi has staged the play with his own troupe of young performers. The production is so meticulously faithful to the words as well as the spirit of the play that it has captured all the evanescent, mystical, ambiguous qualities. I am certainly touched by Du and Liu's deep love, but I am impressed even more by master Tang as the visionary of our time.

Mister Wu [the owner/producer/director of the troupe] is inspired,

---

Excerpts translated from "Qingchi" from *Luanxiao xiaopin*, in *Zhongguo lidai julun xuanzhu*, ed. Chen Duo and Ye Changhai (Changsha: Hunan wenyi chubanshe, 1987), 175–76; "Xiandu," from *Luanxiao xiaopin*, in *Zhongguo lidai julun xuanzhu*, ed. Chen Duo and Ye Changhai (Changsha: Hunan wenyi chubanshe, 1987), 181–82.

but it takes performers like those two youngsters to embody the life and soul of the lovers, and it takes connoisseurs like Bingsheng to appreciate all that is subtle and profound about the play in performance. This production has made me realize how soul stirring is the love and passion in *The Peony Pavilion*. When I first read this play, over ten years ago, I raved about it to everyone as I passed it around, and anyone with a soft spot for love was moved to tears and was completely mesmerized. Later I saw a performance by Taiyi's troupe from Danyang. The young boy who played Liu seemed so possessed by the emotions of his role that his impersonation showed consummate understanding. It is, of course, Du Liniang's love and passion that is the most difficult to convey and explain. Her love is of an unknown source and takes on an uncharted course—real yet intangible, far yet near, departed yet living. Only those who are capable of becoming consumed by love are capable of feeling it deeply and then capable of portraying it. Du's love is genuine and full of fantasy and reverie. Liu's love is equally genuine, but it is bold and unrestrained. One achieves her love through the power of dream; the other expresses his love in real life. Because the love they feel is true and genuine, be it through dream or valor, anything is possible for them. Jiang and Chang, the two young performers from Wuchang, are not only capable of becoming emotionally possessed by their characters' love, but they are also capable of physically enacting their love—one dreamy and ethereal, the other bold and romantic—in a completely natural and unaffected manner.

The owner of the troupe [Wu] Yueshi is a man of great learning and refined taste. He used different experts during the rehearsal process, who took turns helping the performers understand the play, adapted the play for the stage, and planned the mise-en-scène. Through training, the performers' voices are smooth and supple like pearl strings, and their movements are elegant and graceful like divine beings.

Captivating Presence
(actress Yang is the sixth child in her family; her adopted stage name is Chaochao)

It is rare that a skilled performer possesses all three of the following qualities: talent, intelligence, and presence [or charisma].[1] Some have

---

1. Yang Mei was the actress whom Pan Zhiheng admired most. In another essay, "On Five Techniques of Yang Chaochao's Acting," he used Yang as an exemplary model to

talent but lack intelligence, thus rendering their talent witless. Some have intelligence but lack presence, thus rendering their intellect lusterless. It is extremely rare to see brilliance in all its dimensions standing in front of you as big as life.

Yang's stage presence surpasses all, and it is truly captivating![2] Yang is beautifully talented: her nature is pure and charming, her movement is agile and graceful, and her voice is soft and resonant. Yang is truly intelligent: she is quick in memorizing lines (on sight, in fact), grasping the meaning of a play, and making imaginative associations. Without a doubt Yang is stagestruck, always eager to perform and able to enter into an acting mode at the drop of a hat, but once onstage she is completely at ease and natural, in control of her own artistry, and in sync with the entire production. It is the ease of her captivating presence onstage that really sets Yang apart. It is this presence that adds wit to her talent and luster to her intellect.

illustrate some of the crucial points of good acting. In addition to talking about the importance of subtle yet expressive line delivery and stage movement, Pan gave priority to *du* and *si*. By *du* Pan was referring to an actor's appropriate awareness of the paradox of the self and the character. For Pan the better actor is the one who submerges the self in the character. By *si* Pan was concerned with psychologically motivating stage gestures.
2. Here the author made a pun with Yang's stage name, Chaochao, which means "to surpass" or "to be supreme."

WANG JIDE

From *Qu Lü*

Wang Jide (?–1623), also known as Boliang, was born into a scholar-gentry family, which was proud to "have in its library a collection of over a hundred Yuan Plays." He was at one time a student of Xu Wei, who appreciated in him a kindred spirit. While Wang was accomplished as a writer of several literary genres, including drama, his crowning achievement was his *Qu Lü* (*Principles of Lyric Drama*), a comprehensive theoretical book of dramatic aesthetics. The book, which took him over ten years to write and was finished only shortly before his death, in 1623, is the work of a lifetime spent traveling around the country, learning and exchanging views with other artists and scholars. The long-standing friendships he developed with great men of letters such as Shen Jing (1553–1610) and Tang Xianzu also contributed to the richness and depth of the book. Wang intended for his book to address some of the undesirable tendencies of his time, such as writers either not paying sufficient attention to the performance nature of theater or not creating works of high literary quality. Wang saw theater as a total art form that "puts music, lyrics, dance and songs on stage all at the same time." And he believed that a mature theater is characterized by a "written script" that is "presented in the same manner day in and day out." By writing the book, Wang endeavored to elevate the status of dramatic writing so that it would enjoy the same esteem traditionally reserved for poetry and literary prose. In forty chapters Wang dealt with a wide range of subjects in theater history, dramatic structure and technique, and critical theory. Of most theoretical significance are his seminal interpretations of such concepts as *bengse* (literally, "original color," natural quality, basic characteristic, essence, idiosyncracy), *fengshen* (literally, "wind" and "spirit," inspiration, *élan vital*), *xu* and *shi* (literally, "intangible" and "tangible," nonrealistic and realistic, nonmaterial and material, infinite and finite, imaginary and factual, indirect and direct, ambiguous and specific), and so forth. Some of his important ideas would be further elaborated and developed by later theorists, such as Li Yu of the Qing Dynasty.

On Styles

When lyric-drama began *bengse* was the only style of writing. One can see that easily by taking a look at *The Lute Song* or *The Moon-Worship*

Excerpts translated from *Qu lü*, in *Zhongguo xiqu lunzhu jicheng* (Beijing: Zhongguo xiju chubanshe, 1959), vol. 4.

Pavilion (Baiyue ting). But with *The Fragrant Satchel (Xiangnang ji)*, written by a writer of Confucian persuasion, emerged the so-called *wenci* (refined) style. The recent *Jade Pendant (Yujue ji)* by Zhen Luoyong is so intricate and ornate that the true essence is all but eclipsed.

Drama imitates and describes events and situations in life; it should reveal character and values through natural and subtle means of action rather than relying on fancy words. Elaborate stylistic embellishment only diminishes the true natural quality. But many members of the literati are so set in their extravagant ways that this "refined" style of writing is hard to eliminate. This is just like what happened to the classical prose when it gradually changed from the [natural and unaffected] Qin/Han style to the [ornate and artificial] style typical of the Six Dynasties period.

Generally speaking, if a play relies only on the natural simplicity, it can easily become dull; if a play employs only the literary refinement, it is hurt by its own ostentation. *The Moon-Worship Pavilion* excels in its natural quality. *The Lute Song,* however, combines both the natural and the refined; there are natural rustic folksy songs as well as dazzling refined lyrics, which is the right way to go. *The Jade Pendant,* on the other hand, is not without brilliant lyrics, but the play is so full of scholarly cross-references that it utterly confuses the audience. Therefore, it is of foremost importance for a playwright to know first of all the basic direction of the play then flesh out the play and work on the problem areas. The drawback for the *bengse* is that the style is susceptible to vulgarity, while the *wenci* suffers from obscurity. The line between the elegant and the vulgar, between the profound and the shallow, is quite elusive. It all depends on the gifted writers to write carefully and wisely.

On *Fengshen*

Like the ancient rhyme-prose (*cifu*) and the contemporary form of eight-part essay, the lyric-drama has a central core, or design. It has a beginning and an end; it opens and closes. The writer must first establish the structure, the principal idea, and the selection and placement of lyrical modes and tunes; then the writer can start to write the words, lines, and whole speeches. One should not randomly concoct or put up with imperfection. A play should strive to be likened to a *changshan* snake whose head moves in concert with its tail; a good play can also be likened to the silk brocade weaved by the mythical mermaids who tolerate not even a single blemish. A play's idea should be fresh, language splendid, words resonant, and tunes harmonious. When a play is so perfectly put together and assumes a vigorous life of its own, it is fatal even to attempt to add or take away or change the order of a single tune. The wondrous spirit of all this does not reside within certain specific tunes or words but above and beyond. It is inexplicit, inimitable, and inexhaustible. When capturing joy, it is what elevates people to ecstasy, and, when depicting sorrow, it is what breaks people's hearts. It does not just please people; it moves; it touches. It is what we call *fengshen,* or grace or inspiration. The mark of a genuinely inspired work is when no one knows why it is so.

On Playwriting

The northern plays [or *zaju* of the Yuan Dynasty] and our southern plays [or *chuanqi* of the Ming Dynasty] have always been different in their forms. In the northern plays only one character sings, while in the southern plays all characters get to sing. As the only singing part, the talented performer has great freedom to display his virtuosity and emotions. Whereas when lyrics are sung by more than one performer, there are rules and regulations to be observed. No matter how talented, the performer does not have all the free rein. That is the reason it is crucial for the playwright to edit and rewrite. One should keep in mind the whole structure of a play, making each scene a component unit adorned by singing and spoken parts. Don't be predictable or totally off the wall. Don't get carried away by digression, because it slackens the central design, and the actors may take upon themselves to do the cutting. Don't try to rush either because it affects the natural tempo and rhythm. Don't let any character or any scene be out of place. It's essential to highlight and elaborate thoroughly the important actions. In the play *Huan Sha,* however, the critical incidents of the Yue King's tasting of bitter gall and his wife's picking of weeds are left out.[1] Also how could one let pass lightly such crucial actions as Hongfu's eloping or Ruji's stealing of the

---

1. Liang Chenyu's play *Huan Sha* was based on a well-known historical account of Yue King's regaining of power from his enemies and rebuilding his state. During exile he himself slept on the mat made of rough hay and ate the bitter-tasting gall daily. Upon returning home, he ordered his countrymen and women (including his wife) to go deep into the mountains to gather special weeds whose fiber they would weave into cloth to submit to the foreign ruler. All this is acutely to remind himself and his subjects of the humiliation and hardship they had endured under foreign rule.

battle plan?[2] Another mistake of not differentiating the important from the unimportant is to carry on with things that are so insignificant that people get fed up. When using the standard *gong* (palace) musical tunes, one should match them properly with the ongoing action, whether it is sorrowful, joyous, harsh, or happy. For instance, choose tunes such as *xianlu* or *shuangdiao* for scenes depicting sightseeing, and use *shangdiao* or *yuediao* for scenes expressing sorrow and grievance. It is easier to move people when the emotions and the musical tunes are well suited. The best plays are those combining perfectly the high literary value with the keen sense of performance conventions. Such plays do well onstage and are worthy of being passed on to posterity. Plays are merely second rate if they are hard for the general public to appreciate even though they are perfectly and cleverly worded and enjoyable to read over the desktop. If you cannot come up with something either elegant or natural and can only mix clichés with slang, then just don't bother to write.

[The following are selected from the two chapters entitled "Miscellaneous Commentaries" (MC). There are over one hundred short commentaries.]

When poet Bai Letian finishes a poem, he always reads it to some old woman. Then he asks, "Do you understand it?" If the answer is yes, he keeps the poem as it is. If the answer is no, he makes changes. It's the same with plays. They should be understood by old ladies first; then they will be understood by all audience members. That's what we call *bengse* (original color) [MC I, entry 44].

It is crucial that plays are truthful in conception but ethereal in expression.[3] Plays like *Min Zhu, Huan Sha, Hong Fu,* and *Yu He* are *shi,* that is, straightforward or literal, both in conception and execution. [Tang Xianzu's] *Huan Hun (Return of the Soul)*[4] and his two other dream plays, on the other hand, are *xu,* that is, flexible, creative, romantic, fanciful, and subtle in executing truthful *shi* visions. It is easy to use *shi* means to execute *shi* ideas, but it is more desirable and also more difficult to use the *xu* means [MC I, entry 45].

2. Here Wang Jide is referring to the omission of well-known historical incidents in Ming Dynasty dramatist Zhang Fengyi's *Hong Fu* and *Qiefu (Stealing the Battle Plan),* respectively.
3. The opening sentence points to the dichotomy between what is true and what is real. Because of the complex meanings of the words *xu* and *shi,* the opening sentence is sometimes interpreted to mean that, while the idea and vision of a play should be clear, the presentation itself should be flexible, evocative, and inclusive.
4. This is an alternative title often used to refer to Tang Xianzu's *Peony Pavilion* because of the leading female character's coming back from beyond the grave.

The plays by Yuan dramatists consist a great deal of anachronism, [which quite resembles the way of Chinese painting]. For example, Wang Wei puts [the blossoms of] peony, hibiscus, and lotus all into the same frame [even though each flower has a different blooming season]; Mo Ji sports palm trees in a scenic painting of snow. It is, of course, difficult to reason with a common person about this[5] [MC II, entry 9].

---

5. This is one of the earliest discussions of Chinese traditional theater in relation to Chinese classical brush painting, which is known for its *xieyi* (depicting essential meaning) characteristic as opposed to the *xieshi* (depicting surface reality) quality of realistic painting.

YUAN YULING

Foreword to The Story of Burning Incense

Yuan Yuling (1592–1670), also known by numerous pen names, was a late Ming and early Qing dramatist. He was dismissed from his official position when he offended his superior. He often deliberated about the theater in forewords he wrote for other writers' plays. The following is an example in which he discussed the importance of real human feelings and striking dramatic scenes.

The theater has never been flooded with as many inferior plays as today.

When commenting on the great Yuan dramas, Wang Yanzhou placed *The Moon-Worship Pavilion* up there right behind the plays by Wang Shifu and Gao Zecheng.[1] Even for a play like *The Moon-Worship Pavilion* he had a reservation: "It's a pity that the play couldn't bring people to tears." These words were spoken by a true authority on theater. The theater is a world unto itself, and it revolves around nothing but passions and desires. The theater is make-believe, but the passions and desires are real. Those onstage are open to passions and desires, especially the singers; the spectators, the young boys, blind old men, and village crones are open to passions and desires too. But, if the actors do not act with real passions and desires, the spectators cannot be expected to be swept off their feet, and, if the authors do not write about real passions and desires, the actors cannot be expected to deliver soul-stirring performances.

One word is all that is needed to describe *The Story of Burning Incense,* which is *real.* Why? Because nothing is not real in this play, from Guiying's devotion to Wang Kui's breaking up of their marriage, from Jin Lei's

Translated from "Fenxiang ji xu," in *Zhongguo lidai julun xuanzhu,* ed. Chen Duo and Ye Changhai (Changsha: Hunan wenyi chubanshe, 1987), 229. Ming Dynasty dramatist Wang Yufeng's play *The Story of Burning Incense* (*Fenxiang ji*) is a new adaptation of an earlier play, *Wang Kui Betrays Guiying* (*Wang kui fu guiying*). This new version tells a story about how intrigue and greed created rift and eventually destroyed the love between a young scholar named Wang Kui and a prostitute named Jiao Guiying.
1. Wang Yanzhou, also known as Wang Shizheng (1526–90), was a leading member of the Ming Dynasty literary elite. Here Yuan was referring to Wang's evaluations as they appeared in *Qu Zao,* a collection of his critical writings on the theater. Wang Shifu was the author of *The West Chamber Story,* and Gao Zecheng, also known as Gao Ming, was the author of *The Lute Song.*

lechery to Madam Xie's greed. The play so truthfully relates the ups and downs in life that it even brings tears to the eyes of strong men, who are joined by the sobbing young and old. The play should also be noted for several of its strikingly dramatic moments. One of those is the opening scene in which a down-and-out [Wang Kui] attacks the fortune teller with an ax. Another striking scene is the one in which Wang's intended, a former prostitute, feels and acts right at home in the inner chamber of an honorable young maiden. The taking of marriage vows is yet another striking scene. The scenes involving Jin Lei's intrigues—letter fraud, false death notice, and so on—are executed with escalating suspense and drama. From the beginning to the end the play resembles the raging Yangtze River, full of rises and falls and unexpected twists and turns. This is an exemplary play that deals with real passions and desires truthfully and dramatically.

ZHUO RENYUE

Preface to *The New West Chamber Story*

Zhuo Renyue (1606–36?), who also liked to sign his name as "Man in the Moon over the Southern Bank of Yangtze" (*Jiangnan yuezhongren*), was a late Ming literary man. Though a talented poet and playwright, Zhuo was unlucky in the examination halls. His professed pessimistic worldview often leads people to suspect that his early demise at age thirty was the result of suicide.

During his life Zhuo Renyue was in close contact with the leading dramatists of his time, such as Meng Chengshun, Yuan Yuling, and Xu Shijun, and was often asked to write prefaces to and critiques of plays. His preface to his own play *The New West Chamber Story* is a rare piece of classical tragic theory. The play itself is now lost, but the preface makes it clear that Zhuo rewrote the well-known play as a gesture of defiance against the propensity for bestowing happy endings or poetic justice to otherwise tragic plays.

In this world happy days are short and sad days are long, just as life is fleeting and death is eternal. It is all predestined. There is no stopping sadness from following in the wake of happiness or death in the wake of life. Plays nowadays, however, all begin with misfortunes, worries, and tears of partings but end with feasts and laughter of reunions. As if suffering would bring about endless happiness, as if encountering death would guarantee eternal life. It is utterly absurd!

The theater is supposed to do good for the world. The biggest good it can do is to help people rise above their fortunes and misfortunes and rise above life and death. Life and good fortune weaken us; death and tragedy strengthen us. No matter how appalling the suffering or how horrifying the death, if the theater keeps attaching happy endings to tragedies and offering life after death, what good does it do for the people and the world?

The ending of the original story of Cui Yingying was tragic,[1] so was the ending of Huo Xiaoyu, who died a tragic death.[2] There are countless

---

Translated from "Xin xixiang xu," in *Zhongguo lidai julun xuanzhu,* ed. Chen Duo and Ye Changhai (Changsha: Hunan wenyi chubanshe, 1987), 246.
1. This refers to the Tang Dynasty novel *The Story of Yingying* by Yuan Zhen. In the novel Zhang Sheng is forced to leave Yingying, who then has to enter into a marriage with Zhen Heng, whom she does not love.
2. This refers to the Tang Dynasty novel *The Story of Huo Xiaoyu* by Jiang Fang.

examples of such tragic endings in the genre of novel. Then why could not even dramatists as great and wise as Wang Shifu and Tang Xianzu be free from the convention [of happy endings]? When I read the novels I find my thoughts transported to the world beyond, but when I read the stage versions I find myself tied to mundane existence. It is clear which experience is more beneficial.

[Tang Xianzu's play] *The Purple Hairpin* is, generally speaking, still quite faithful to the novel on which it is based, except for the resurrection scene. *The West Chamber Story* has completely departed from the original novel. If the part that Wang Shifu wrote still retains some of the spirit of the novel, the part that Guan Hanqing supposedly wrote definitely does not.[3] In dramatizing my *New West Chamber Story,* I followed the original novel's story line, which is backed up by the discovery of Cui and Zhen's tombstone[4] and corroborated by the *Weizhi Chronicle.*[5] I dare not to compete with [the authors of various previous versions of *West Chamber Story* such as] Dong, Wang, Lu, and Li. Neither do I dare to appropriate one single word of theirs.[6] I am just presenting the unembellished story, which gives the audience more than enough to commiserate. What the two leading characters say in the novel by Yuan [Zhen] points to the inevitable ending of the story: Cui herself says: "It begins in chaos and ends in abandonment, just the way it goes." [Zhang] says this exceptionally beautiful creature "will bring catastrophe to either herself or others." It is ever so true, and it is what I want to reveal.

---

3. At one time it was popularly believed that Wang Shifu only finished the first four acts of *The West Chamber Story,* and it was Guan Hanqing who wrote the final fifth act.
4. Apparently, during the Ming Dynasty a tombstone bearing the words "Mr. Zhen of Yingyang and his wife Cui of Boling," inscribed by Qing Guan of the Tang Dynasty, was excavated in Henan Province. Because the names Cui and Zhen coincided with the characters Cui Yingying and Zhen Heng, some people assumed that they were the same couple.
5. This refers to the *Yuan Weizhi Chronicle* compiled during the Song Dynasty by Wang Xingzhi.
6. Here Zhuo Renyue is referring to Dong Xieyuan of Jin, Wang Shifu of Yuan, and Li Rihua and Lu Cai of Ming.

ZHANG DAI

From *The Tao Hut Dream Memoirs*

Zhang Dai (1597–1685?) was best known as a literary essayist of the late Ming and early Qing periods. Zhang was also deeply interested in the theater of his time and had written or adapted scripts for the stage on many occasions. One of his many books, *The Tao Hut Dream Memoirs* (*Taoan mengyi*), is a collection of short essays and observations about the theater. It is a rare, historic document that vividly recorded the theatrical activities and practices of the late Ming Dynasty period. Two of the following excerpts are about two distinctive approaches to acting by two great performers to whom Zhang was very close. One developed complete emotional identification with her characters, while the other cultivated a detached and critical method of presenting his characters. In the third piece Zhang describes favorably scenic practices developed by some theater practitioners to create spectacular stage illusions.

Actress Zhu Chusheng

Zhu Chusheng was an actress of regional opera *diaoqiangxi* [in Zhejiang Province]. Her acting was vastly superior to her peers in the same profession . . . Though no great beauty, Chusheng had clear and striking features, and the beauty of her bearing was peerless. Her acting was noted for both subtlety and expressiveness: the movement of her eyebrows and eyelashes could poignantly convey arrogant aloofness or intense love. Her sensitive eyes and eloquent body language brought her characters to life physically and emotionally. Theater was her life, and she gave it all she could. She was always improving herself, never allowing a mistake to repeat itself. Chusheng loved to sit quietly by herself, letting her imagination carry her away. Sometimes she became so involved with the emotional life of her characters that she forgot herself. One day I was with her at Dingxiang Bridge: the sun was setting, the smoke [from kitchen chimneys] was rising, the trees and other vegetation were disappearing into shadowy obscurity. Chusheng lowered her head and was

Excerpts translated from "Zhu Chusheng," Peng Tianxi chuanxi," and "Liu Huiji nuxi," from *Taoan mengyi*, in *Zhongguo lidai julun xuanzhu,* ed. Chen Duo and Ye Changhai (Changsha: Hunan wenyi chubanshe, 1987), 251–53.

very quiet, tears pouring down. When I asked her what was wrong, she did not answer me directly. Chusheng experienced such vast emotions so deeply that she eventually died from them.

Actor Peng Tianxi

Peng Tianxi is well-known for his marvelous acting. Everything that he does or says, however, is thoroughly studied and well founded in its source or reason. Once, in order to do a play right, he spared no money or assets in retaining a master teacher. During his three springs in the West Lake area Tianxi toured to Shaoxing five times and gave fifty to sixty performances at my home alone; still, he did not exhaust his repertoire of talent.

Tianxi mostly plays clown and painted-face [villain] roles. When he impersonates those highly placed treacherous villains throughout history they become all the more ruthless, cunning, and dangerous. He gets inside the characters in order to externalize their evil through artful uses of his face, voice, and body. He characterizes the ultimate evil. Deceptive smiles and subtle spasms of the eyes and brows all help to capture the evil at its most heinous, menacing, and deadly. Being well versed in history and literature, widely traveled, and a discerning man of the world, Tianxi resents not being fully validated because evil and injustice is rampant. He finds in theater a means to venting his indignation and castigating corruption.

When I see a play so masterfully performed, I feel the urge to wrap it up in the best silk and keep it forever. It is just like enjoying a perfect moonlit night or savoring a cup of exquisitely brewed tea. You can only experience it for a fleeting duration, but you will treasure the moment forever.

Liu Huiji and His Women's Troupe

The appeal of women's troups seems always to come solely from the performer herself—her beauty, grace, mystique, and pleasing voice. It is quite different, however, with Liu Huiji's troupe. Liu sets out to create the kind of fantasy and spectacle that the theater has been lacking. The staging of one scene in *Emperor Tang Minghuang's Excursion to the Moon* (*Tang minghuang you yuegong*) is such an example. When Ye Fashan enters, the stage becomes instantly enshrouded in pitch darkness. With the sounding of a powerful thunderbolt a black curtain is drawn back to reveal a bright full moon. Sitting in the moon by the sweet osmanthus tree is the goddess Chang-e, accompanied by Wu Gang and the white rabbit, making the elixir [of eternal youth]. The moon is veiled with a sheer silk scrim and seems to be floating on multicolored clouds created by the lighting effect of goat-horn lamps in five different shades. Inside, several flares branded "Brighter than Moonlight" (sai yueming) are lit to achieve the brilliance and coloring of sunrise. A huge ribbon turns lavishly into a bridge to the moon. It is so miraculously spectacular that one forgets it is just a play. There are many other remarkable moments, for instance, the lantern dance. About a dozen people carrying one lantern appear and disappear, producing incredibly enchanting, dreamlike, and outlandish illusions. If Emperor Tang Minghuang were to witness this, he would surely be astonished and ask where all these glowing spirits onstage have come from! Peng Tianxi once made this remark to me: "When we have women's troupes like Liu Huiji's, why do we still need men's troupes! Why do we still need an actor like me, Peng!"[1] Tianxi is a theater man of very high critical standards and rarely gives endorsement. When he praises Huiji's troupe, his opinion is certainly not carelessly given.

---

1. Peng Tianxi was the same renowned kunqu actor of the late Ming and early Qing periods discussed by Zhang Dai earlier.

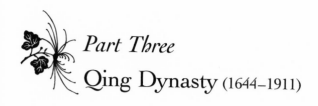

Part Three
Qing Dynasty (1644–1911)

DING YAOKANG

Some Notes on Playwriting

Ding Yaokang (1607–78), also called Xisheng and Yehe, was an early Qing Dynasty dramatist from Zhucheng, in Shangdong Province. Only four of his thirteen plays are extant. When one of his surviving plays, *Red Pine Journey* (*Chisong you*), was published, around 1649, Ding included with it a preface and a short essay entitled "Some Notes on Playwriting." These succinctly stated notes—"Three Difficulties," "Ten Don'ts," "Seven Musts," and "Six Pairs of Reversals"—proved very influential among the Qing dramatists as well as theorists interested in playwriting guidelines and techniques.

There are three difficulties in playwriting:

1. Developing a *structure* that is well proportioned with complicated scenes and simple scenes.
2. Creating a musical *rhythm* that is neither too fast nor too slow.
3. Making the *language* appropriate to given emotions and situations.

There are ten don'ts in playwriting:

1. Don't choke the life out of your work by merely reproducing the outward appearance of a calabash, so to speak.
2. Don't load your writing with fancy expressions that ring false in real human situations.
3. Don't develop too many plot lines lest they should crowd out the main action.
4. Don't use a dull and flat narrative that does not create spirit or mood.
5. Don't rhyme with words that are hard to enunciate or unsuited to standard musical tunes.
6. Don't write lyrics that are overly ornate and difficult to sing.
7. Don't try to dress up the vernacular and cause the unnatural union between the character and his speech.

Translated from "Xiaotai ouzhu cilie," in *Zhongguo lidai julun xuanzhu*, ed. Chen Duo and Ye Changhai (Changsha: Hunan wenyi chubanshe, 1987), 269.

8. Don't choose a subject matter that is too vulgar and offensive to good taste.

9. Don't be pretentious.

10. Don't show sorrow or joy so excessively that the audience gets fed up.

There are seven musts in playwriting:

1. You must have complications—ups and downs, twists and turns. They should not only be alive and well in the center of the play but also in each and every part, that is, in individual scenes, in individual arias, and in individual lines.

2. You must have composure. This applies not only to the regular male and female roles but also to the clowns and painted faces, because self-awareness does not disappear entirely when buffoonery and exaggeration take over.

3. You must have relevance. The story and the way in which it is communicated should be beneficial to our world, fostering good morals and values.

4. You must have loud and clear lyrics and tunes. You should eliminate obscurity and discord and create clarity and harmony like that of flowing water and singing nightingale.

5. You must have real situations. Anything that can be added on or removed is bound to smack of triteness. Cohesive plot lines and situations do not come from patchwork.

6. You must astonish people with the way you connect and juxtapose one scene to the other. You have to amaze people in order truly to touch and move them.

7. You must tightly unify your play. You are a true master when you take care to weave all the loose ends, clues, hints, innuendos, and so on into a logical web.

There are six pairs of reversals in playwriting:

1. Peace and turmoil.
2. Joy and sorrow.
3. Fortune and misfortune.
4. Virtue and vice.
5. Union and separation.
6. Prosperity and desolation.

LI YU

From *Li Liweng on Theater*

Li Yu (1611–80?), also known as Li Liweng, was a famous early Qing Dynasty writer, scholar, and man of the theater. Early in life Li was known as a prodigy, well versed in the classics and gifted in poetry, drama, and fiction. When Li passed, with flying colors, his first degree (*xiucai*) examination at age twenty-four, the Ming Dynasty was in its last years of sociopolitical instability before being toppled by the Manchus, a non-Han Chinese tribe from northeastern China, who established the Qing Dynasty. Caught in social turmoil, disappointed in the examination halls, and constantly beset by financial difficulties, Li, however, never lost interest in life and developed a reputation as a consummate connoisseur of the art of living. He took to writing in earnest, he opened the famed bookshop the Mustard Seed Garden, and he formed his own theater company of female performers, for which he acted as producer, manager, playwright, and director. Although both his plays and his company enjoyed considerable success, Li was not satisfied because he felt he had to make concessions to popular demands and financial constraints. Li's own ideas about theater and drama are well presented in his book *Casual Notes in a Leisurely Mood* (*Xianqing ouji*).

Casual Notes in a Leisurely Mood, first published in 1671, is considered by many critics as a book on the art of living, a comprehensive guide to dealing with the problems of human conduct. Li stresses that happiness is not a ripe fruit that drops into one's mouth by chance but is, rather, something to cultivate, to strive for. In eight chapters and two hundred and thirty-four subtopics ranging from playwriting, acting, architecture, gardening, landscaping, interior design, and culinary delights to clothing, personal grooming, and sexual needs, Li maps out a commonsense route by which he believes the average man and woman can live life to the fullest despite the vicissitudes of life. It is his views on theater, however, that have made the book an influential classic of aesthetics. In fact, the chapters on theater have often been grouped together to become an individual book, *Li Liweng on Theater.*

Li Yu's theory of the theater as stated in *Li Liweng on Theatre* is divided into three main sections: playwriting (*ciqiu*), the performance (*yanxi*), and performer's voice and appearance (*shengrong*). As for playwriting, Li deals chiefly with plot construction, the use of language, music, and prosody, dialogue, comic elements, and overall dramatic structure. Regarding performance and

Excerpts translated from *Xianqing Ouji,* ed. Shan Jinhang (Hongzhou: Zhejiang guji chubanshe, 1985).

performers, Li discusses the selection of scripts, adapting scripts, directing techniques, the selection and training of performers. Behind the appearance of disorganization and rambling, we see a knowledgeable man of the theater speaking about the importance of drama as a literary genre, the unique qualifications of a playwright, the consequences of the concept that a play is to be performed in front of an audience, the choices of subject matter and theme, plot development, characterization and language, the use of dialogue, and the use of comic elements. Furthermore, as a practical man of the theater, Li also deals with many of the problems related to the staging of plays and the training of performers. Both in scope and depth, *Li Liweng on Theater* was unprecedented in the history of Chinese theatrical criticism.

The Chapter on Playwriting (*Ciqu bu*)

Playwriting has been considered as the least important of literary skills, ranking just slightly higher than the hobbies like horseracing, swordfighting, wine tasting, or gambling. . . . I say a skill is a skill, big or small, and it should be valued by a person's proficiency in it. If you are really good at what you do, you can make a name for yourself . . . The writing of drama not only made writers famous, but it also captivated the attention of some former emperors, and, because of their skill in this literary genre, their names and statecraft have been remembered by posterity. Let history speak for itself: writers like Gao Zecheng and Wang Shifu were noted scholars of the Yuan Dynasty, but their fame rests primarily with their plays. Had the first not written *The Lute Song* and the second *The West Chamber Story,* who would have remembered their names today? It is *The Lute Song* and *The West Chamber Story* that have kept their names alive. Tang Xianzu, a genius of the Ming Dynasty, is noted for his poetry, essays, and correspondence, but he is a household name today not because of those works but because of his play *Return of the Soul* [another title of *Peony Pavilion*]. Had he not penned the play, Tang would not have been remembered. Each dynasty has been outstanding in one particular type of literary genre, as indicated by the pet but true phrases "Han History," "Tang Poetry," "Song Prose," and "Yuan Drama." Were it not for the tremendous output of plays including *The Lute Song* and *The West Chamber Story,* the memory of the Yuan, which was intrinsically wanting in any other achievements, would have quickly faded and certainly wouldn't have stood a chance of being esteemed by the learned together with the other three great dynasties. A dynasty's position in history rests on the plays that it produced. Therefore, while different from other genres, the art of playwriting is not a minor skill but ranks high, along with history, biography, poetry, and prose.

The Central Brain (*Li zhunao*)

What is the central brain of a play? It is nothing but the germ from which the author develops the work. In a play there are many characters, but they are all playing supporting roles to the single leading character, with whom the play originates. It is this character's experience of life's vicissitudes that unites the play from the beginning to the end; everything else, no matter how sensational, colorful, or complex, is there merely as an accompaniment. A play not only germinates from one single character; it comes from one single inciting incident related to that character. Taken together, this character and this incident make up the central brain of the play. Only when this character and this incident are truly extraordinary can this play be worthy of passing from generation to generation, resulting in the eternal life of the character, the incident, and the author.

Let's take a look at *The Lute Song*. The leading character here is Cai Bojie, and the inciting incident is his taking as a second wife the daughter of the [powerful] Niu family in the capital.[1] It is from this single incident alone that many other subordinate incidents or plot lines develop—for instance, his parents' starving to death in the famine, his first wife Wuniang's fulfilling of her filial duties, his being deceived by a crook who did not deliver money, jewels, and letters to his parents, and Zhang Dagong's acting generously to the needy. [Cai's] second marriage to the Niu daughter is the central brain of *The Lute Song*. *The West Chamber Story* is another good example. Here the leading character is Zhang Junrui, and the inciting incident is his White Horse Rescue of [Cui Yingying],[2] from which all the other plot developments stem—such as the mother's promising of marriage, Zhang's expecting the blessed event to take place, [Yingying's maid] Hongniang's helping the lovers, Yingying's eloping with Zhang, and even the former suitor Zheng Heng's trying to break up the lovers. The White Horse Rescue is the central brain of *The West Chamber*.

Many of today's playwrights may know to write about one all-

---

1. For a brief plot summary, see page 41.
2. Early in the play Cui Yingying's mother promises her daughter's hand in marriage to whoever succeeds in saving her honor from the bandits. Zhang Junrui, who is already secretly courting Yingying, succeeds by getting his friend, the White Horse General, to undertake the rescue. Then the mother goes back on her word. The story goes on from there.

important character, but they often do not know how to start from one inciting incident. They enumerate this character's deeds one by one, as though they were spreading pieces of gold and jade all over the place. As individual pieces they are all fine, but they don't make a good full-length play, because they are loose pearls without a string, a house without a beam. When the author doesn't know where to begin, naturally the audience doesn't know what to follow. No wonder theater lovers have drifted away! Many writers make this mistake. Now that I have pointed it out, I hope the number will get smaller and smaller.

Unity and Wit (*Zhong jiqu*)

Unity and wit (*jiqu*) are two indispensable qualities in drama. The former is the internal spirit of drama; the latter is its external manifestation. Lacking these two qualities, a play is like a clay man or a clay horse, possessing only the shape of a living form without the breathing spirit— clearly, the result of a playwright's inferior craftsmanship. Such a playwright pads out his play line by line, forcing his audience to remember the play section by section. If the audience becomes in the least inattentive, it will be impossible to recall what the previous song or scene is about. Watching the second act, the audience will have no idea what is likely to happen in the next act. A play put together in such a disconnected and disunified manner is a waste of time both for the writer and the spectators, who suffer pain from having to strain their ears and eyes too much.[3] Eliminate disunity; eliminate pedantic and affected ways.

When I use the word *unity,* I don't simply mean that one scene follows another or that a single actor plays one character. Rather, I mean that the action of the play should be unified, coherent, and connected as the veins are by the blood that flows through them. Even seemingly unrelated incidents should have hidden connections to the main action that gradually become evident, just as the fibers of the lotus root remain intricately interconnected even though it has been snapped in half. Unity is essential.

When I say use wit and eliminate pedantry and affectation, I'm not just talking about romantic love stories. The same principle also applies to subject matters concerning loyalty, filial piety, moral integrity, and righteousness or dealing with the emotions of grief, pain, sorrow, and enmity. Wit refers to the ability to challenge authority, to do the unexpected, to make people laugh through their tears. . . .

---

3. For this particular paragraph, I have consulted extensively the translation by Nathan Mao and Liu Ts'un-yan in their book *Li Yu* (New York: Twayne Publishers, 1977), 118.

It takes a special gift to be a playwright. If someone is not endowed with this gift, he is simply not suited to be a playwright, no matter how hard he tries. It's really not hard to tell if someone is gifted or not. You will know by observing how this person speaks and writes. If his conversation is not pedantic, he will show his inventiveness in one or two sentences out of every ten; if his writing is not wooden, he will have one or two paragraphs that are truly inspired in every essay. If he is also endowed with great imagination, then this person is suited to write plays. If one is not born with such gift, he is far better off doing something other than trying to write plays.

Beware of the Superficial (*Jie fufa*)

Drama is the most complex form of writing. There are so many different things to attend to, for instance, creating distinct characters who come to life on the stage and developing credible situations and actions. I feel that the ability to handle "emotion" (*qing*) and "scene" (*jing*) constitute the two most important challenges for a playwright. Emotion is what is felt in each character's heart, whereas a scene is what is observed by everyone in the external world. One comes from the inside; the other comes from the outside. It is easy to depict a scene, but it is difficult to describe emotions. These two things are as far apart as heaven and earth. A person's emotions are his alone. Zhang San [Tom] feels differently from Li Si [Dick], and therefore their emotions have to be described differently. The external scenes, however, are shared by many. In describing spring and summer, a playwright needs only to distinguish them from autumn and winter. Gifted playwrights naturally devote themselves more to the hard work of conveying inner emotions and less to the easy job of describing external scenes. Those who excel in depicting mountain and river excursion scenes, in depicting moonlight and flower garden excursion scenes, will only succeed partially if they cannot handle the emotions of each of their characters.

The Truth of Language (*Yu qiu xiaosi*)

Of all literary endeavors playwrighting is the most heroic, most magnificent, most satisfying, and it even does wonders to one's physical well-being. Without this genre the gifted and talented would feel suffocated; the brave and the gallant would feel trapped. I was born into turmoil and accompanied by hardship from childhood to old age. Worries and anxieties temporarily leave me only when I write plays. On those occasions I feel not only that I am releasing my frustrations, but also that I am secretly becoming the happiest man between heaven and earth, reveling in so much luxury and glory that what is desired in real life all seems paltry compared to the illusions I create. If I fancy being a mandarin, I am gloriously promoted to the top at once. If I desire to leave office and live like a recluse, in a wink I am transported to the wooded hills. If I desire to be a genius poet, I become the reborn Du Fu or Li Bai.[4] If I desire to marry the most beautiful woman, I become the husband of Wang Qiang or Xi Shi.[5] If I desire to be a celestial being, I can make the Western Paradise[6] or the holy *Pengdao*[7] appear right in my study. If I desire to show loyalty and filial piety, I can make an emperor greater even than Yao and Shun,[8] and I can make a parent live even longer than Peng Jian.[9]

Writing in other literary genres, you can make an allegory only through various implicit means. If you have ten points of grievance, you can only express three or four directly. If you have eight buckets of talent, you can only pour out two or three. If you are just a bit unconventional and unhampered in expressing yourself, you are considered lacking in the proper Confucian composure, accused of being reckless and frivolous, thus ruining your chance of having your work reach every household. To write a play, on the contrary, is to say what you mean to say and to say all you want to say. The worst enemy for a playwright is the implicit and restraint.

To speak without inhibition is not as easy as it sounds. Language is the expression of the feelings of the heart. If you are to speak for a character, you must first explore the feelings of the character you are going to portray. And how can you put yourself in someone else's shoes without experiencing his dreams and obsessions? I put myself in my character's shoes and try to feel and think like him when I write the words for him to speak. I do this not only for upright characters but also for wicked characters. Thus, a virtuous character should speak like a virtuous character, and a vicious character should use language that reveals the evil thoughts he harbors.

In short, all subtleties of human emotion and thought should be evident in the kind of language a character uses. The words should ring

---

4. Du Fu and Li Bai, living in the Tang Dynasty, are considered the two greatest poets in the history of China.
5. Wang Qiang and West Shi are two legendary beauties.
6. A Buddhist term.
7. *Pengdao* refers to the Penglai Island, a fabled abode of immortals in Chinese mythology.
8. Yao and Shun are the first two great idealized kings in Chinese legend.
9. Peng Jian, known for his longevity, is said to have lived eight hundred years, according to ancient mythology.

true and be unique to the character. Do not use stereotypes or generalizations. Follow the lead of the narrative in *The Water Margin* (*Shui hu*)[10] and the drawings of Wu Daozi,[11] which are the best in this respect. Once a play is written in that way, it will certainly become popular, even if you do not intend it to.

The Chapter on Performance (*Yanxi bu*)

The only reason for writing a play is to have it performed onstage, and here success or failure depends on many factors.
[. . .]

Understanding the Play (*Jieming quyi*)

The meaning and the feeling of the arias should come across in the singing. Meaning comes from the plot, the action of the play. Having understood the plot and its meaning, a performer can then sing the words with conviction—a question is a question, an answer is an answer; a sad person looks distraught, a happy person seems exuberant, not vice versa. Moreover, there are all kinds of nuances in the use of the voice that affect the meaning and the feeling of a play. Nowadays, all an actor does in preparing to perform a play is to read it and then to sing it, no understanding actually being required. Some actors can perform the same play all day long for months, or even all their lives, and still not understand what or whom they are singing about. They only sing with their mouths, without using their minds. An aria that comes straight from the mouth but is not reflected in the facial expressions or body movements deprives the play of its meaning and feeling. Like children reciting the classics by rote, it is forced and unnatural. Even if the melody and rhythm are extremely precise and the elocution absolutely clear, such a performance is not of the highest quality, only second-rate or worse.

Any actor wishing to perform a play well must ask a good teacher to explain its meaning clearly. If the teacher is not clear, ask the author or a good scholar for help. Start singing the words only after clarifying what they mean. While performing, concentrate on the spirit of the play throughout and strive for maximum truth and naturalness. . . .

---

10. *The Water Margin* (*Shui hu*), written in the early Qing Dynasty by Shi Nai'an, is one of the best classical novels in China.
11. Wu Daozi was a famous painter from the Tang Dynasty.

Coaching Speech (*Jiaobai*)

Almost all acting coaches and their students agree that learning to sing arias is difficult and learning to speak dialogues is easy. It seems that, if you can read a dialogue fluently, you can speak it well too. As for an aria, you have to read the lyrics fluently and sing it dozens of times before you can really sing it well. Therefore, it seems obvious that singing is much more difficult than speaking. I, however, do not think this is true. Singing is difficult but also easy. Speaking is easy but also difficult. To know that speaking is difficult will actually make it easier, whereas to assume that speaking is easy will make it more difficult. In singing an aria, the pitches, tones, and rhythms have fixed rules for one to follow, because they are written precisely in the scores and taught strictly by teachers. Once accustomed to these rules through standard training, a performer will naturally do things the right way. But, in delivering a spoken passage, the pitches, tones, and rhythms are not governed by fixed rules. One can imitate teachers, who, unfortunately, most likely learned the speeches only haphazardly on their own when they them-selves were neophytes. So how can they teach their students properly? Vagueness vaguely taught becomes a vicious cycle. The proper ways of delivering dialogue are not clearly explicated. No wonder people assume that speaking fluently is good enough and quite easy. As far as I can tell in the Pear Gardens,[12] at least 20 to 30 percent of the performers are good singers but only 1 or 2 percent of the performers are good speakers. The one or two are good at delivering speeches not because they themselves are actually knowledgeable but because their teachers are well grounded. The choice of a good teacher is crucial. . . .

The spoken words of a play are just ordinary speech, but there are principles governing its delivery. Let's look at everyday speech. When a learned person speaks, one sentence is worth ten; when an ignorant person speaks, ten sentences may not be worth even one. It is all a matter of conviction, the ability to convey precisely one's point. The speech of a play is fictional, but the delivery also requires the ability to convey the point precisely. It is like asking someone to pass along a message: if the messenger delivers your message properly, he helps the matter; if not, he wrecks it. Proper speech delivery is possible if the following principles are correctly applied. . . . We know that speech varies in pitch and cadence. As for when it should be high and rising or low and falling, the answer is the same as that for singing. In an aria

---

12. The Pear Garden (*Liyuan*) refers to the theater academy and the acting profession.

there is the difference between the primary words and secondary, or subordinate, words. When singing, the primary words are sung with a higher pitch and given more emphasis, while the secondary words receive a lower pitch and less emphasis. The same principles also apply to the delivery of spoken words. The primary words should be spoken emphatically with a higher pitch, whereas the secondary words should be spoken in a lower and more subdued tone. This is a golden rule as well as the most workable and simple approach to speech delivery.

Getting Rid of Senseless, Old Clichés (*Tuotao*)

There are countless clichéd practices in the theater, some of which are very odd. It is particularly ridiculous that some extremely trite and vulgar devices are imitated by thousands of theater people, becoming fixed conventions. If it is ludicrous to try to look beautiful by imitating West Shi's famous melancholic countenance, it is even more absurd to copy East Shi's infamous frown. Theater depends on novelty and freshness to keep from being predictable to the audience. If every actor performs in the same way and everything looks the same, the audience does not need to see the performance to know the play. When clichés are used, the suspenseful scenes would not arouse suspense, nor would the touching scenes move the audience. Some long-established comic routines can still make people laugh, but the laughter comes from the recognition of the expected, seen before in other plays, not the pleasure of seeing the novel or unexpected.

Recently costumes in the theater have become excessively extravagant and ostentatious. Generally speaking, it seems unreasonable to ask for frugality and modesty in a business that is meant to dazzle and entertain. What is peculiar, however, is that women's dancing costumes, which are supposed to be light and soft, have become as bulky and hard as suits of armor—they boast of wide and thick shoulder pads, double-layered dresses with additional gold embroidery and silk brocade, and "modesty" shields for the back and front of the lower body. This is sheer madness.

Costumes should be light and soft, easily flowing along with the moving body. As for the embroidery on costumes, only two patterns are appropriate: the phoenix and birds for the upper part, and white and rosy clouds for the lower part—the well-established "clouds-and-feathers-costume." Mixing with gaudy colors and ornaments is not acceptable. I am making no innovation here; I am simply trying to restore a good and sound tradition.

The Chapter on Actor Training (*Shenrong bu*)

Literacy and Artistry (*Wenyi*)

To acquire artistry one must acquire literacy first. It is not that one should learn the difficult subject first so that what comes next becomes easy; it is, rather, that mastering the easier subject will help one tackle a more difficult one later on. Everything under heaven has a key that opens it. What is the key? It is literacy and reason. One key usually opens only one door, yet the key of literacy and reason can open thousands of doors. It is because every profession between heaven and earth has its key in literacy and reason. I advocate this idea not only for the women I am training. In fact, it is applicable to everyone—scholars, farmers, workers, merchants, and so on.

It may already seem rather simplistic to think that the two words *literacy* and *reason* can solve all the problems in the great big world. But I still wish to point out that one of the two words is more fundamental than the other. People acquire literacy not for its own sake but as a step toward reason. Once a person enters the door of reason, the key of literacy can be put aside. There are countless numbers of trades and professions under heaven, and the ability to understand reason is the key to every one of them. To acquire artistry or skill is easy for those who understand reason and very hard for those who do not; the disparity is comparable to that between heaven and earth. And, if one is illiterate or does not read, how can one understand reason? That is why to acquire artistry one must first acquire literacy.

To help the female performers understand poetry one must ask them to read a lot. Once an actress has read so much that she sounds as if poetry rolls naturally off her tongue, the poetic mood and emotion will spontaneously come through. The development of both her wit and reason all depends on the quality of poetry that she reads.

Singing and Dancing (*Gewu*)

In the old days the masters of song and dance taught their girls singing and dancing not for its own sake but to help enhance their vocal abilities and natural gracefulness. Singing helps to cultivate a sweet and clear voice. Once having learned to sing well, the actress, even when speaking casually, will sound like a mesmerizing nightingale, there is music and song in the spoken words. Dancing helps to train a graceful and flexible body. Once having learned to dance well, the actress, even when walking or turning casually, will move like dancing willows and smiling flowers; there is grace and rhythm in the movement itself.

I have said that the way a woman carries herself is something she is born with, not something she can learn. Then why am I talking about studying *tai* [manner, attitude, posture, carriage, or bearing]? Because there is a difference between manners in real life and those on the stage. A girl at home conducts herself freely and naturally, but on the stage her bearing only seems natural but is actually carefully controlled. This is the result of study and training.

Everybody knows that a *sheng* (male character type) has a *sheng's* prescribed manners, a *dan* (female character type) has a *dan's* prescribed manners, and so do the other stock character types. While it is the same for male performers, I am here mainly talking about female performers. When a male performer impersonates a woman character, he has to accentuate his transformation, manners and all, or else he cannot pretend to be a woman. When a female performer plays a woman character, it's very important for her not to be artificial but, instead, natural and subtle; otherwise, she would be like a man playing a woman. Someone may ask how can a woman be artificial when she is playing a woman? This person doesn't know that oftentimes when a female performer goes onstage she self-consciously assumes a reserved and dignified manner. While she sees herself as being reserved and dignified, the audience sees her as being artificial. She must be asked to forget that she is acting on the stage and to imagine that she is at home going about her usual business. Only in this way can she avoid being artificial. If it takes some doing for a female performer to play a woman character well, it is even harder for her to play a male character, particularly the minor male character types such as an old man or a clown. It is not hard to play those male types in situations in which the male character is sitting, lying in bed, or happily chatting away. What is hard is when action requires that the male character move about or cry big tears. Female performers cannot make strides because of their bound feet, and they cannot look wan and sallow because of their pretty young faces. The old saying goes: "One playing a dragon should look like a dragon, and one playing a tiger should look like a tiger." But, rather than having people laugh at her because outwardly she does not resemble the male character type she is playing, a female performer should try to get closer to her character inwardly. If she puts herself in her character's shoes and lives the part, the female performer will win praises because she embodies his spirit and expresses his emotions truthfully and accurately.

LI YU

A Monologue from *The Flounder*

The following excerpt is a monologue from Li Yu's play *The Flounder* (*Bimuyu*), a love story about the actress Liu Miao Gu, who delivers the speech, and the scholar-actor Tan Chuyu.

Ever since I became secretly engaged to Mr. Tan, I have been so happy that I have finally found the man to spend the rest of my life with. What makes me even happier is that he has changed from playing *jing* [painted-face roles] to playing *sheng* [young male roles]. Contrary to other performers who much prefer loafing off the stage to performing on the stage, we are really pleased when we get to go on the stage and truly dread it when we have to get off. It is because off the stage we have to stay apart to guard against gossip, but on the stage we are together as husband and wife. On the stage he adores me as his real wife, while I love him as my real husband, and everything comes deep from the heart and goes deep into the heart. The others think we are just acting, but he and I are doing it for real. When a performance becomes real life, when the performers are the happiest doing it, how could it help but be the best performance there is? No wonder this troupe's reputation is getting better and better every day.

Translated from "Bimuyi liumiaogu bai," from Bimuyu, in *Zhongguo lidai julun xuanzhu,* ed. Chen Duo and Ye Changhai (Changsha: Hunan wenyi chubanshe, 1987), 308.

JI YUN

From "Actor and Character"

Ji Yun (1724–1805), also known as Xiaolan, was a prominent scholar of the Qing Dynasty. For over a decade he was the editor-in-chief of the famous *Siku Quanshu* (*Great Encyclopedia* [1772]), personally responsible for the *Siku Encyclopedia Catalog Abstract* (*Siku quanshu zongmu tiyao*) and the *Siku Encyclopedia Concise Catalog* (*Siku quanshu jianming mulu*). Ji Yun also wrote numerous verses and short essays and recorded fictional or actual stories, mostly supernatural tales.

In the year 1747 a dignitary once asked an actor whom he really admired: "There are so many of you in your profession; why are you the only one who is really good on the stage?" The actor replied: "When I impersonate a female on the stage, I not only try to look like a female in my physical appearance; I also try to feel like a female in the depth of my heart. It's the tender emotions together with the sweet and delicate demeanor of a female that enthralls the audience. If I keep my male feelings, even just a trace, it will betray my true self; then how can I compete for the audience's affection for feminine beauty and guile? When I play a chaste female, I fill my heart with purity and virtue, so, even if I am having fun joking and laughing I do not lose my chaste inner core. When I play a morally loose female, I fill my heart with lust, so, even if I am sitting stately, I cannot hide my loose nature. When I play a noble female, I fill my heart with dignity, so, even if I am dressed in plain clothes, I retain my nobility. When I play a plebeian female, I fill my heart with pettiness, so, even if I am outfitted in grandeur, I still personify vulgarity. When I play a kind female, I fill my heart with loving tenderness, so, even if I am angry, I do not behave harshly. When I play a fiery female, I fill my heart with willful hot temper, so, even if I am obviously in the wrong, I cannot be humble in my words. I always put myself in the shoes of my characters, completely identifying with their emotions: happiness, anger, sorrow, or joy as well as kindness,

Excerpt translated from "Xinxin zaiyiyi," from *Yuewei caotang biji,* in *Zhongguo lidai julun xuanzhu,* ed. Chen Duo and Ye Changhai (Changsha: Hunan wenyi chubanshe, 1987), 336.

resentment, love, or hate. When I don't simply play the role but really live the part of my character, the audience accepts me as such too. The reason I am the best on the stage is because I am different from the other female impersonators, who may look and move like their female characters but do not feel like them."

JIAO XUN

From *Huabu Nongtan*

Jiao Xun (1763–1820), also known as Litang, was a prominent Qing Dynasty philologist whose encyclopedic scope of knowledge also branched into history, theater, mathematics, and phonology, among other things. Residing serenely in a rural village for more than ten years, he wrote over forty books on various subjects, including two on theater, *Ju Shuo* (*On Theater*) and *Huabu Nongtan* (*Peasants on Regional Folk Theater*). The former is a six-volume selection of critical writings on the subject of theater throughout Chinese history; the latter is a collection dedicated to the "lowbrow" regional folk theater. Jiao was the first theorist to laud the merits of the diverse, vital, and popular regional theater forms.

Preface to *Huabu Nongtan*

It is the vogue in theater circles to admire the accent and tunes of *kunqu* opera.[1] *Huabu,* the collective label for various regional operas using local accents and tunes, is dismissed as gibberish because of their popular nature. I for one, however, am particularly fond of *huabu*. It is true that *kunqu's* accent and tunes are delicate, intricate, soft, and harmonious, but the listeners can hardly understand what is being said without the help of a written script. Also, except for about ten plays such as *The Lute Song, Killing a Dog* (*Sha gou*), *The Dream of Handan* (*Handan ji*), and *A Handful of Snow* (*Yipeng xue*), *kunqu's* repertoire is not all that worthy because it consists mostly of ignominious affairs between the sexes, as in the likes of *The West Chamber Story* and *The Red Pear Blossom* (*Hong lihua*). *Huabu,* on the other hand, descends directly from the Yuan drama and mostly deals with compelling issues of loyalty, filial piety, chastity, and righteousness. Even women and children can understand *huabu* because the language is natural and straightforward. People are moved and excited by *huabu* because the musical tunes are invigorating and generous.

Excerpts translated from *Zhongguo gudian xiqu lunzhu jicheng* (Beijing: Zhongguo xiju chubanshe, 1959), 8:225, 230–31. The heading is added by the editor/translator.
1. Because *kunqu* was first established in the Wuzhong area in southern Jiangsu Province, people sometimes referred to it as *Wuyin* (Wu-accent), as Jiao did in this preface.

It has been a long tradition that in the second and the eighth month of the year the villages outside the city would host performances, one after another. Old peasants and fishers all come to enjoy themselves on these occasions. Since the success of the popular actor Wei San from Sichuan, other performers like Fan Da [*sic*] and Hao Tianxiu have followed his suit and have even brought popular folk theater to the outlying villages. I am very pleased that the popular regional operas have seen a revival in recent years. I often take my old wife and young grandchildren with me on a little boat, rowing along the lake to catch various performances.

During work breaks in the heat of the summer the villagers gather in the shades of willow trees and beanstalk sheds. They tell stories, which more often than not come from the *huabu* plays they have seen. When I join them and clarify a few things for them about the plays, they always show their appreciation with warm applause and big smiles. A village scholar has taken notes of these gab sessions and has shown them to me. These are just some *nongtan,* or peasants' talk, not to the level of refined readers, I say. After some cutting and trimming, here is what is left of the notes.

This preface is written by me, the master of the house named Diaogulou,[2] on the first day of autumn, the eighteenth of the sixth month in the lunar calendar, of the year 1819.

A Review of *Sai Pipa*

The *huabu* play that I like best of all is *Playing the Lute (Sai Pipa),* the story about Chen Shimei deserting his wife.

Chen has elderly parents and is married with children when he leaves home to take the imperial examination at the capital. After he passes the exam with flying colors, he accepts the emperor's daughter's hand in marriage. He abandons not only his wife but his parents as well. His wife cares for the parents when they are living and gives them proper burials when they pass away, just like lady Zhao in *The Lute Song.* She then takes the children with her to the capital, but Chen refuses to recognize her and the children. He is so infatuated with the prestige and privilege of being the son-in-law of the emperor that he certainly does not want to risk losing them by acknowledging his wife and children. In

2. Jiao spent the last decade of his life writing in this country house away from the distractions of cities and towns.

return for food the wife plays the lute on the streets of the capital, singing about her abandonment by her husband. This catches the attention of Prime Minister Wang. When attending Chen's birthday party, Wang says: "There is a woman very good at playing the lute. Let's bring her in here for the celebration." Chen is stunned when the lute player turns out to be his country wife. He harshly orders her out and gives Prime Minister Wang a good tongue lashing. Once back at home Wang sends his attendant with all the gifts given him by Chen to the inn at which Chen's wife and children are staying. Wang also has the attendant tell her: "Your husband cannot very well acknowledge you in public, but, if I bring you to him in the dark of the night, he will take you back for sure." She enters Chen's new residence undeterred. This is not only because the gatekeeper dares not disobey Prime Minister Wang's order but also because Chen experiences momentarily a sentimental attachment to his past.

In the end, however, he decides that his imperial alliance is more valuable, so he rejects his wife. The wife falls on her knees as she pleads: "I can go away, and you don't have to worry about my life or death, but these children are your own flesh and blood, please keep them and take care of them, I beg you." Chen gets all choked up at first, but upon further deliberation he turns nasty and orders the gatekeeper to throw his wife and children out. Considering his wife and children huge inconveniences to him, Chen sends assistants to kill them at the inn late at night. As soon as he gets wind of the plot, the innkeeper helps the wife and the children escape and hide in the temple of the Three Warrior Gods. The wife takes off her own clothes to cover the children and proceeds to commit suicide by hanging herself. She is saved by the three warrior gods, who also teach her and the children the secrets of warfare. Because of their meritorious service to the Xixia military expedition, the wife and the children all receive high honors and great fortunes. In the meantime Prime Minister Wang is outraged when he hears about Chen's assassination attempt, so he brings charges against Chen for concealing from the emperor the fact of his previous marriage. Chen is promptly sent to jail. When the wife returns triumphantly from the battle with her children, she is asked to pass rulings on a few cases, including Chen Shimei's. The wife is sitting high on the chair reserved for generals, while Chen squirms on the floor of the court room in ropes and prison garb. When he recognizes that the judge is his former wife, Chen is so ashamed that he wishes that he could find a hole to crawl into. The wife cites his crimes one after another, reprimanding him on and on to her heart's content.

I have never seen anything more satisfying than the "Woman Judge" scene in *Playing the Lute,* not even the "Interrogation of Maid Hong" scene in *The West Chamber Story,* in which the maid turns on the old mistress, to everyone's delight. *The West Chamber Story* is really not to the taste of the respectable because of its salacious sexual nature. *Playing the Lute,* on the other hand, up until the turning point in the Three Warrior God's temple we endure with the protagonist all her misery, hardship, and unspeakable indignity; now that we hear her vindication clear and loud, it is like instant recovery from a long illness; it is like having the ultimate scratch of an unbearable itch; no words can describe this kind of pleasure and satisfaction, which *The Lute Song*[3] does not provide. The audience of *Playing the Lute* should not only see Chen's contemptibility but also his remorse at times. It is not difficult for a good actor to play how cruel he is toward his wife and children, but the true challenge lies in how convincingly he can convey his sense of guilt. It only increases his self-loathing by lashing out at Prime Minister Wang and trying to kill his wife and children in the dark of night. One false step brings ever-lasting grief. The warning bell is sounded loud and clear for all to take note. In this respect *The Lute Song* by Gao Ming is also found wanting.

---

3. For a brief plot summary, see page 41.

LI DOU

From *Yangzhou Memoirs*

Li Dou, also known as Beiyou and Aiyi, was an eighteenth-century dramatist, active around the time of Emperor Qianlong and Emperor Jiaqing. His eighteen-volume *Yangzhou Memoirs,* written during a period of over thirty years, is a collection of personal observations of social, cultural, and economic activities in his hometown, Yangzhou, an important center of arts and commerce. The fifth volume of the book is on theater, in which Li pays attention not only to performances of both the elite *kunqu* and various popular *huabu* forms but also to some little-known but interesting information of the behind-the-scenes activities, internal organization of theater troupes, the makeup of the orchestra, the troupe's wardrobe, and so on. In the following excerpt Li talks about the prominence of young female and clown roles in the popular *huabu* theater and the wide range of the clown's comic line of business.

Of all lines of business in *huabu* the young female roles and clowns, especially the acrobatic clowns, are the most prominent. The roles of young warriors and painted faces are next in the hierarchy. In contrast, the roles of elderly and middle-aged men do not even have separate categories, simply designated as male parts. Likewise, the roles of elderly and proper women are jointly labeled female parts.

The clowns specialize in generating comical gags, both verbal and physical. The characters they create range from wily tricksters to vulgar philistines, from bumblers to slow-wits, from cunning merchants to shameless rascals, all spouting some hilarious mixture of regional dialects that just keeps the audience in stitches. The limitation of local colors and dialects, however, also contributes to each individual regional folk theater's not having influence as widespread as that of *kunqu*. The Beijing school is an exception, since mandarin is used in delivering comic speeches, thus making its clowns the most favored. For instance, whenever Lin Yunpu appears on the stage in his clown getup the audience cheers incessantly. By the way Lin also happens to be a masterful poet and calligrapher from a prominent family. Likewise, Liu Ba from

Excerpt translated from *Yangzhou huafang lu,* in *Zhongguo lidai julun xuanzhu,* ed. Chen Duo and Ye Changhai (Changsha: Hunan wenyi chubanshe, 1987), 362–63.

Guangdong province is an accomplished scholar and equestrian who comes to the capital for the imperial exams but falls in, instead, with the Beijing troupe and becomes a consummate clown. I have personally witnessed the supreme caliber and broad popularity of these clowns, far surpassing other indigenous regional performers. Our own local clowns, from Zhang Podou, Zhang Sanwang to Dou Zhanger and Zheng Shirun, all had followed in the footsteps of Wu Chao and Wan Dacha, limiting themselves to amusing only the villagers with local tales in regional dialects. The practice remained in this fashion until last spring, when the local company engaged Liu Ba, and the other clowns began to imitate him by learning to use mandarin and expanding repertory.

Here are a couple of examples of Liu Ba's exceptional artistry. One play that showcases his talent is *The Senior Scholar from Guangdong* (*Guang ju*). The story goes: on his way to attend an imperial exam the senior scholar from Guangdong finds himself in the company of a debauched scholar staying in the same inn. When lured by a group of prostitutes, the senior scholar first resists in the name of morality and superiority. Bit by bit, however, he succumbs to sexual temptation and ends up losing literally even the shirt off his back. Liu vividly personifies the foolishness of the old pedant. Liu's superb handling of an elaborate range of comic stage business in *Officer Mao Takes a New Post* (*Mao bazong shangren*) is another remarkable example. Officer Mao is newly appointed to the post of provincial deputy chief because of his meritorious service in flood control. In the presence of his superior commander he plays the mousy clown; in front of ordinary soldiers he acts the part of a haughty clown; when passed over in promotion by his subordinate, he alternately impersonates the clowns of envy, jealousy, and embarrassment; upon hearing his own promotion, he becomes the grateful clown; when in the company of fellow officers, he puts on the face of a self-satisfied clown; when talking about his past, he parodies being hardworking; when coaching soldiers in archery, he mimics irritation; when greeting guests, he simulates the lack of proper protocol; when called upon by the superior commander, he turns into the clown in a stupor with shaky knees. Liu Ba is just so vivid and versatile as a clown.

HUANG FANCHUO

From Pear Garden Basics

Huang Fanchuo was an eighteenth-century theatrical actor, performing around the time of Emperor Qianlong and Emperor Jiaqing. Based on his lifelong experience onstage he wrote a book about acting, which became well-known as *Pear Garden Basics* (*Liyuan yuan*) after his friend Zhuang Zhaokui helped to revise and expand it. Later Huang's students also put out a new edition based on the original manuscript. The book existed only in handwritten copies until 1917, when the first typeset printed version was published. The book remains valuable because it was written by an accomplished actor who was able to articulate the guiding spirit of the art he practiced. The book has four main sections. The "Ten Mistakes in Acting" ("Yibing shizhong") deals with what Huang considers the ten most common malpractice in acting—namely, "not standing straight," "over-acting," "not knowing the true meaning of the words," "mispronouncing words," "weak enunciation," "stiff neck," "raised shoulders," "inflexible waist," "moving around too much," and "vacuous facial expression." The "Eight Principles for Movement and Expression" ("Shengduan bayao") is excerpted here. Two sections are devoted to the "Six Principles for Spoken Words" ("Qubai liuyao") and the "Six Key Points from Treasure Mountain Collection" ("Baoshanji liuze"). The latter is apparently a selection of remarks on acting from a book entitled *Treasure Mountain Collection,* which Huang deems valuable.

Eight Principles for Movement and Expression

[The eight principles are as follows:] Distinguish the eight chief character types; understand the four major emotional states; let the eyes lead; sway the head slightly; take steady steps; articulate with hand gestures; watch yourself in the mirror; and finally do not allow any idle day. [Now I will discuss each of them one by one.]

You should carefully distinguish the characteristics of the following eight types of individuals.

Excerpts translated from "Shenduan bayao," from *Liyuan yuan,* in *Zhongguo lidai julun xuanzhu,* ed. Chen Duo and Ye Changhai (Changsha: Hunan wenyi chubanshe, 1987), 366–67.

The noble: dignified in appearance; looking straight into people's eyes; deep voice; firm and commanding steps.

The rich: jovial in appearance; smiling eyes; pointing fingers; speaking in a relaxed and unhurried manner.

The poor: frail in appearance; eyes transfixed; hands wrapped around the shoulders; nose running.

The vile: ostentatious in appearance; casting wicked glances sideways; shrugging shoulders; moving swiftly.

The imbecile: vapid in appearance; eyes rolling upward; mouth open; head shaking.

The mad: fit to be tied; menacing stares; laughing and crying at the same time; moving about erratically.

The sick: languid in appearance; teary eyed; panting; trembling.

The drunk: listless in appearance; misty eyed; lethargic body; stiff feet.

You should understand the four major emotional states—that is, happiness, anger, sorrow, and shock.

To show happiness: the key is the wagging head, followed by beaming eyes, a smiling face, and a voice sounding of joy and jubilation.

To show anger: the key is the glaring eyes, followed by knitted brows [squeezed nose?], stick out chest, and a voice sounding of fury and rancor.

To show sorrow: the key is the teary eyes, followed by stamping feet, lifeless facial expression, and a voice sounding of anguish and bereavement.

To show shock: the key is the gaping mouth, followed by flushed cheeks, quivering body, and a voice sounding of tension and bewilderment.

(You can observe children: when affected by certain things, their emotions are clearly written on their faces and emitted from their mouths. Happiness, anger, sorrow, or shock are right there on the faces; joy, hatred, grief, or bewilderment come right out of their mouths.)

You should let your eyes take the lead—that is, to give priority to using your eyes expressively to indicate emotions as well as situations. The old saying is right: "When the eyes are expressive, the face becomes the window of your heartfelt sentiment."

You should sway your head slightly because it creates liveliness. But remember to sway only slightly, not too vigorously or randomly.

You should keep your steps steady. Everybody knows that big strides are not for the stage, but steps too small will not do either. Adhere to the golden mean, and the key is to keep steady. Even when moving quickly and busily, each step should be clearly defined.

You should articulate with expressive hand gestures. Use hands to communicate various emotions and conditions.

You should watch yourself in the mirror. You will improve your acting by practicing in front of a mirror, because it helps you to discover your own strengths and weaknesses.

You should not allow one idle day to slip by. Keep training and practicing every day, because the damage done by one idle day will take more than three days to repair. Please do remember this.

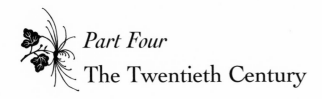

Part Four
The Twentieth Century

Wang Guowei on Theater

Wang Guowei (1877–1927) was a brilliant and multifaceted modern Chinese scholar. He was in the vanguard of the watershed generation of modern Chinese thinkers who reached intellectual maturity around the time of the 1894–95 Sino-Japanese War. Galvanized by the humiliating defeat by Japan, fearful that China would soon be completely "cut up like a melon" by foreign powers, the concerned members of the Chinese intelligentsia threw themselves into a fury of reform activities that would last till the collapse of the Qing Dynasty in 1911. To preserve China from the threat to her integrity posed by foreign scourge, they began to reassess critically the values of the culture in which they themselves had been raised and to take up seriously the study of the so-called practical knowledge of the West and Japan so as to make China "wealthy and powerful" (*fu qiang*). Wang Guowei, however, was highly skeptical of a technological solution to the fundamental problems of the human condition. Believing in the importance of satisfying humanity's deepest spiritual and philosophical yearnings, Wang launched his own ambitious project to modernize China by championing Western ideas, particularly the "pure" philosophical tradition of German thinkers such as Kant, Schopenhauer, and Nietzsche, as differentiated from the British philosophical doctrines of "utilitarianism and evolution." His essays on German philosophy and philosophical aesthetics, his poetry, literary criticism, and aesthetic theory, and his works on ancient Chinese history and drama exerted groundbreaking and lasting influence on the Chinese literati.

Wang Guowei's interest in drama developed as a result of having been made aware, through his reading in German philosophy and aesthetics, of the esteem in which fiction and drama are held in the modern West. Between 1908 and 1912 Wang produced no fewer than eight studies on the latest subject of his intellectual fascinations, Chinese drama: *Catalogue of Plays* (*Qu lu* [1908]), *On the Origins of Drama* (*Xiqu kaoyuan* [1909]), *The Register of Ghosts: A Collation* (*Lugui bu jiaozhu* [1909]), *Anecdotes about Actors* (*Youyu lu* [1909]), *On the Great Melodies of Tang and Song* (*Tang song daqu kao* [1909]), *Miscellaneous Observations on Drama* (*Luqu yutan* [1910]), *On the Role System in Ancient Drama* (*Guju jiaose kao* [1911]), and *Song and Yuan Drama* (*Song yuan xiqu kao* [1912]).

Song and Yuan Drama was Wang's last and most important work on drama,

Excerpts translated from "Taohua shan yu honglou meng," from *Honglou men pinglun,* in *Zhongguo lidai julun xuanzhu,* ed. Chen Duo and Ye Changhai (Changsha: Hunan wenyi chubanshe, 1987), 439–40; "Yuanju zhi wenzhang," from *Song Yuan xiqu kao,* in *Wang guowei xiqu lunwenji* (Beijing: Zhongguo xiju chubanshe, 1984), 84–90.

of which he had a very high opinion. He rightly declared in his preface to the work: "All of the material [used in this work] have been collected by me, and the theories advanced in it for the most part have also been conceived by me. The world's study of this subject has begun with me, and the greatest contribution to this subject has been this work." Unlike his predecessors and older contemporaries, who, as Wang put it, "all despised drama and would not discuss it," Wang was enabled by his study of Western philosophy and philosophical aesthetics to free himself from what he perceived as the traditional contemptuous Chinese view of drama.

As the modern pioneer of thoroughgoing research on ancient Chinese theater and drama, Wang was not only avidly interested in investigating the origins and interpreting the evolution of Chinese theater, but he was also intensely concerned with the form and content of the plays whose history he was studying. A number of his studies are classics in this field, and much of the later Chinese investigation has built upon rather than radically restructured them. In many ways they have yet to be superseded. Wang's *Song and Yuan Drama,* in particular, is considered with Lu Xun's *Concise History of Chinese Novel* (*Zhong-guo xiaoshuo shilue*) as one of the "twin peaks" of studies on Chinese literary history, for both are not only pioneering but also authoritative.

In their effort to preserve the endangered centuries-old Chinese civilization Wang Guowei and many of the 1890s generation of intellectuals had turned to the West for new blood. Some of them, however, later came to realize and to regret that, by espousing Western ideas at variance with Confucian wisdom, they had unwittingly contributed to the subversion of traditional Chinese culture.

This was the irony, indeed the tragedy, of the watershed generation of Chinese intellectuals: having themselves set the empire on a radical course that would lead eventually to the demise of Confucian China, they lived to decry many of the features of the new society whose emergence was due in no small measure to their own youthful examination of foreign strands of thought. No one better exemplifies this type of transitional intellectual, the type who helped to subvert a culture that he would later cherish above all else, than Wang Kuo-wei [Guowei].[1]

Wang was unhappy in later life and committed suicide at age forty-nine.[2]

---

1. Joey Bonner, *Wang Kuo-wei: An Intellectual Biography* (Cambridge: Harvard University Press, 1986), chap. 16, p. 216.
2. Wang was a brilliant and complex thinker and scholar with a wide range of intellectual interests and a gentleman of lofty ethicoreligious convictions. He lived in a most tumultuous age of Chinese modern history, a life with many contradictions and tragic ironies. For instance, he was the first one to proclaim the dignity of traditional literary works that are written in a vernacular style, such as novels, or that contain vernacular elements, such as lyrics and plays. By doing this, he inadvertently paved the way toward

The selection of the following excerpts is partly intended to illustrate Wang Guowei's evolving conception of theater in general and tragedy in particular. The first of the excerpts was from chapter 3 of his *Critique of Dream of the Red Chamber*[3] (*Honglou meng pinglun*) written in 1904. In his analysis of the novel Wang paused long enough to make some observations on Chinese drama. It was written during a time when Wang had studied more of Schopenhauer than Chinese drama. Hard-pressed by Schopenhauer's criteria, the thrust of Wang's remarks on that occasion was the suggestion that Chinese drama, unlike its Western counterpart, lacks a tragic dimension. And he attributed this fatal flaw to the perpetual optimism of the Chinese people. By the time he was writing *Song and Yuan Drama,* in 1912, Wang had already outgrown many of the Schopenhauerian ideas. Although he appears still to put much stock in suffering, Wang no longer insists that suffering must have the purpose of inducing resignation in the hero. His growing appreciation of Song and Yuan drama also helped him to widen his own Schopenhauerian definition of tragedy to include any play that contains a sense of injustice or ends on a note of despair. The second excerpt is from chapter 12, "The Language of Yuan Drama" ("Yuan ju de wenzhang") of *Song and Yuan Drama.*

Dream of the Red Chamber and *Peach Blossom Fan*

The spirit of our people is this—worldly and optimistic. Plays and novels of ancient times that exemplify this spirit are, without exception, all infused with this optimism; they begin sadly but end happily, they begin with separation but end with reunion, they begin with hardship but end with good fortune. Unless he writes according to this [formula, a Chinese writer] finds it difficult to satisfy the cravings of his public.

The most conspicuous examples [of dramatists conceding to this formula of the happy ending] are *The Peony Pavilion* and *The Palace of Eternal Life* (*Changsheng dian*), the former with its return of the soul and the latter with its reunion. *The West Chamber Story* was an unfinished work whose last part was completed by another author. But, even if this play had been completed [by the original author, Wang Shifu, himself],

---

the general acceptance of the May Fourth revolutionary proposal that all Chinese literature in the future be written in the vernacular, which is completely unacceptable to Wang, the intellectual elitist, who only wrote in the elegant classical Chinese. Being a proponent of free will, Wang nevertheless adhered to the Confucian ethic of loyalty to one ruler even after the demise of the Qing court in 1911. When he drowned himself, in 1927, in the Kunming Lake in the former imperial Summer Palace, he was still wearing his queue and old-fashioned clothes, symbols of his loyalist sympathies.
3. *Dream of the Red Chamber* (*Honglou meng*), the novel, was the literary masterpiece written by Cao Xueqin (1715?–63).

I wonder whether his ending would not have been as superficial and commonplace as the "Continuation" to *The West Chamber Story*. . . .

In all our literature only *The Peach Blossom Fan (Taohua shan)*[4] and *Dream of the Red Chamber* are imbued with a spirit of pessimism and resignation. [But in the final analysis] the resignation depicted in *The Peach Blossom Fan* is not pure. Despite all the changes that he either witnessed or experienced, [Hou Fangyu] was unable to attain final enlightenment on his own, and he became enlightened only on hearing the words of Zhang, the Taoist monk. That [Hou] should suddenly give up [Li Xiangjun] because of Zhang's one sentence after he has, for her sake, willingly undergone the rigors of hundreds of miles of travel, taken unpredictable risks, and even landed in jail strains the credulity of all but a three-foot-tall small child. Therefore, whereas the resignation depicted in *Dream of the Red Chamber* is convincing because it comes internally [from the free will], the resignation in *The Peach Blossom Fan* is implausible because it comes from an external source. Furthermore, the author of *The Peach Blossom Fan* was using the story of Hou and Li to express his anguish over the loss of his country, and it was not his objective to delineate the human experience. Therefore, whereas *The Peach Blossom Fan* is a work of politics, nationalism, and history, *Dream of the Red Chamber* is a work of philosophy, universality, and literature. Where *Dream of the Red Chamber* contradicts the spirit of our people is precisely where lies its value. [Revisionist plays such as] *The Southern Peach Blossom (Nan taohua shan)*[5] and *New Dream of the Red Chamber (Honglou fu meng)*[6] are products of the spirit of optimism of our people.

The Language of Yuan Drama

The unrivaled exquisite excellence of Yuan drama was not recognized in its own days. It was not until the Ming Dynasty that some scholars started to become enthusiastic about it and even compare it to great literature from other eras. In the past three hundred years most scholars, however, still tend to ignore Yuan drama, but those who actually had a taste of it have been, without exception, overwhelmed with admiration.

4. *The Peach Blossom Fan,* a classic in the Chinese dramatic repertoire, was written by the Qing Dynasty dramatist Kong Shangren (1648–1718).
5. Written by Kong Shangren's friend Gu Cai, *The Southern Peach Blossom* ends with Hou and Li getting married and living happily ever after.
6. It is one version of many happy or at least cheerful "continuations," or sequels, to *Dream of the Red Chamber.*

All literature is superior because of its naturalness, and nowhere is this more evident than in the case of Yuan drama, particularly its dramatic songs. None of the Yuan dramatists were of high social standing or even greatly learned; their purpose in writing plays was not to store them in famous mountains for posterity. They simply wrote as the spirit moved them in order to amuse themselves and others. They did not think about the clumsiness of their plots, did not avoid expressing vulgar ideas, and did not pay attention to the contradictions they created in their characters. They merely wrote down the emotions they felt inside them and recorded the circumstances of the age, with the result that frequently genuine truths and an elegant style can be found in their works. Yuan drama may thus be called China's most natural literature. Naturalness of language was a necessary result of these characteristics of Yuan dramatists and their method of composition.

Although from the time of Ming Dynasty onward all plays (*chuanqi*) have been comedies, the Yuan Dynasty produced some tragedies. As regards those that are still extant, plays such as *Autumn in the Han Palace* (*Han gong qiu*), *Raindrops on the Parasol Tree* (*Wutong yu*), *Dreams of Western Shu* (*Xishu meng*), *Jie Zitui on Fire* (*Huoshao jie zitui*), and *Zhang Qien Kills the Wife of a Sworn Brother* (*Zhang qien ti sha qi*) are not written according to [the conventional formula] beginning with separation but ending with reunion, beginning with hardship but ending with good fortune. Those plays most imbued with the tragic spirit are Guan Hanqing's *Injustice to Dou-e* (*Dou-e yuan*) and Ji Junxiang's *Orphan of the Zhao Family* (*Zhaoshi guer*). While these plays contain scheming villains, courageous acts are still performed through the heroes' assertion of will. They may be deservingly ranked among the world's greatest tragedies.

The clumsiness of the plots of Yuan drama will not concern us here. Such clumsiness arose from the fact that in those days this aspect of drama was not stressed. [Dramatists] therefore often modeled themselves on one another or simply wrote not very carefully. . . .

The most sublime feature of Yuan drama, after all, is neither its ideas nor its structure but its language. Where does its distinction lie? It lies, in a word, in its *yijing*. What is *yijing*?[7] It is the ability of the Yuan plays [to communicate ideas, desires, emotions, situations vividly, movingly and with great verisimilitude]. In describing emotions they pierce one to the heart, in describing scenes they bring them right before one's

---

7. *Yijing* is sometimes roughly translated as "artistic conception." Based on Wang's other writings, it refers to an artist's ability to depict not only external reality but also internal feelings—something at once objective and subjective, realistic and expressionistic.

eyes and ears, and in narrating events they make one think that the actual personages themselves are speaking. . . .

[. . .]

In ancient literature the classical language (*gu yu*) was generally used to describe things; the colloquial language (*su yu*) was hardly ever used. The number of words used in a piece of ancient literature, moreover, was never very great; only in Yuan drama and its songs, because of the permissibility of using nonmetric words (*chen zi*), was it suddenly possible to describe things with many colloquial words and natural sounds. This is something that had never occurred before in ancient literature.

[. . .]

As regards Yuan drama, truly a new language was freely employed in a new genre. This is only the third time such a thing has occurred in our country's literary history aside from the poetry of Chu (*chu ci*) and the Buddhist scriptures (*nei dian*).

[. . .]

As regards [great] Yuan dramatists, they have been customarily ranked in such an order since the Ming Dynasty as Guan [Hanqing], Ma [Zhi-yuan], Zheng [Dehui], and Bai [Renfu]. Based on chronology and degree of excellence, I feel it would be more appropriate to name them in this order: Guan, Bai, Ma, and Zheng. Guan Hanqing was an absolute original whose language deftly describes every human emotion, and every word is a bona fide natural (*bengse*); he may therefore be regarded as the greatest Yuan dramatist. Plays by Bai Renfu and Ma Dongli [Zhiyuan] are elegant and powerful; their emotions are profound and their language lucid. Zhen Dehui's style is delicate and his sentiments romantic, distinctly his own. All four are dramatists of the first class. The works of all other dramatists never went beyond the greatness of these four individuals. . . .

The language of Yuan drama alone more than qualifies it as a literary peak. Because it is so natural, it could address the political and social situations of the time, inadvertently providing a great deal of material for historians and social commentators. Also, because of the frequent use of vernacular language, colloquial expressions from the Song, Jing, and Yuan dynasties are abundantly well preserved in the plays. There definitely is a book on the subject if somebody would collect those [colloquial expressions], sort them out, and make a study of them. Well, of course, linguistics is not the business of this book.

LIANG QICHAO

Popular Literature in Relation
to the Masses

Liang Qichao (1873–1929), also known by many aliases, such as "Master of the
Ice Drink Café," was a prominent activist of the 1898 Constitutional Reform
and Modernization. When the reform attempt failed, Liang went into exile in
Japan, where he continued his activities as a leading proponent for reforming
arts and letters by writing, publishing new journals, such as *New Novel*,[1] and
introducing Western ideas. As a reformer and a loyalist—like his friend Wang
Guowei—Liang was completely against violent revolution. He served briefly in
the Restoration government of Yuan Shikai. Liang devoted the rest of his life to
teaching, researching, and writing. The following excerpt from "Popular Literature in Relation to the Masses" was originally published in the first issue of *New
Novel*, in 1902. In this article Liang emphasized again and again the vital importance of popular literature—chiefly the vernacular novel and drama. It is also on
this occasion that he formulated his theory of popular literature's four powers:
xun, jin, ci, and *ti* (to permeate, to immerse, to shock, and to transcend).

If you wish to reform the citizens of a country, you must first reform the
popular literature of the country. To reform ethical standards, you must
reform the popular literature; to reform religion, you must reform the
popular literature; to reform the political system, you must reform the
popular literature; to reform customs, you must reform the popular
literature; to reform learning and improving technology, you must reform the popular literature; to reform people's hearts and characters, you
must reform the popular literature. Why? Because popular literature
wields incredible influence over the way of the world.

Popular literature influences the way of the world through four powerful
means. The first power is *xun* (to fumigate or permeate)—that is, to be
omnipresent, to influence people gradually and imperceptively by what

Translated from "Lun xiaoshuo yu qunzhizhi guanxi," in *Zhongguo lidai julun xuanzhu,*
ed. Chen Duo and Ye Changhai (Changsha: Hunan wenyi chubanshe, 1987), 385–90.
1. In historical context the word *xiaoshuo* (novel) in the original title actually refers to all
popular literary and performative genres, including the vernacular novel and drama. The
word's closest equivalent today would probably be *mass media.*

they constantly see and hear. When a person reads a popular novel, his perspective, mind, and consciousness are involuntarily affected without himself knowing it. Little today, little more tomorrow, eventually the point of view of the novel assumes a place in the person's heart, becoming a seminal seed that thrives upon further reinforcing. From one seed to another and another, disseminated into one person's heart one after another and another, this kind of seed can propagate all over the world and in every domain.

The second power is *jin* (to soak or immerse). While *xun* operates in space (the breadth of the influence determines if its power is big or small), *jin* works in time (the depth and length of the influence determines if its power is big or small). *Jin* is to become completely absorbed. Oftentimes when a person reads a good novel, he cannot extricate himself afterward from that fictional world for days and days on end. Those who read *Dream of the Red Chamber* undoubtedly experience lingering infatuation and melancholy; those who read *The Water Margin* surely are left with the persisting sense of outrage and justice. As great works go, the longer they are, the more drenching the power they have. It is like wine, if you drink it continuously for ten days, the intoxication will last you one hundred days.

The third power is *ci* (to spur or pierce)—that is, to provoke and shock. While *xun* and *jin* work slowly and steadily, *ci* acts quickly and impulsively. While *xun* and *jin* influence people with the power of imperceptibility, *ci* arouses people with the force of shock. *Ci* can take over your body and mind in an instant; you may suddenly develop unfamiliar feelings over which you have no control. . . . *Ci* works better when words are spoken rather than written, but written form is used more often so that the words can reach more people and have more lasting value. In written form the colloquial is better than the formal; the allegorical is better than the theoretical. Therefore, nothing delivers the astounding *ci* more powerfully than popular literature forms such as vernacular novel and drama.

The fourth power is *ti* (to transcend or rise above). Unlike the three earlier powers, whose influence on people all come from the outside, *ti* works from the inside out, which is the best way, according to Buddhist teachings. People who read novels often find themselves shedding their own ordinary existence and taking on the identities of the heroes. By identifying with the central characters, the readers are lifted out of their own reality and become one of them, be it Washington, Napoleon, Buddha, or Confucius. Talking about the Buddhist out-of-body experience—is there any better way?

These four powerful means can be used to change and mold the world. The clergy use them to help establish religious institutions, and politicians use them to help organize political parties. If a man of letters enjoys one of the four powers, he is a master. If he possesses all four powers, he is a god. Putting the four powers to good use, the world will be a blissful place for millions of people; putting the four powers to evil use, the curse will last tens and thousands of years. Nothing possesses the four powers like the popular literature does, which is to be loved and feared at the same time!

LIU YAZI

Foreword to The *20th-Century Grand Stage*

Around the same time when Liang Qichao and others were advocating reforming popular literature and drama, Chen Qubing (1874–1933), a poet active in
the progressive literary group Southern Society (*nan se*) published *The 20th-
Century Grand Stage* (*Ershi shiji dawutai*), the first professional theater journal in
China, in 1904. For the journal's first issue Chen asked his friend Liu Yazi
(1887–1958) to write a foreword, which was considered a manifesto of revolutionary theater. Because of its revolutionary nature and radical tone, the journal
was shut down by the Qing authorities after only two issues.

Liu Yazi was a poet, lyricist, and essayist. As a late Qing classical scholar
(*xiucai*) turned revolutionary, Liu was an activist in the movement that overthrew
the feudalistic Qing Dynasty and established the republic (1911). He worked at
one time as Sun Zhongshan's presidential secretary. After the People's Republic
of China was established, in 1949, Liu Yazi was a member of the People's
Congress.

Open your eyes and look around: the mountains and rivers are as
good as dead. The country is cut up by warlords and bandits, as it has
been for a long time. The people are demoralized and dispirited, as
they have been for a long time. Communities are doomed without
public morality; words sound more vacuous without real action. There
is no good news in this vast land; still in their prime, men of letters are
plunged into deep despair. Into this world shrouded in darkness comes
a bright beam of hope; it is from the theater in the south—using
colorful costumes to wake up those slumbering in their dreams of
yesteryear, using beautiful songs and graceful dances to call back our
nation's soul. The revolutionary army of the Pear Garden is waving the
tricolored flag of America![1] The foundation is laid, organization is
ready, and to sustain its growth and spread its influence comes this
journal. . . .

Excerpt translated from "Ershi shiji dawutai fakanci," in *Zhongguo lidai julun xuanzhu,* ed.
Chen Duo and Ye Changhai (Changsha: Hunan wenyi chubanshe, 1987), 419–21.
1. The flag was used as a symbol of revolution.

Huigu does not know spring or autumn; *zhaojun* does not know morning or night.[2] They live a short life and have shallow thoughts. *Lin Jing* by [Confucius] deals with three worlds: the world seen, the world heard, the world passed down from the past.[3] The ignorant multitude are usually buried in the muddy present up to their neck; they do not know if they have a future, and they know nothing about the past. The events of the past 261 years [under Manchu rulers of the Qing Dynasty] have wiped the past out of the people's minds. They have forgotten their ancestors' style of attire and taken to pigtail as the essence of Chinese culture. The Manchu rulers are public enemies of us Chinese people, but they are being revered as the rightful master. Faced with a populace of so little intelligence and knowledge, it is utterly useless trying to arouse them by repeating such slogans as "Drive out [the barbarian invaders]" (*quchu* [*dalu*]) and "Reclaim [China]" (*guangfu* [*zhonghua*]). What we should do [first] is, through singing and dancing, to reenact the history of upheaval and occupation, showing vividly and without reserve the ten-day massacre in Yangzhou, the ten thousand–family bloodbath in Jia-ding, the hideous crimes of the occupying force, and the dignity of the martyrs and victims, then we can make our case for retaliation clearly and quickly.

The traffic between Asia and Europe has been going on for a number of centuries, but most of our people know nothing of the outside world. Those of us who believe in the republic and welcome reform are often avid about men such as Rousseau, Montesquieu, Washington, and others. It is again useless trying to get our countrymen to understand [these men's ideas], because to them they are just too far-fetched. What we should do [next] is have actors dressed up as foreign nationals to act out their histories: French Revolution, American Independence, the glory of the unification of Italy and independence of Greece, and the misery in occupied India and Poland. If we can impress all this on our countrymen, they are bound to be inspired. This is what theater reform can do, and this is the objective of *The 20th-Century Grand Stage*.

---

2. Here the author is citing Zhuangzi's *Xiaoyao you*. *Huigu* is the kind of insect that is born in summer and dies when autumn arrives. *Zhaojun* comes to life after sunrise and dies before nightfall.

3. *Lin Jing* is another title given to *Chun Qiu* (*Spring and Autumn Annals*).

LIN SHU

Preface to *Tales from Shakespeare*

Lin Shu (1852–1924), also known by many aliases, was a prominent writer, scholar, and translator of his time. He had a *juren* degree from the Qing Dynasty imperial exams, and he taught at Beijing University, among other prestigious institutions of higher learning. Lin did not know any foreign languages, but, with the help of friends, colleagues, and missionaries who orally related to him the well-known works of Western literature, he "translated" into classical written Chinese over one hundred and eighty works of Western literature. His translations, or renditions, were very influential and popular. His *Tales from Shakespeare* (1904), which contains twenty stories based on the Bard's plays, was the second earliest introduction of Shakespearean works into China. Until 1921, when the great dramatist Tian Han translated from the English originals *Romeo and Juliet* and *Hamlet,* almost all the so-called Shakespearean plays on the Chinese stage were dramatized versions based on Lin's book.

W hen the Europeans criticize our country, they usually say that China is becoming increasingly weak and ill-fated because she is narrow in her view of the world, outdated in her thinking, allowing her past to dominate her present, and too fond of gods, fairies, ghosts, and demons. The young and audacious in our country are going all out for reform and change. They embrace only the new, mocking the old tradition and practice and discarding past history and heritage.

There are certainly justifications in what these people are doing. But, if they think that all things Western are new to China, they are wrong, for it would be like glorifying somebody by exaggerating his merits or destroying somebody by magnifying his faults. Aren't Hardy and Shakespeare literary giants of the great civilized England? Look at Hardy's books that I have translated; there are taboo snakes and condemned ghosts all over the place. Shakespeare's poetry is quite comparable to that of our [great poet] Du Fu, but he often conjures up images of gods, fairies, ghosts, and demons. If the Westerners are so civilized,

Translated from "Yin bian yan yu xu," in *Zhongguo lidai julun xuanzhu,* ed. Chen Duo and Ye Changhai, (Changsha: Hunan wenyi chubanshe, 1987), 457–58.

then maybe these works mentioned should be banned and burned so as not to interfere with scientific knowledge. As far as I know, however, Shakespeare's poetry is held in high esteem among the well bred [in the West]. There his works are not only read and recited in every household but also performed in theaters, where men and women are moved to tears as they hold each other's hands listening to every word, where no one is ever tempted to call him old-fashioned or accuse him of having a fetish about gods, fairies, ghosts, and demons. Why is this the case? Certainly, many old things are useless today, for example, the cooking vessels and drinking cups from the Bronze Age, heavy and rust eaten. But no expense should be spared to obtain, preserve, and display, say, a distinguished suit of armor once worn by a great personage from an illustrious family. People who are affluent and not troubled by the material needs of everyday life turn their interest to the past in pursuit of new personal enrichment. This is just like what [Su] Dongpo said, that when one has had enough rich meats and fine grains he starts to miss the snails and clams [of the old days].

Running a country and educating its people are two important matters that do not depend on arts and literature. When all is well with the country and its people, good arts and literature can add more luster; but when good arts and literature is all a country has, they do not benefit either the governing or educating. That's why the Westerners make government and education their priorities, gathering wealth and building military strength. They are so rich and powerful that no outsiders dare to humiliate them. It is only then they begin to enjoy arts and literature in their leisure time. Maybe Mr. Hardy and Mr. Shakespeare are old-fashioned and using gods, fairies, ghosts, and demons too much, but the civilized Westerners are certainly not complaining.

I am old, and I do not use the same language as Hardy and Shakespeare, but I am particularly fond of these two gentlemen's works. My good friend Mr. Wei Chunshu, from Renhe[1]—young, erudite, and a master of Western languages—and I teamed up to do translations at the Translation Studio of the Jingshi Daxuetang (Capital University). After Mr. Wei orally translated the works to me, I put them into [Chinese] literary form. In about two years we translated about three or four works, of which the most massive one is the *Biography of Napoléon*. We are about to graduate from the studio early this coming autumn. When free one night, Mr. Wei picked up some Shakespeare by chance; I started scrib-

1. Renhe is today's city of Hangzhou, in Zhejiang Province.

bling away by the night lamp. Twenty days later we have a book of Shakespeare's poetic tales.

The British certainly embrace new ideas in running their country, but they do not discard Shakespeare's poetry. Now that I have translated the book of Shakespeare's poetic tales, won't those believers in new things reject it?

There are some different versions of Shakespeare's poetic tales coming into our country. There are similarities and differences in the selections of tales as well as in the contents of actual tales themselves. My book contains twenty tales, each of which has a new title by me for the purpose of highlighting.

Prefaced by Lin Shu from Ming County,[2] May 1904.

---

2. Ming County is today's city of Fuzhou, in Fujian Province.

CHEN DUXIU

On Theater

Chen Duxiu (1800–1941) was a leading figure in the May Fourth new cultural movement. Chen was a founding member of the Chinese Communist Party (CCP) and served as the first general-secretary of the party's central committee, but he was later expelled from the CCP due to internal political strife. "On Theater," written under Chen's pen name, Sanai, was first published in 1904. In the article Chen, who considered the theater as an important didactic tool, clearly stated that "theater is in fact a great big school for all the people under heaven; theater workers are in fact influential teachers of the people." In order for theater to play a truly positive role in society, Chen put forth five suggestions for reform.

Theater is what people love to see and hear most. It is an art form that can easily get into people's heads and touch their hearts. People may choose to stay away from the theater, but once they are inside a theater their thoughts are without a doubt controlled by what is going on onstage. Theater has the power to take possession of its audience, making it happy and joyful one moment and sad and mournful the next, making it dancing in delirium one moment and crying in a flood of tears the next. It doesn't take much time to make incredibly great changes in people's minds. It is thus no wonder that *Long Plank Hill* (*Changban po*) and *Village of the Evil Tiger* (*Ehu cun*) spur heroism; *Story of Burnt-Bones* (*Shaogu ji*) and *Red Plum Pavilion* (*Hongmei ge*) arouse lamentation; *Wen Zhaoguan* and *Ten Stories of Wu Song* (*Wu shihui*) incite vengeance; *Selling Rouge* (*Mai yanzhi*) and *Swingboat on a Lake* (*Danghu chuan*) entice erotic desire. There are many other plays dealing with the supernatural, the rich, and the famous, all capable of changing people's beliefs and disposi-tions. From this perspective theater is in fact a great big school for all the people under heaven; theater workers are in fact influential teachers of the people.

In the eyes of those pedantic and stuffy scholars, of course, why

Translated from "Lun xiqu," in *Zhongguo lidai julun xuanzhu*, ed. Chen Duo and Ye Changhai, (Changsha: Hunan wenyi chubanshe, 1987), 460–62.

should anyone be interested in theater, which has a reputation for being vulgar, bawdy, licentious, wasteful, and useless, while there are many useful things to learn and do in the world? Furthermore, entertainers who are considered no better than prostitutes are not permitted by the court to become government officials through civil exams, so why would anybody in his right mind not dismiss theater as a profession? My lauding the importance of actors would seem quite absurd. But people who hold this view are prejudiced, because whether a person is noble or base depends on his moral character and not on the high or low of his profession. In our country, China, actors are looked down upon and deprived of equality with other citizens. In the countries in the West the situation is just the opposite: the actors are equals of the literary and the learned, because it is believed that theater is extremely important in fostering morals and values and that the performers are not to be slighted.

When we look back to the beginning of theatrical activities in our own country, we can also see that acting or performing is not unworthy. In the ancient time the sagacious and the worthy all performed musical rituals, such as *Yunmeng, Xianchi, Shao, Dawu,* and others.[1] They performed in the temples or in the streets and were looked up to as the standard. In the Zhou dynasty the musical rituals developed [poetic quality] into *Ya* and *Song.* And theater evolved gradually through the dynasties of Han, Tang, Song, Yuan, till roughly about two hundred years ago, to become what we know it today. Theater today is a descendant of the ancient *yue,* the musical rituals. . . . Confucius said: "Nothing is better than *yue* at transforming social conventions." And Mencius said: "Today's *yue* is the ancient *yue.*" Theater is today's *yue.* For those who feel the compulsion to scorn theater while insisting on paying homage to the ancient *yue,* it is like asking people to abandon today's regular script and take up the ancient calligraphy of seal characters. Can this be done? It doesn't take a wise man to give the answer. Music changes over time; today's certainly differs from that of the ancient times. Listening to the ancient music today, people will find it unfamiliar; even the much recent tunes of *kunqu* cannot find more than a handful of true connoisseurs. Why did Wei Wenhou fall asleep when he heard the ancient *yue,* while King Zhuang of Chu became so moved when he saw the performance by the actor Meng?[2] It is all because the conventions have changed from

---

1. These four musical rituals, together with *Shaojian* and *Daxia,* make up a group of six standard musical rituals representing six different ancient periods, from the time of the legendary prehistoric Huangdi to the beginning of the West Zhou Dynasty (1066–771 B.C.E.).
2. You can find these two well-known historical incidence by referring to "Wei Wenhou" and Sima Qian's "Anecdotes of Comedians" in the first part of this book.

the time of the ancient *yue;* one gets bored when he cannot understand or recognize it. If you play the ancient *yue* today, people will not like it because the language and tunes are obscure. On the other hand, because today's theater in its typical forms of *xipi* and *erhuang* uses the familiar standard speech, it is easier to reach and touch the audience. Some may consider it ordinary and common, but it is the way to make the ordinary and common people understand. Some may consider it frivolous and useless, but theater is for making up stories of the past to teach the audience of today. Furthermore, theater can offer things that you do not get in everyday life—namely, classical costumes, heroic outlaws, and women warriors. All this shows that theater plays beneficial functions. Knowing that makes it easier to see the biased and presumptuous nature of the objections of theater raised by those pedantic and stuffy scholars.

Theater does have beneficial functions, yet there are also shortcomings in the way theater is practiced today. It is thus not surprising that there are criticisms against theater as it really is not perfect. The imperfection should not lead us to negate the positive role of theater. What is needed is to correct the mistakes and make improvements by examining the theater's strengths and weaknesses.

First of all, our theater should create more new plays that foster high morals and values. In our Chinese history we have great heroic figures like Jing Ke, Nie Zheng, Zhang Liang, Nan Jiyun, Yue Fei, Wen Tianxiang, Lu Xiufu, Fang Xiaoru, Wang Yangming, Shi Kefa, Yuan Chonghuan, Huang Daozhou, Li Ding-guo, Qu Shisi, and many more. We can turn their stories into new plays, singing and performing passionately of loyalty, filial piety, righteousness, and heroism. This will benefit our world and our people tremendously. Some old plays, such as *Human Flesh (Chi renrou)*, *Long Plank Hill (Changban po)*, and many others, are also good for arousing feelings of loyalty and righteousness.

Second, our theater should adopt some Western techniques. It is very effective to have characters engage in debates or give speeches in order to expand the audience's perspective. It pays to implement the latest devices of lighting, sound, electricity, and many other scientific breakthroughs.

Third, our theater should not perform plays featuring gods, fairies, ghosts, or demons. As the supernatural is incomprehensible, it can stir up the ignorant masses and cause a great deal of trouble. The 1900 Boxers were definitely influenced by the supposedly invincible troops and generals from heaven as seen in the stage plays. Plays like *Sizhou City (Sizhou cheng)*, *The Battle Array of Five-Land-Mines (Wulei zhen)*, *The Gate of*

Southern Sky (*Nantian meng*), and so on are exceedingly ludicrous. It is worse when gods and spirits are thrust into such plays as *Wu Song Kills His Sister-in-law* (*Wu song sha sao*), which originally is a good revenge play. Wu Song, a man of exceptional ability, can certainly defeat his enemy, Ximeng Qing, on his own. By having gods and spirits assist him only renders his powers worthless. We should immediately get rid of such irrational elements of gods and spirits.

Fourth, our theater should not stage sexually obscene plays. Plays such as *Marrying Yuehua* (*Yuehua huan*), *Swingboat on a Lake* (*Danghu chuan*), and so on offend public decency. This is the reason that theater is considered by some as being licentious and acting profession as being inferior. It is bad enough when young men and women see obscene plays with male performers impersonating female characters. It is really shameless when female performers actually play the indecent scenes, arousing uncontrollable desires. Such plays should be banned.

Fifth, our theater should free itself from the convention of lauding personal wealth, fame, and success. Throughout their lives many of our countrymen are concerned with only achieving their own personal wealth, fame, and success, but they do not care about our country by either looking for ways of maintaining national stability or by bringing useful sciences to this land. The reasons why this country is losing its strength is because it lacks [unselfish] people with true visions and real talents. It will be a step in the right direction if we radically revise plays such as *Feng Long Tu, Hui Long Ge, Hong Luan Xi, Tian Kaibang, Shuang Guan Gao*.[3]

Theater will never again be considered vulgar, bawdy, licentious, wasteful, and useless if these five suggestions for reform are implemented. Right now our country is facing serious crises, and the interior provinces are backward and demoralized. Some concerned people are hoping to solve the problems by establishing schools, but they can only educate a limited number of students, and it takes time to see results. Some are promoting social reform by writing new novels or publishing their own newspapers, but they have no impact on the illiterate. Only the theater, through reform, can excite and change the whole society— the deaf can see it, and the blind can hear it. There is no better vehicle for social reform than the theater.

---

3. This group of plays all deal with personal ambitions and success stories.

WU MEI

Foreword to Playwriting Techniques

Wu Mei (1884–1939), a teacher all his life, was a professor of classical Chinese literature at universities in big cities like Beijing, Nanjing, and Guangzhou. As an artist-scholar sympathetic to the revolution and active in the progressive literary organization Southern Society, Wu wrote over ten plays in support of social reform. For instance, his *Wind Cave Mountain* (*Feng dong shan*), set in late Ming, was a heroic drama about resistance against the Qing; his play *Chang Hong Blood* (*Chang hong xue*) was written in memory of the six executed leaders of the aborted *Wuxu* Reform. Wu distanced himself from politics in his later years.

Wu Mei's most outstanding scholarly achievement is his work on dramatic theory. Some Chinese critics feel Wu Mei is comparable in importance to Wang Guowei, believing that, wheareas Wang Guowei's emphasis is mostly on the history of drama, Wu's focus is more on the drama itself, specifically the lyrics.[1] Among his many books on theater are *Fireside on Theatre* (*Guqu chentan*), *Chinese Theatre: A Survey* (*Zhongguo xiqu gailun*), *Yuan Drama: A Study* (*Yuanju yanjiu*), and many textbooks and lecture notes. Wu Mei was at his most original when he was doing comparative analysis of plays, the composition of lyrics, and various stylistic features. The following excerpt is taken from chapter 2, part 1, of Wu's earlier book *Fireside on Theater*. Here Wu identifies truth and wit as the key ingredient of a good play and regards beauty, or the aesthetic pleasure, as the sole purpose of playwriting.

Generally speaking, a play is good when it is characterized by the word *zhen* (real, or true). To be real is to be realistic and not superficial and to touch and move people truly. [Things on stage] are getting more and more indiscriminate these days because people are easily tempted by new fads and exotic vogues. Moral instruction is theater's function, but one cannot expect to make the world better by simply citing traditional morals, ancient teachings, and dated truisms. In order to instruct in an unobtrusive way that people enjoy, we may adopt some of the popular fads and help the people to improve gradually. As long as the [play's]

Translated from "Lun juzuofa yinyan," in *Zhongguo lidai julun xuanzhu,* ed. Chen Duo and Ye Changhai, (Changsha: Hunan wenyi chubanshe, 1987), 480–81.
1. Such as literary historian Pu Jiangqing. See Ye Changhai, *History of Chinese Theatre Studies* (*Zhongguo xijuxue shigao*) (Shanghai: Shanghai wenyi chubanshe, 1986), 503.

emotions and reasons stay true, when the new and exotic are properly done, the audience will heed the moral teaching and think twice before acting immorally. One cannot expect the people to return to the golden means by issuing stern warnings. Replacing the new that is mindless with the intelligent kind, substituting the exotic that is reckless with the thoughtful kind, it will please both the audience and the author, for it enhances the stage performance as well as the playwriting. This is what I mean by *zhen*.

The next thing a good play needs is *fengqu* (wit, or humor). People nowadays are fond of light reading and averse to solemn teaching. The great historian once said: "Laughter and wit [are the best medicine, and they] can also solve disputes."[2] This works the best in the theater. [The following is] recorded in the Song Dynasty documents. Qian Weiyan and Yang Yi were fond of poetry in the style of [the great poet Li Shangyin, also known as] Yuxi, so they [imitated him and] came up with their own so-called Xikun style, which in turn started a whole tidal wave of imitations. One day an actor playing Li Yuxi entered the stage dressed in [uncustomary] rag and looking rather thin and pallid. He brought the entire house down when he said to the audience: "I'm picked clean by all those gentlemen in their den." . . . Wit of this kind critiques social manners in the best possible way. If you were there, you would have for sure laughed up your sleeve. This is wit, quite different from dirty jokes of the street. Wit is indispensable, and it is necessary to link it to moral instruction. If circumstances are such that you cannot speak frankly, you may want to use the allegorical world of plants and insects to get your point across. This is what I mean by there is more than one way to speak your mind. This is what I mean by *fengqu*.

I have talked about *zhen* and [*feng*]*qu*. A playwright has to know these two. That *zhen* and [*feng*]*qu* can benefit society and amuse people is because the playwright's ultimate aim is to create *mei* (beauty, or aesthetic pleasure). That is all.

---

2. See Sima Qian's "Anecdotes of Comedians" in this book.

ZHUO YAN

From Xiqingzhai Notes

Zhuo Yan, a classical scholar from Fujian province, earned his *jiuren* rank in 1893. Zhuo specialized in dramatic lyrics and songs. His manuscript *Xiqingzhai Notes* was not published and is today archived in Fujian Province Library. In the following excerpt Zhu joined the debate then going on among playwrights and scholars over the relative importance of words and tunes. It was in fact a debate started way back in the Ming Dynasty between dramatists Tang Xianzu and Shen Jing (1553–1610). The audience's perspective is one of the new contributions that Zhuo Yan made to this ongoing debate.

Learned elder Lin Shu once remarked: "Lyrics in plays are often poorly written. If real poets are to write them, going to the theater may become worthwhile." I smiled and said: "My teacher, you are emphasizing the words of the lyrics, but in theater it is the tunes of the music that is more important. Sometimes the words in a play may be rather crude, but they rise and fall in perfect cadence with the music notes. If you have poets to refine and polish the lyrics, the words will be brilliant for sure, but I'm afraid they may not be suited to set into musical tunes. . . . As a child, I loved to listen to theatrical tunes; I often squeezed my way through the standing crowd to listen to temple performances, sometimes just to catch a certain aria, sometimes just to enjoy two or three particular lines of singing. I didn't know that much about musical measure or rhythm, but what came into my ears went straight to touch my heart, taking over my whole being completely. Musical tunes in plays may commend small respect, but they affect people in subtle yet profound ways. It is ample proof that playwrights must know how to choose tunes."

This excerpt, from the unpublished manuscript, can be found in *Zhongguo lidai julun xuanzhu,* ed. Chen Duo and Ye Changhai (Changsha: Hunan wenyi chubanshe, 1987), 519.

LI LIANGCAI

From "Examine the Old Plays"

Li Laingcai (1860–1932) was an activist in the movement against the Manchu rulers. After the 1911 revolution, which ended the Qing Dynasty, Li held several important positions in the new government of Shanxi Province, such as chief historian and advisor. In 1912 he cofounded a theater society, *Yisu Linxueshe,* expressly aimed at changing old social and cultural habits and customs. Li contributed to the group in his various capacities as chairman, playwright, critic, and editor of the organizational journal *Yisu Journal* (*Yisu zazhi*). It was in this journal that the following piece was originally published. By examining over two hundred plays in traditional repertoire in the spirit of "taking away the blemishes and keeping the jewel" and putting them into three categories—plays to discard, plays to revise, plays to adopt—Li embarked earnestly on a journey of modernizing traditional theater, even though his reasoning or proposals may not all be acceptable.

In our country only 1 or 2 percent of the population can read books, but theater is an entirely different matter; from the court and the gentlemen to the lowly, the ignorant, the poor, and even women and children, nobody does not know theater. It is universally recognized around the world that theater is a natural means for educating the public, for it can inspire and bring out goodness in the virtuous and punish and frustrate wickedness in the evil. That is the reason we cannot afford not to be careful about the plays. How to be careful? We have to look at each play and what influence it has on people. I have set out to examine the old plays and have divided them into the ones to discard, the ones to revise, and the ones to adopt.

The plays to discard can be subdivided into six types: (1) sexually obscene; (2) illogical; (3) bizarre; (4) mundane; (5) unexemplary; and (6) historically untrue.

This article by Li Liangcai was so popular that it was published several times. The existing versions all have various types of errors, mostly in the examples of plays listed under each category. The editors Chen Duo and Ye Changhai, in *Annotated Writings on Theatre in Chinese History* (*Zhongguo lidai julun xuanzhu*) (Changsha: Hunan wenyi chubanshe, 1987), 525–27, omitted all the examples. This translation is based on their edited version.

1. Sexually obscene. Classics like *Airs of the States* (*Guofeng*)[1] contain songs depicting promiscuity and impropriety as well as chastity and propriety, so that the good can be praised and the vile can be condemned. Plays do serve some form of admonition, but, as a rule, it does not happen until the final act; in the meantime actors pull out all the stops, performing the sexually provocative scenes in the middle section to satisfy popular taste. The scum of society certainly cannot comprehend that these acts are morally punishable! The country is suffering from moral decay. Since these plays do far more harm than good, let us discard them entirely.

2. Illogical. Some plays are concocted by men of extremely shallow intellect that may fool the ignorant peasants and savages with their completely improbable and illogical stories. If we allow this type of play to spread, ignorance will increase among the people. If the people are ignorant, the country has no hope for progress.

3. Bizarre. Ghosts and spirits, I am not here to discuss whether they exist. The ancients practiced spirit worship to teach what the law could not reach; they were able to do that because the people were kind and honest. Today people are not morally grounded; some commit crimes in the name of spirit worship, which no longer benefits the society the way it used to. It is not unfounded when people say that the troubles with the Boxers originated in the theater. To serve the people's interest let us not use the plays [with ghosts and spirits in them].

4. Mundane. What gets recorded in books and histories are all extraordinary tales (*chuanqi*). Because they are extraordinary (*qi*), they get handed down (*chuan*); if not extraordinary, they would not get handed down. Had his father and stepmother not been so cruel and mean to him, Xun's filial piety would not have become that famous. Novels and plays are meant for extraordinary happenings. Plays about mundane, ordinary, everyday occurrences pose no harm to the world, but they do not benefit it either. Not doing good hampers doing good, so let us discard [mundane plays].

5. Unexemplary. The great Way (*dao* or *tao*) is that which can be shared by other people. When you lead the way and people do not follow, you the leader may say it is not your fault. But, if what you pontificate is beyond what the people can comprehend, [then the fault is

---

1. "Airs of the States" (*Guo feng*) is the first of the four sections in the Confucian classic *Book of Odes* (*Shi jing*). It contains 160 folk songs depicting various aspects of the lives of common people. The "airs" touch upon subjects common to folk poetry the world over—courtship and marriage, the harvest and the hunt, games and festivals.

yours]. And [worse still] if you glamorize wild and illicit exploits. Why misuse the learning on the unenlightened?

6. Historically untrue. The illiterate common people do not read books, and what meager little they know about the world all comes from the theater. It is already a great pity that they cannot see the whole picture of history; how can we allow what they do see to be false? If you are teaching the masses, you might as well give them correct information. There are many versions of history plays; let us get rid of the erroneous ones.

The types of plays mentioned here should be discarded because they have a detrimental influence on people. Taking a look at the popular plays, nearly six or seven out of ten smack of the mentioned faults. It would be a real shame if we dispose of all these plays because of their defects regardless of the fact that they also exhibit outstanding good features. We can take away the blemishes and keep the jewel by revising these plays so that we can continue to use them. Correct the one or two flaws embedded in a fundamentally fine play by checking against the six categories listed here; in this way the fine tree gets to stand tall in its grandeur, the beautiful bamboo gets to show its elegance, and the extraordinary rock gets to express its uniqueness.

The plays to revise are in three groups: (1) plays that have become distorted in circulation; (2) plays that have fallen victims to clichés; and (3) plays whose good ideas are impeded by the six defects.

1. Plays that have become distorted in circulation. I will not point to a specific play or a specific group of plays. It is up to judicious people constantly to keep a watchful eye.

2. Plays that have fallen victims to clichés. Very few popular plays have not fallen victims to clichés. [Here are some common clichés,] for instance, (a) in order to usurp power, the treacherous man stabs the loyal and virtuous in the back and gets in cahoots with foreigners and faithless clergy, and the rightful ruler is rescued only by the sudden appearance of a chivalrous expert swordsman; (b) the imperial concubine residing in the West Palace connives to frame up the empress in the Central Palace and in the process endangers the well-being of the crown prince; (c) boy meets girl, falling instantly in love, but only after many complications do they achieve union; (d) foreign princesses coerce Chinese generals to marry them; (e) someone looks down upon the poor and rejects his spouse of humble origins; or (f) someone relies on power and position to

snatch somebody else's sweetheart. Plays containing clichés like these are not completely worthless in themselves. But, if they are also coupled with the six detrimental defects, then they would not be worth keeping [without revision]. Such plays are too numerous to mention.

3. Plays whose good ideas are impeded by the six defects. There are many plays that belong to this category. I will cite some familiar examples. . . .

Somebody once said: Writing a play (*kunqiang xi*) is as hard as writing an eight-part essay (*bagu wen*), because it is impossible to be perfect. If I may say so, there is no play that cannot use a rewrite. Whether the theme is shallow or profound, whether the structure is loose or tight, whether the characters are well matched, whether the spoken dialogues are too many or too few, whether the plot is ordinary or extraordinary, whether the onstage scene and offstage scene follow each other—about all this everybody on the street corner has an opinion, but is anybody the final authority? How dare I say which play is a fine play? But, since I am engaged in this task [of examining the old plays], I have to identify the good plays, recognizing that my field of vision is limited.

The plays to adopt can be put into roughly four categories: (1) plays that arouse people's conscience; (2) plays that instill wisdom and knowledge; (3) plays that showcase acrobatic skills and martial arts for a good cause; and (4) plays that use humor and wit appropriately.

1. Plays that arouse people's conscience. The conscience is to the human heart like fire is to flint; it appears only when aroused or impacted. Eyes become bright upon seeing light, and ears become astute upon hearing sound. Without light or sound eyes and ears will fall into disuse and lose all their brightness and astuteness. So that which sparks and arouses is what keeps things alive and growing. When we have plays that spark and arouse conscience and keep it alive and growing, shouldn't they be treasured? There are many plays in this category, and I cannot name them all.

2. Plays that instill wisdom and knowledge. The saying goes: When there are ten thousand things to do, to know is the first thing. Another saying goes: When you know well, you will do well. The *Great Learning* (*Daxue*)[2] explicates the whole world, but it all starts from precise

---

2. *The Great Learning* (*Da xue*), together with *The Analects of Confucius* (*Lunyu*), *The Doctrine of the Mean* (*Zhongyong*), and *Mencius* (*Meng zi*), make up the "Four Books" (*Sishu*), required reading of a classical scholar.

knowledge. Knowledge is power! Some may say that common people do not have the luxury of being knowledgeable about a great many important things; all they can expect is some elementary knowledge or common sense. What is elementary knowledge or common sense? Real reasons and true facts relevant to their daily existence will guide people to the right path. It is acknowledged that "extraordinary tales" make good plays, but being extraordinary does not mean being untrue or making up fantastic tall tales to mislead the people.

3. Plays that showcase acrobatic skills and martial arts for a good cause. This type of play delights the people because it rights the wrongs of this world. It is poetic justice that delights the people, and that is why the chivalrous warrior who upholds justice deserves respect.

4. Plays that use humor and wit appropriately. Inserting some humor and wit in the middle of a serious and gloomy play provides comic relief. It may not be profound, but it certainly is good for mental health. Furthermore, very often sarcasm and irony work a lot better than solemn words and even better than acrobatics or martial arts.

MAO ZEDONG

From "Talks at the Yan'an Forum on Literature and the Arts"

Mao Zedong (1893–1976)—guerrilla fighter and grand strategist, peasant orga-
nizer and oracular Marxist philosopher, radical architect of China's social revolution and dreamy poet of allegorical musings—does not require introduction.
Collectively known as "Talks at the Yan'an Forum on Literature and Arts",
Mao's talks delivered during the Yan'an Forum (three sessions between 2 and 23
May 1942) have remained the single most important document, an "ideological
guide" for the Chinese Communist Party in regard to matters of arts and
literature. In his philosophical, dialectical, and didactic top form Mao developed
some of the most important critical concepts that would dominate the Chinese
literary, artistic, and critical scene for a half-century and beyond: standpoint,
attitude, and audience, form and content, intention and effect, "popularization"
and "elevation," "from life" and "higher than life," "criticism" and "self-
criticism," and so on. The subtitles are the editor's.

Comrades! You are invited to this forum today to exchange views and
ascertain the proper relationship between our work in the artistic and
literary fields and our revolutionary work in general, to determine what
is the proper path of development of revolutionary arts and literature and
how they can better help the other revolutionary activities, so that we
can overthrow the enemy of our nation and accomplish the task of
national liberation.

. . . The purpose of our meeting today is precisely to fit arts and
literature properly into the whole revolutionary machine as one of its
component parts, to make them powerful weapons for uniting and
educating the people and for attacking and annihilating the enemy and to
help the people to fight the enemy with one heart and one mind. What
are the issues to be addressed in order to achieve this objective? I think

Excerpt translated from "Zai yan'an wenyi zuotanhui shangde jianghua," *Mao zedong
xuanji* (Beijing: Renmin chubanshe, 1966), 3:804–35. The editor/translator checked this
translation against the one in *Mao Tse-tung: An Anthology of His Writings* (New York:
New American Library, 1962).

they are the issues of standpoint, attitude, and audience of the artists and writers and of how they should work and how they should study.

Standpoint, Attitude, and Audience

Standpoint: Our standpoint is that of the proletariat and the broad masses of the people. For members of the Communist Party this means that they must adopt the standpoint of the Party and adhere to Party spirit and Party policies. Are there any of our artists and writers who still lack a correct or clear understanding on this point? I think there are. Quite a number of our comrades have often drifted away from the correct standpoint.

Attitude: Our specific attitudes toward specific matters arise from our standpoint. For instance: Should we praise, or should we expose? This is a question of attitude. Which of these two attitudes should we adopt? I should say both, and it all depends on whom you are dealing with. There are three types of people: the enemy, the allies in the united front, and our own people—namely, the masses of the people and their vanguard. Three different attitudes must be adopted toward these three types of people. With regards to our enemies—that is, the Japanese imperialists and all other enemies of the people—the task of revolution-ary artists and writers is to expose their cruelty and treachery, point out the inevitability of their defeat, and encourage the anti-Japanese army and people to fight them with one heart and one mind and to depose them resolutely. In our attitude toward our various allies in the united front, we ought to promote unity as well as criticism, and there should be different kinds of unity and different kinds of criticism. We support their resistance against Japan and commend them for their achievements. But we ought to criticize them if they do not put up an active resistance against Japan. We must resolutely censure anyone who opposes commu-nism and the people and moves closer and closer toward the reactionary path with each passing day. As to the masses of the people, their toil and struggle, their army and their party, we should of course praise them. The people also have their shortcomings. Many among the proletariat still entertain petit bourgeoisie notions, while the peasantry and the urban petit bourgeoisie still harbor backward ideas—these are the bur-dens handicapping them in their struggle. We should take time patiently to educate them and help them to remove the burdens from their backs and overcome their own shortcomings and errors so that they can make big strides forward. In the course of their struggles, if they have changed or are changing themselves, our arts and literature should depict this process of change. Unless they persist in their errors, we should not take a one-sided look at them, ridicule them or even act in hostility toward them. What we produce [as artists and writers] should enable them to unite, to progress, and to stride forward with one heart and one mind, discarding what is backward and promoting what is revolutionary; it certainly should not do the opposite.

Audience: For whom are the artistic and literary works intended? . . .

The audience for our arts and literature is made up of workers, peasants, soldiers, and their cadres; thus, the problem arises of how to understand these people and to know them well. A great deal of work has to be done in order to understand them and to know them well. . . . Our artists and writers should work in their own field, which is arts and literature, but what they should do first of all is to understand and know the people well. How did they stand in this regard in the past? I should say that they failed miserably, and they were like heroes with no place to display their heroism. What did they fail to know well? They failed to know the people well. They did not know well either whom they were depicting or the intended audience; they were practically perfect strangers to both. They did not know well the workers, peasants, soldiers, and their cadres. What did they fail to understand? They failed to understand their language; that is, they lacked an adequate knowledge of the rich and lively language of the masses of the people. Many artists and writers, living a barren existence away from the people, are of course unfamiliar with the people's language. As a result, their works are not only written in a dull and dry language but often contain awkward expressions of their own coinage that don't fit in with popular usage. Many comrades love to talk about "doing it the popular way" (*dazhong hua*), but what does the term mean? It means that the ideas and feelings of our artists and writers should be fused with those of the broad masses of workers, peasants, and soldiers. In order to do so one should conscientiously learn the language of the masses. If one does not understand much of the language of the masses, how can one talk about creating works of art and literature? When I say heroes with no place to display heroism, I mean that the masses do not appreciate your empty lengthy talk. The more you put on airs as veterans, as "heroes," and the harder you try to pitch a sale, the more the people refuse to be impressed. If you want the masses to understand you and if you want to become one of them, you must be determined to undergo a long and even painful process of transformation.

Source versus Flow

What, after all, is the source (*yuan*), or fountainhead, of any kind of art and literature? A work of art or literature is ideologically the product of the human mind reflecting the life of a given society. Revolutionary arts and literature are the products of the mind of revolutionary artists and writers reflecting the life of the people. In the life of the people itself lies a mine of raw material for arts and literature, namely, things in their natural state, things crude but also most lively, colorful, rich, and fundamental; in this sense they outshine arts and literature and also provide for them a unique and inexhaustible source. Some may ask: Is there not another source in the books, in the artistic and literary works of ancient times and foreign countries? As a matter of fact, artistic and literary works of the past are not the source but the flow (*liu*); they are products that the ancients and the foreigners created out of the artistic and literary raw material they lit upon in the people's life of their own times and places. It makes an enormous difference whether or not one has such examples to look up to, a difference that explains why some works are refined and others crude, some polished and others coarse, some superior and others inferior, some smoothly done and others laboriously executed. Therefore, we must not refuse to inherit the legacy from the ancients and the foreigners and learn from such examples, even if feudal or bourgeois. But inheriting a legacy and learning from examples should never take the place of creating our own work, for nothing can take its place. In arts and literature the uncritical appropriation and imitation of the ancients and foreigners represent not only a shameful lack of originality but also the most harmful doctrinairism. All revolutionary artists and writers in China, all artists and writers of high promise, must, for long periods of time, unreservedly and wholeheartedly go into the midst of the masses, the masses of workers, peasants, and soldiers; they must go into the heated struggles, go to the only, the vastest, and the richest source to observe, experience, study, and analyze all men, all classes, all types of people, all the vivid forms of life and struggle, and all raw material for arts and literature; then and only then can they proceed to create their own work. Otherwise, you will have nothing to work on and will turn into the kind of "empty-headed" artist or writer against whom Lu Xun, in his will, so earnestly cautioned his son.

Life versus Art

Although man's social life constitutes the only source for arts and literature and is incomparably more vivid and richer than arts and literature as such, the people are not content with having only the former; they demand the latter. Why? Because life as reflected in artistic and literary works can and ought to be on a higher level, more powerful, better focused, more typical, nearer the ideal, and therefore more universal than everyday life. Revolutionary arts and literature should create all types of characters on the basis of actual life and help the masses to push history forward. For example, on the one hand there are people suffering from hunger, cold, and oppression, and on the other hand there are people exploiting and oppressing other people—a contrast that exists everywhere and seems quite commonplace; artists and writers, however, can create works of art and literature out of such daily occurrences by organizing them, bringing them to a sharp focus, and making the contradictions and struggles in them typical, thus creating works of art and literature that can awaken and arouse the masses and motivate them to unite and fight to change their environment. If there were no such works of art and literature, this task could not be accomplished or at least not effectively and speedily accomplished.

Popularization versus Elevation

What are popularization (*puji*) and elevation (*tigao*) in arts and literature? What is the relationship between the two? Works for popularization are simple and clear and therefore more readily accessible to today's broad masses of people. Works of a higher level are more refined and therefore more difficult to produce and less likely to win the ready acceptance of today's broad masses of people. The problem facing the workers, peasants and soldiers today is this: engaged in a ruthless and bloody struggle against the enemy, they remain largely illiterate and lack cultural sophistication as a result of the prolonged rule by the feudal and bourgeois classes. And, consequently, they badly need a widespread campaign of enlightenment, and they are eager to have literacy, knowledge, arts, and literature that meet their immediate need and are readily accessible to them and which can heighten their passion for struggle and confidence in victory, strengthen their solidarity, and enable them to fight the enemy with one heart and one mind. In meeting their basic needs, we are not "adding flowers to the brocade" but "sending charcoal in snowy weather." Under the present conditions, therefore, popularization is the more pressing task. It is wrong to despise and neglect this task.

But popularization and elevation cannot be rigidly separated. It is possible to popularize even now a number of works of a higher order, because the level of sophistication of the broad masses is also steadily rising. If popularization remains always on one level—for one, two, or three months or for one, two, or three years, circulating always the same stuff like *Little Cowherd* (*Xiao fangniu*)[1] or the same characters like "human, hand, mouth, knife, cow, goat"[2]—will not the educator and those being educated remain much the same? What is such popularization good for? The people need popularization, but along with it they need elevation too, elevation from month to month and from year to year. Such elevation does not take place in midair nor behind closed doors but on the basis of popularization. It is at once determined by popularization and gives direction to it. In China the revolution and revolutionary culture are uneven in their stages of development, and they spread and expand only gradually; thus, in one place not only the work of popularization may have already been accomplished but also the popularization-based elevation, while in other places the work of popularization may not yet have even begun. Therefore, the helpful lessons of popularization-based elevation in one place may be applied in another, serving as guidance to the work of popularization and elevation there and saving a lot of trial and error. Internationally, the helpful lessons of foreign countries, especially the experiences of the Soviet Union, can serve as our guide. Our elevation is on the basis of popularization, while our popularization is under the guidance of elevation. This being the case, the work of popularization not only constitutes no obstacle to elevation but offers a basis for our work of elevation on a limited scale at present and prepare the necessary conditions for our far more extensive work of elevation in the future.

---

1. A popular Chinese operetta with a cast of only two characters, a cowherd and a village girl, carrying on a dialogue in song and dance. With its songs reworded for the purpose of anti-Japanese propaganda, it enjoyed much popularity in the early days of the War of Resistance against Japan.
2. In Chinese these are written characters of few simple strokes, usually taught in the first lessons of old primers.

Besides the elevation that directly meets the needs of the masses there is also the elevation that meets their needs indirectly, namely, the elevation needed by the cadres. Being advanced members, the cadres are generally better educated than the masses, and arts and literature of a higher level are entirely necessary to them; and it would be a mistake to ignore this. Anything done for the cadres is also entirely done for the masses, because it is only through the cadres that we can educate and guide the masses. . . .

Since we have addressed the issue of the relationship between popularization and elevation, the issue of the relationship between experts and popularizers can also be settled. Our experts should serve not only the cadres but chiefly the masses. Our literature experts should pay attention to the wall newspapers of the masses and the reportage literature in the army and the villages. Our drama experts should pay attention to the small troupes in the army and the villages. Our music experts should pay attention to the songs of the masses. Our fine arts experts should pay attention to the fine arts of the masses. All these comrades should stay in close contact with the popularizers of arts and literature among the masses, help and guide the popularizers as well as learn from them, and through them draw nourishment from the masses to develop and enrich themselves and to prevent their specialties from turning into hollow and lifeless castles in the air away from the masses and reality. Experts should be respected; they are very valuable to our cause. But we should also remind them that no artist or writer can produce any work of significance unless he or she is in touch with the masses, gives expression to their thoughts and feelings, and acts as their faithful spokesperson. Only by speaking for the masses can he help educate them, and only by becoming their pupil can he become their teacher. If he regards himself as the master of the masses or as an aristocrat lording over the "lowly people," then, no matter how great his talent, he will not be needed by the people, and his work will have no future.

Critical Criteria: Political versus Artistic

There are two criteria in art and literary criticism: political and artistic. According to the political criterion, all works are good that facilitate unity and resistance against Japan, that encourage the masses to be of one heart and one mind, and that oppose retrogression and promote progress; on the other hand, all works are bad that undermine unity and resistance against Japan, that sow dissension and discord among the masses, and that oppose progress and drag the people backward. And how can we tell the good from the bad here? By the motive (subjective intention) or by the effect (social application)? Idealists stress motive and ignore effect, while mechanical materialists stress effect and ignore motive; in contrast, we dialectical materialists insist on the unity of motive and effect. The motive of serving the masses is inseparable from the effect of winning their approval, and we must unite the two. The motive of serving the individual or a small clique is not good, nor is the motive of serving the masses good if it does not lead to a result that is welcomed by the masses and confers benefit on them.

In examining the subjective intention of an artist—that is, whether his motive is correct and good—we do not look at his declaration but at the effect his action (mainly his work) produces on society and the masses. Social application and its effect are the criteria for examining the subjective intention or the motive. We reject sectarianism in our art and literary criticism and, under the general principle of unity and resistance against Japan, we should tolerate artistic and literary works expressing all kinds of political attitude. But at the same time we must firmly uphold our principles in our criticism, adhere to our standpoint, and sternly criticize and repudiate all works containing views against the nation, science, the people, and communism, because such works, in motive as well as in effect, are detrimental to unity and resistance against Japan. According to the artistic criterion, all works are good or rather good that are comparatively high in artistic quality; bad or rather bad that are comparatively low in artistic quality. Of course, this distinction also depends on social effect. As there is hardly an artist who does not consider his own work splendid, our criticism ought to permit the free competition of all varieties of artistic works, but it is entirely necessary for us to pass correct judgments on them according to the criteria of artistic standard, so that we can gradually raise the art of a lower level to a higher level and change the art that does not meet the demands of the struggle of the broad masses into art that does meet them.

There is thus the political criterion as well as the artistic criterion. How are the two related? Politics is not the equivalent of art, nor is a general worldview equivalent to the method of artistic creation and criticism. We believe there is neither an abstract and absolutely unchangeable political criterion nor an abstract and absolutely unchangeable artistic criterion, for every class in a class society has its own political and artistic criteria. But all classes in all class societies place the political criterion first and artistic criterion second. The bourgeoisie always rejects proletarian artistic and literary works, no matter how great their artistic attainment. As for the proletariat, they must treat the arts and literature of the past according to their attitude toward the people and whether they are progressive in the light of history. Some things that are basically reactionary from the political point of view may yet contain certain artistic merits. But the better such a work is artistically, the greater the harm it will do to the people, and the more reason for us to reject it. The contradiction between reactionary political content and artistic form is a common characteristic of the arts and literature of all exploitative classes in their decline. What we demand is unity of politics and art, of content and form, that is, the unity of revolutionary political content and the highest possible degree of perfection in artistic form. Works of art, however politically progressive, are powerless if they lack artistic quality. Therefore, we are equally opposed to works with the wrong political approach and to the tendency toward the so-called poster and slogan style (*biaoyu kouhao shi*), which is correct only in political approach but lacks artistic power. We must meet a two-front challenge in arts and literature.

Both of these tendencies can be found among many of our comrades. The comrades who tend to neglect artistic quality should pay attention to its improvement. But, as I see it, the political side is more of a problem at present. Some comrades lack elementary political common sense, and consequently all kinds of muddled ideas arise. Let me give a few examples found here in Yan'an.

"The theory of human nature." Is there such a thing as human nature? Of course there is. But there is only human nature in the concrete, no human nature in the abstract. In a class society there is only human nature that bears the stamp of a class but no human nature transcending classes. We endorse the human nature of the proletariat and of the great masses of the people, while the landowning and bourgeois classes endorse the nature of their own classes as if—though they do not say so outright—it were the only kind of human nature. The human nature advocated by certain petit bourgeois intellectuals is also divorced from or opposed to that of the great masses of the people; what they call human nature is in substance nothing but bourgeois individualism, and consequently in their eyes proletarian human nature is contrary to their human nature. This is the human nature theory promoted by some people here in Yan'an as the so-called basis of their theory of arts and literature, which is utterly misguided.

"The fundamental point of departure for arts and literature is love, the love of mankind." Now love may be one point of departure, but there is still a more basic one. Love is a concept, a product of objective practice. Fundamentally, we do not begin from a concept but from objective practice. Our artists and writers who come from the intelligentsia love the proletariat because their social life has made them feel that they share the same fate with the proletariat. We hate Japanese imperialism because the Japanese imperialists have oppressed us. There is no love or hatred in the world that does not have its cause. As for the so-called love of mankind, there has never been such all-inclusive love since humanity was divided into classes. All the ruling classes in the past liked to advocate it, and many so-called sages and wise men also did the same, but nobody has ever really practiced it, for it is impractical in a class society. Genuine love of mankind will be born only when the class distinctions have been eliminated throughout the world. The classes have caused the division of society into many opposites, and, as soon as they are eliminated, there will be love of all mankind, but not now. We cannot love our enemies, we cannot love social evils, and our goal is to exterminate them. How can our artists and writers fail to understand such common sense?

"Arts and literature have always depicted the bright as well as the dark side of things equally, on a half-and-half basis." This statement contains a number of muddled ideas. Arts and literature have not always done so. Many petit bourgeois writers have never found the bright side, and their works are devoted to exposing the dark side, the so-called literature of exposé. There are even works specializing in propagating pessimism and misanthropy. On the other hand, Soviet literature during the period of socialist reconstruction portrays mainly the bright side. It also depicts shortcomings in their work and includes villainous characters, but such depiction serves only to point up the brightness of the whole picture and not to be on a so-called half-and-half basis. Bourgeois writers of reactionary periods portray the revolutionary masses as ruffians and depict the bourgeois as saints, thus reversing the so-called bright and dark sides. Only truly revolutionary artists and writers can correctly solve the problem whether to praise or to expose. All dark forces endangering the masses of the people must be exposed, while all revolutionary struggles of the masses must be praised—this is the basic task of all revolutionary artists and writers.

"The task of arts and literature has always been to expose." This sort of argument, like the one mentioned earlier, arises from a lack of knowledge of history. We have already shown that the task of arts and literature does not consist only of exposure. For the revolutionary artists and writers the object of their exposé can never be the masses of the people but only the aggressors, exploiters, and oppressors and the harmful influences they leave behind among the people. The people have their shortcomings too, but these are to be overcome by means of criticism and self-criticism among themselves, which is also one of the most important tasks of arts and literature. We should not, however, call that "exposing the people." For the people it is basically a question of how to educate them and raise their consciousness. Only counterrevolutionary artists and writers describe the people as "born ignorant" and revolutionary masses as "tyrannical mobs."

"This is still an era of essays in the style of Lu Xun." Living under the rule of dark forces, deprived of freedom of speech, Lu Xun had to fight with freezing irony and burning satire in his particular style of essays, and in this he was completely correct. We too also must dish out piercing ridicules of the fascists, Chinese reactionaries, and anything harming the people. But in our border region of Shanxi-Gansu-Ningxia and the anti-Japanese base areas in the enemy's back, where revolutionary artists and writers enjoy full freedom and democracy and only counterrevolutionaries are denied them, essays should not be written only in the style of Lu Xun. Here we can shout at the top of our lungs and need not resort to obscure and cryptic expressions that would make it hard to understand for the broad masses of the people. In dealing with the people themselves and not the enemies of the people, Lu Xun, even in his "essay period," did not mock or attack the revolutionary masses or revolutionary parties, and his writing style was also entirely different from that used in his essays aimed at the enemy. We have already said that we need to criticize the shortcomings of the people, but we must do that from the standpoint of the people and out of the wholehearted eagerness to protect and educate them. If we treat our comrades like enemies, then we are standing on the enemy side. Are we then to give up satire all together? No. Satire is always necessary. But there are all kinds of satire: the kind for our enemies, the kind for our allies, and the kind for our own legions; each assumes a different attitude. We are not against satire as a whole, but we must oppose its abuse.

"I am not given to praise and eulogy; works by those who extol the bright side are not necessarily great nor are works by those who depict the dark side as necessarily paltry." If you are a bourgeois artist or writer, you will extol not the proletariat but the bourgeoisie; if you are a proletarian artist or writer, you will extol not the bourgeoisie but the proletariat and the other working people: you must choose one or the other. Works by those who extol the bright side of the bourgeoisie are not necessarily great, while works by those who depict its dark side are not necessarily paltry, and works by those who extol the bright side of the proletariat are not necessarily great, but works by those who depict the so-called dark side of the proletariat are undoubtedly paltry. Are these not the facts in the history of arts and literature? Why should we not praise the people who are the creator of the human history? Why should we not praise the proletariat, the Communist Party, the New Democracy, and socialism? Of course, there are some people who have no enthusiasm for the people's cause, who stand aloof, looking with cold indifference on the struggle and victory of the proletariat and its van-guard; they are only interested in themselves and tirelessly singing praises of themselves and maybe a few cronies. Petit bourgeois individualists like this are naturally unwilling to sing praises of the meritorious deeds of the revolutionary masses or to hearten their courage in their struggle and confidence in their victory. People like this are the black sheep in the revolutionary ranks, and the revolutionary masses have indeed no use for such "singers."

"It is not a matter of standpoint; the standpoint may be correct, the intention and idea good, but the presentation is flawed and thus produces a bad effect." I have already spoken about the dialectical materialistic view of motive and effect, and now I'd like to ask: Is the question of effect not one of standpoint? A person who, in doing a job, minds only the motive and cares nothing about the effect is very much like a doctor who hands out prescriptions and does not care how many patients may die taking what he prescribes. Suppose, again, a political party keeps on making pronouncements while paying no attention to their actual realiza-tion. Is such a standpoint correct? Are such intentions good? Of course, a person is liable to make mistakes in anticipating the result of an action before it is taken, but are his intentions still good if he persists in the same old rut even when facts prove that it leads to a bad effect? In judging a party or a doctor, we must look at the practice and the effect, and the same applies in judging an artist or a writer. One who has a truly good intention must take the effect into consideration by gathering experi-ences and studying methods or, in the case of creative work, the means of expression. One who has a truly good intention must criticize most candidly the shortcomings and mistakes in his own work and resolutely correct them. That is the way the Communists practice self-criticism, which is the only correct standpoint. At the same time, it is only through such a process undertaken conscientiously and responsibly that we can gradually understand and hold onto the correct standpoint. If one refuses to do this in practice, then he is really ignorant of the correct standpoint, despite his conceited assertion to the contrary.

"Asking us to study Marxism is to repeat the mistake of making us follow the creative methodology of dialectical materialism, and it will do damage to creative spirit." To study Marxism is to help us look at the world, the society, and arts and literature from the perspective of dialectical materialism and historical materialism, it is not to require us to write philosophical speeches in works of art and literature. Marxism can only guide, but not substitute, realism in artistic and literary creation, just as it can guide, but not substitute, atomic theory or electronic theory in physical science. Empty and dry doctrine or formula will definitely be destructive to creative spirit, but the creative spirit is not the only thing that is being damaged; Marxism is the first that is being damaged here. Dogmatic "Marxism" is not Marxism; it is anti-Marxism. Does it mean that Marxism doesn't do damage? Oh yes, it decidedly does damage to the creative mood that is feudal, bourgeois, petit bourgeois, liberal, individualistic, nihilistic, art-for-art's-sake, aristocratic, decadent, pessimistic, or any other kind of so-called creative mood that is alien to the broad masses of people and the proletariat. For a proletarian artist or writer shouldn't these moods be destroyed? I feel they should be destroyed and completely so. New things can be built on the site of demolition.

MAO ZEDONG

A Letter after Seeing
Bishang Liangshan

After seeing a Beijing opera performance of *Driven to Join the Liang Mountain Rebels* (*Bishang liangshan*), a revised version of an old play based on the novel *The Water Margin* (*Shui hu*), Mao wrote an enthusiastic letter, on 9 January 1944, to leaders of the company at the Central Party School in Yan'an. This letter was to have a lasting impact, especially during the Cultural Revolution (1966–76), the peak of "revolutionizing traditional theater."

January 9th, 1944

Comrades [Yang] Shaoxuan and [Qi] Yanming,[1]

I saw your play; you have done a great job. I thank you, and please tell the actors I thank them! History is created by the people, but on the stage of the old traditional theater (in the literature and arts that have been separated from the people) the people have been turned into the dregs of society, while the Masters, Madames, Young Masters, and Young Misses have dominated the stage. This reversal of history has now been reversed again by you; you have restored history to its true face, and you have given the old traditional theater a new beginning. For this I congratulate you. Guo Moruo has done a lot in history plays in the area of spoken drama; now you have done so in the old traditional theater. What you have begun is an epoch-making beginning of revolutionizing old traditional theater. I am very pleased when I think of this. Hope you write more and perform more, building up the momentum and making it the order of the day across the land!

With high respect,
Mao Zedong

Translated from *Yan'an shinian xiju tuji: 1937–1947*, ed. Zhong Jingzhi (Shanghai: Shanghai wenyi chubanshe, 1982), 61.
1. Yang Shaoxuan and Qi Yanming participated in rewriting the new Beijing opera version of the play, and Qi also directed the production that Mao Zedong saw.

142

MEI LANFANG

From "A Talk on the Art of Acting"

Mei Lanfang (1894–1961) came from a family of theater artists. Both his father and grandfather were accomplished female impersonators of *Kun* opera and Beijing opera. His uncle, who was responsible for raising Mei Lanfang, whose father passed away early, was a well-known Beijing opera musician. Mei himself made his first stage appearance at age eleven. The world-famous Beijing opera female impersonator, Mei Langfang, was not only a master of the theater form he inherited, but he was also a bold and visionary innovator, for he was concerned with keeping his theater a living art form sensitive to the changes of time. Among many of his contributions Mei was credited for upgrading the literary standards of the plays with strong women characters and for combining and developing techniques for better showcasing the performers' versatility in singing, dancing, movement, speech, and acrobatic skills. As a result, Mei helped to turn the young female characters on the stage into more respected, intelligent, talented, cultivated, and dignified human beings. Mei's brilliance as a performer not only won him personal fame at home and abroad; his visits to Japan, United States and the former Soviet Union helped to establish Beijing opera's status as a relevant and distinctive theatrical form in the consciousness of the world literary and artistic community. The following excerpts are taken from a talk Mei gave to the students at the China Academy of Traditional Theatre in May 1960. Here Mei Lanfang was calling people's attention to the importance of emotional authenticity, psychological truth, and social realism.

Every play has a story; every story has its characters; and every character, whether male or female, has a different social status, age, personality, and living environment. We actors should get to know clearly the historical background of each story first, then we should carefully analyze and deeply experience the characters we play in all four distinct aspects mentioned earlier [social status, age, personality, and living environment]. This is an area directly related to an actor's intellectual sophistication and political consciousness. A play script stipulates whether a character is good or bad and whether his actions are good or bad, but it is ultimately up to the actor

Excerpts translated from "Guanyu biaoyan yishyde jianghua," *Mei lanfang wenji* (Beijing: Zhongguo xiju chubanshe, 1962), 48–59.

to bring the play and the character to life. The higher the actor's political consciousness, the more vivid the character he portrays, and the better can the play's educational function be fulfilled. It is not an easy task; only through continued hard study can it be done well.

There are generally four principal role categories in the Beijing opera: male (*sheng*), female (*dan*), painted face (*jing*), and comic (*chou*); and within each category there are a number of variants. What distinguishes these variants? It is the four aspects. In short, there were certain types of characters before there were role categories, each with fixed conventions. For example, a play called for a young boy to play a singing part; thereafter the variant, or subcategory, "male child" (*wa-wa sheng*) came into existence. In today's new society a great number of new heroes have emerged, and there are no precedents for such character types on the Beijing opera stage. For that matter we may very well break away from the confines of the old role categories and invent new ones. For instance, we cannot present the character of the "White-haired Girl" [simply in the conventional] *qingyi, guimendan, or huadan*.[1] The White-haired Girl we now have on the stage is a very good new creation.

My line of business has been playing female roles, concentrating only on the four classifications: *qingyi, guimendan, huadan,* and *daomadan*.[2] Just a few days ago I played Du Liniang, a *guimendan*, in the scene of "Dream in the Garden" ["Youyuan jingmeng," from *The Peony Pavilion*]. Now I will talk about this classification first.

It is clear from the word *guimendan* that this type of role portrays unmarried or just-married young women in the old days. Du Liniang in "Dream in the Garden" and Wang Baochuan in "The Wager" ["San ji zhang," from *The Red-Maned Steed (Hongzong liema)*] are both *guimendan*, but they should be performed differently. Both characters are struggling

---

1. White-haired Girl (*Baimao nü*) is the title heroine of a popular story about oppression and class struggle; the story has been made into plays, films, a song-drama (*geju*), a dance-drama (*wuju*), a ballet, and a modern Beijing opera.

   Qingyi, literally "blue-clothed," is one classification in the traditional female role category, which symbolizes women of virtue, dignity, and strong character, loyal to their family obligations and often portrayed in moods of anguish and adverse situations. The subjects are usually filial daughters, distressed lovers, and faithful wives.

   Guimendan, literally "in the girl's chamber dan," is another classification in the traditional female role category. The subjects are young girls and unmarried women.

   Huadan, literally "flower dan," is yet another classification in the traditional female role category. The subjects are young coquettish women or their vivacious soubrettes, who are full of charm, provocativeness, and mischief.

2. *Daomadan*, literally "sword-horse dan" (sometimes also called *wudan*, meaning "military dan"), is yet another classification in the traditional female role category. The subjects are young women skilled in fighting and horseback riding, who are accustomed to robust action without dispensing with their feminine charm.

against the feudal marriage conventions, but, while Du Liniang battles only in her own mind, Wang Baochuan has put her ideas into action. Consequently, the presentation of these two should not be the same. Wang Baochuan has had physical contact with her lover, and in the course of the action she rises to resist openly her father's oppression. Therefore, we can present her struggle in an impassioned and vehement manner. Du Liniang, on the other hand, has been kept in her insulated chamber under feudal coercion. She has never had any real lover; her struggle is only in her head, for she has never had the chance to act upon her ideas. Accordingly, the way we present her deep dissatisfaction should be diametrically different from the way we present Wang Baochuan's. Du's struggle is internal, whereas Wang's is external. One requires one to be subtlely implicit, the other vividly explicit. In acting, implicitness seems more difficult to achieve than explicitness. We have to present the forbidden secret angst of a young girl living in feudal times while always keeping in mind a sense of subtle propriety so that a young girl's anxiety about love would not be misinterpreted as a young woman's sexual desire. You see, this is quite a delicate job, isn't it?

Kun opera is an older theatrical tradition [than Beijing opera]. Its vocal styles and movements are very rich and beautiful, yet its lyrics can be very elusive. If an actor does not fully understand the meaning of the lyrics, he cannot empathize with the true character of the role he plays. Take myself for an example: I learned "Dream in the Garden" first from Master Qiao Huilan, and I also received frequent notes from Master Chen Delin. At first I was just simply imitating what my teachers were doing, without fully understanding the meaning of the lyrics. Later on several good friends well versed in poetry and literature elucidated to me over and over again in great detail the nuances of the scene, which helped me tremendously. Still, I had to overcome a lot of difficulties to further my studies, because I began learning acting at a very young age, and I did not have a good foundation in classical literature. After I understood the meaning of the lyrics, it still took me a long time fully to understand and identify with my character. I have done this scene many times in the past decades. I still study it and work on it every time I do it. Last year before filming the piece for the big screen, I again studied all the lyrics word by word, line by line, with a few friends, and I felt that I had again gained some new understanding. That is why you may notice that my characterization of Du Liniang was somewhat different from before. The old proverb goes: Live and learn. This is really a wise saying based on experience.

A JIA

From "Truth in Life and Truth in Art"

A Jia (1907–), born Fu Luheng in Jiangsu Province, is a well-known theorist, playwright, and director of the Chinese traditional theater. His interest in painting and the traditional theater started when he was a young child. In 1937 A Jia went to Lu Xun Academy of Arts and Literature (Lu xun yishu wenxue yuan) in Yan'an, and shortly after he became the head of the Beijing Opera Studies division. It was while in Yan'an that A Jia achieved fame as a talented playwright, director, and actor of Beijing opera. After the Communist victory, in 1949, A Jia was appointed to many important leading positions in the arts, including deputy president and chief director of the preeminent China Beijing Opera Company.

A Jia was very interested in the theoretical research on traditional theater. The following speech was given in 1956, during a time when the Soviet-style socialist realism was achieving prominence not only in modern spoken drama (*huaju*) but also in other theatrical forms. In his speech A Jia warns against blindly applying realistic doctrines to the nonrealistic traditional theater and discusses the relationship between life and art in general and the distinctive characteristics and aesthetic principles of the Chinese traditional theater in particular.

In recent years, while dealing with the issue of improving the art of traditional theater acting, there has been a tendency among many of our comrades who want to use Stanislavsky's theory of theater to solve the problems in acting in our traditional theater. Their intention is good; in the process of learning from this advanced practice, however, they start with precepts and forget to use the reality of Chinese traditional theater as the point of departure. The initial purpose is to use Stanislavsky to help get rid of some formalistic elements in the acting of traditional

---

Excerpts translated from "Shenghuode zhenshi he xiqu biaoyan yishude zhenshi," *Zhongguo xiqu lilun yanjiu wenxuan* (Shanghai: Shanghai wenyi chubanshe, 1985), 45–69. This piece, originally a lecture given at a workshop for actors of the traditional theater sponsored by the Ministry of Culture in October 1956, was published in the first issue of *Study of Traditional Theatre* (*Xiqu yanjiu*) in 1957. Some paragraph divisions have been added to avoid excessively long paragraphs.

theater, but, because of some mistaken notions, now the presentational form of traditional theater itself is being attacked.

What is formalism in acting? Where is it? It is very easy to talk about it in the abstract, but once in the rehearsal hall in a hands-on situation some people are no longer that clear-headed. They often go all out trying to impose naturalism on the traditional theater, and they have ready-made theoretical support, namely "content determines form" or "begin with life," two ironclad principles that no one dares to question. These two universally valid principles have been misinterpreted by the dogmatists. In applying them to the traditional theater, they demand that the actors not use *chengshi* (formalized stage conventions), for they believe that a play's style and a character's personality and disposition will emerge naturally only through a director's responsive guide in rehearsal and an actor's inner connection with the character. This is called "from the inner heart to the outer form" (*cong neixin dao waixing*), which means that once you have the "internal action" (*neixin huodong*) the perfect "external action" (*waixing dongzuo*) will follow naturally. If [anyone demands that] actors first master some acting techniques, which we call *chengshi,* he is typically considered to have committed formalism, a serious mistake in principle, because he is not doggedly following the so-called principles of "first inside then outside" or "starting from life itself" or "letting content determine form."

Under the dominance of this way of thinking—that inner connection will automatically produce technical skills—the directors and actors find it unnecessary to study the unique features of acting in traditional theater as well as a whole set of many related stage rules and, of course, it seems unnecessary for the actors to practice their daily technical and physical routines. Some people really believe that the purpose of theater reform is to break away from this kind of traditional practice. These people consciously or unconsciously use the principles of naturalism for spoken drama to judge whether the acting in traditional theater is valid or not and to critique the traditional means of expression. When they encounter something that they cannot explain, instead of admitting their own ignorance, they assume these things have no connections to real life and thus should be eliminated. Sometimes they will isolate an individual dancelike movement (e.g., *yunshou, woyu, yaozi fangsheng, titui,* or *cuobu*) and ask the actors to trace it back to an actual movement in real life; if they cannot, then it is proof enough that such *chengshi* belongs to formalism. Some old actors cannot endure this type of prodding and questioning, so they quickly admit fault and stop teaching the techniques to their students. Some very good actors, who used to seem like the real dragon or tiger when they play one, now feel lost and ill at ease on the stage, because they do not want to be accused of practicing formalism.

When I saw some famous actors at a performance recently, they did not pause where there ought to be a pause, and they dragged where they ought not; [a *chengshi* such as] "da beigong" was done half-baked, and they dared not to face the audience squarely in the eye; gestures and rhythms were ambiguous, the statuesque posturing in stillness disappeared, and all the stylized movements were executed hesitantly. A usually very good play just went by loosely and vapidly. As I found out later, apparently it was the result of trying to create realism on the stage, trying to experience deeply the internal action, and trying to break away from the tradition of *chengshi*.

Of course, when I am pointing out all these problems I am not saying that traditional theater acting, because of its unique characteristics, should be allowed not to experience real life or be allowed to disregard the idea of letting content determine form or be allowed to be negative about the creative methods of realism or even be allowed to dismiss the advanced lessons from the Stanislavskian school. No, absolutely not. When I am praising the outstanding features of the traditional theater, I am not saying that it is perfect and has nothing wrong with it. No, that is not true either. The issue here is, no matter whether you are espousing experiencing life or promoting the working method of realism, as a theater worker, especially if you are a director, you should understand the intrinsic laws governing the particular art form you practice. Painting, music, dance, literature, and theater all need experiences of life, all can learn something from realism, and that is what all these art forms have in common. In the actual creative process, however, each art form works with its own special standards and means of expression. Otherwise, what is there to say about artistic forms? There is no creative method in this world that exists without specific artistic practice, and no artistic practice exists without its own particular means of expression. Life is the source of art; naturally, art cannot disregard the truth of life—but, in reflecting life, each art has to use its own particular form and develop its own characteristics. Because different art forms have different means of expression and, in depicting life, they have different perspectives and methods and they all have their own strength and limitations, so there should not be a uniform standard. . . .

The practice of constructing a play performance on a series of scenes (*fenchang*) is the structural basis of the traditional theater. . . . The importance of using entrances (*shangchang*) and exits (*xiaxhang*) to indicate scene changes onstage mainly lies in the unique handling of space and time onstage. The key point is that, as soon as the actors evacuate the stage space, it no longer exists as any specific locale in a specific time. In spoken drama there are also entrances and exits, but they function differently than in the traditional theater. For instance, in spoken drama, as long as the set is not changed, no matter how often the characters enter and exit, the locale stays the same. In fact, even before the characters make their entrance, specific time and locale (indicated by scenery and lighting) already exist onstage. It is not so with the stage of the traditional theater; if there is no character on it, the stage does not represent any locale or environment. In the past there was usually in the middle of the stage a table and two chairs, which are just abstract ornaments having no relation whatsoever with the action of the play. Only when the character enters, a specific locale is assumed; when the character exits, the locale again disappears along with him. For instance, in the play *The Sword of Universe* (*Yuzhou feng*) it is not until Zhao Gao enters that the stage becomes the minister's residence, and in the second scene it is not until Emperor Qin enters that the stage space becomes the Golden Palace. The locale changes not only from one scene to another, even within the same scene. For instance, in a recent performance of the scene *Search of the Du Residence* (*Sou dufu*) three ministers were searching the Du residence, from the front hall to the backyard, from the barn to the stable, and all the way to the water dungeon; it seemed to move really fast and suspenseful as they were combing every place, but all those specific locations were indicated in the same space of the same scene. . . .

Time is handled with similar principle as space. If the distance of scores of miles is covered by circling the stage once, then the time to cover that distance (approximately several hours) is now only several minutes. Over ten years have elapsed between the scenes *Switching Sons on the Execution Ground* (*Fachang huanzi*) and *Holding up the Vessel to See the Picture* (*Juding guanhua*), but on the stage of the traditional theater all it takes are two scenes. In the "study" scene of *Inquiring the Woodcutter and Raising Hell* (*Wenqiao naofu*), the actor who plays Fan Zhongyu, through three short arias and a few stylized movements, in a matter of three to five minutes, is able to convey how a grief-stricken scholar endures a long and lonely night lamenting the loss of his wife and children. . . . Examples like this are too numerous to mention one by one, and this type of means of expression can only be realized through the special *fenchang* structure [I've been talking about].

If we adopt [from the realistic spoken drama] the act division and realistic scenery, the traditional theater's characteristic means of expression will be completely destroyed. . . . [Let's just take a hypothetical look at this hybrid form]. In physical movement there might be a bit more stylization allowed than in the spoken drama, but the stylized movement and posture would be limited to only those that help the actors express their characters' moods and emotions; totally lost would be those imaginary yet convincing pantomime and postures that help the actors create and communicate with the nonmaterial physical environment. There might still be singing and musical accompaniment, but the vocal stylization and percussion segment developed with the *fenchang* structure would have no reason to exist. I am not being stubborn or conservative; I am simply explaining the characteristics of the traditional theater as an art of synthesis (*zonghe xing*).

Fenchang structure is just a structure; it takes bringing together singing, doing, reciting, and fighting (*chang, zuo, nian, da*) to begin completing a concrete stage image, to begin creating a given situation in space and time. In *Beating the Drum and Scolding Cao* (*Dagu macao*) the song goes:

> Murderous air hovering over Prime Minister's front gate,
> Swords and spears standing like trees in a thick forest,
> Double phoenix coiling around ornamental colonnade,
> Awe-inspiring like Emperor's Nine-dragon court.

The Prime Minister Cao Cao's residence on the stage is not at all ostentatious like that, but [a good actor who plays] Mi Heng can conjure it all up vividly through his stirring singing and acting. This is descriptive singing (*shuochang*). Paddling a boat down rapid water in *Autumn River* (*Qiu jiang*), looking for the missing letter throughout the house in *Killing Xi* (*Sha xi*)—all these actions take place on a stage without scenery or set; [the good actors who get to play] the old boatman, Chen Miaochang and Song Jiang, communicate them effectively through pantomime and movement. This is the doing part. In *Seven Heroes Join Forces* (*Qixiong juyi*) the twilight time is brought to life as [the actor who plays] Zhu Tong moves elegantly and recites expressively:

Green hills piercing the clouds, as
Birds of pine-cypress forest frolicking in their nests;
Rosy rays shimmering around the setting sun, as
Travelers of long journey raising their weary gaze.

This is the reciting part. The acts of charging ahead on land or overturning rivers and seas are accomplished with all kinds of skills in martial acrobatics. This is the fighting part. If the *fenchang* structure is to be replaced by one based on acts, then all these acting skills will be out of commission; if not exactly like heroes with no place to exercise heroism, the skills will be at least not fully utilized. Separating the *fenchang* structure from the singing, doing, reciting, and fighting, the stage is just an empty space.

The *fenchang* structure, on the one hand, provides tremendous freedom and opportunity for utilizing the acting techniques. On the other hand, it also demands meticulous execution of and perfect coordination between all the technical skills. For instance, if the movement in acting (mainly the pantomime) is not precisely, clearly, and perfectly performed, then what is required by the *fenchang* structure cannot be fulfilled. If you are climbing the stairs, the audience has to feel as if the stairs were there. If you are paddling a boat, the audience has to feel as if the water were actually there. Therefore, on the traditional theater stage, aside from the issue of the playscript, technical skills in acting are decidedly most important.

Between *chengshi* and life there are always going to be contradictions; we should all know that. *Chengshi* comes from life, and yet it is not the same as life, just as the truth of art comes from the truth of life, and yet is not the same as the truth of life. Looked at in this way, they are opposites. From the perspective of life it is all natural, innocent and pure, free and spontaneous; a square is a square, a rectangle is a rectangle; life wants to keep the truth in its natural state and resists the rules and regulations of stage conventions like *chengshi*. From the perspective of *chengshi*, or art, the life onstage has to have strict regularity and precise control in every aspect—entrances and exits to be accompanied by music; words to be delivered in perfect rhythm, and every move to be in sync with gongs and drums. Life is always flesh and blood; *chengshi* is always relatively static. Life invariably wants to break away from the confines of *chengshi*; *chengshi* invariably wants to impose structure on life.

The case is never closed between the two. The correct way to work out the contradictions or conflicts is not mutual concession but mutual infiltration. On *chengshi*'s part it should use life as the basis, tapping into its positive energy, appreciating its distinctive characteristics, conceding to its reasonable demands, amending the parts of conventions that are unreasonable, and overcoming its own rigidity. On life's part it should rise above its own disorganized and less-than-striking natural state, learning the artistry of elegance and control without submitting to *chengshi*'s tyranny or dispensing with life's own natural spontaneity . . . This is the unity of opposites between life and *chengshi* in the traditional theater. They will always have contradictions and conflicts, but they have to strive for unity. . . .

Comrade Liu Chengji says: Stylized movements onstage can be likened to [the strokes that produce] the black-inked dragon in [traditional Chinese] painting: parts of the dragon are hidden behind the clouds, while parts of it are clearly shown; some scales here and a few claws there, together it is a complete picture of the dragon. I find this analogy most interesting. The acting in the traditional theater has that quality of "showing the head and not the tail of the celestial dragon." What should be conspicuous is conspicuous, what should be omitted is omitted, what should be succinct is succinct, what should be copious is copious; some places are merely lightly touched upon, while other places are repeatedly emphasized. Let's look at *The Yellow Crane Tower* (*Huanghe lou*). In the play Zhou Yu attends Liu Bei with the uttermost ceremony and courtesy—the way he bows to him when they meet, the way he dusts the seat for him at the banquet, the way he beckons "after you," the way he proposes a toast. All these acts are performed emphatically and repeatedly, but they are not seen as trivial or repetitive, because this whole series of actions are connected to one objective, that is, the assassination of Liu Bei. Underneath Zhou Yu's formality and civility is the insidious bloodthirst. The traditional theater acting concentrates on crucial moments like that, playing them up, piling them on, and pulling out all the stops. As for things like "there is wine but no dishes" or "there are cups but chopsticks are missing," they are all not important, for they take away nothing that matters to the truth of art. Next let me give an example that shows how acting can be succinct and effective at the same time. In *Borrowing Boots* (*Jie xue*), to show how much the miser prizes his new boots, the actor holds the boots with a fan that is very exquisite; instantly the boots' value is raised. After putting on the boots, in fear of damaging them, he crawls on his knees. These techniques are succinct and profound.

To understand fully the truth in life and the truth in the art of traditional theater acting is to enhance the creativity and development of the traditional theatrical art. We must ask ourselves to understand the distinctive characteristics and intrinsic principles of the art we practice. We must guard against the current form of formalism, particularly the tendency toward naturalism.

HUANG ZUOLIN

From "On Mei Lanfang and Chinese Traditional Theater"

Huang Zuolin (1906–94) was a leading director of Chinese modern theater. As a young man, Huang Zuolin went to study in England on two different occasions. While he was there as an undergraduate, between 1925 and 1929, Huang wrote, directed, and performed his first plays and got to know Bernard Shaw, who encouraged him to become China's great dramatist. During his second sojourn in England, from 1935 to 1937, Huang studied directing with Saint-Denis at the London Theatre Studio while completing his master's thesis on Shakespearean productions at Cambridge. Shortly after the Japanese invasion Huang returned to China to help develop modern spoken drama (*huaju,* as differentiated from the traditional theater, *xiqu*). There are many "firsts" associated with Huang in Chinese theater: he and his wife, Danni, were the first to teach Stanislavsky techniques in China; he founded one of the first successful professional modern drama companies in China, the Bitter Toilers (*Kugan*); as artistic director of the premier Shanghai People's Theater, Huang was also the first theater artist to introduce both Brecht's theories and plays to China. In 1962 he delivered the now famous speech "On Conceptions of Theater" ("Mantan xijuguan") to advocate a kind of modern spoken drama that blends elements of Chinese traditional theater and the Brechtian model. Huang's plea for a more open-minded approach to diverse forms of theater was unanswered because of the tight rein of socialist realism at the time and the ensuing ten-year Cultural Revolution, during which Huang lost more than just the privilege to direct plays. It was during the opening up of the 1980s that Huang's ideas truly caught fire. An artist and a teacher, Huang was not a theorist and never presumed to be one, but his ideas of a modern theater, which he called *xieyi,* launched a heated nationwide theoretical discussion and inspired and continue to influence new generations of Chinese theater artists. Today one could not participate in any good conversation about theater without hearing terms such as *xieyi* or *xijuguan,* which Huang made popular.

In 1980 Huang wrote an article entitled "Mei Lanfang, Stanislavsky, Brecht: A Study in Contrasts," in which he incorporated a generous portion of his 1962 speech "On Conceptions of Theater." The following excerpts are taken from Huang's own English version of the article, with only very minor editorial changes. The headings for the excerpts are Huang's.

Excerpted from an article in *Peking Opera and Mei Langfang* (Beijing: New World Press, 1981).

Endless Search for New Theatrical Truth

The history of the theater is a summary of man's endless search for new dramatic means of expression and new theatrical truths. The valuable experiences have been preserved and the worthless ones discarded. In the twenty-five centuries of the theater's history innumerable dramatic methods have come into being; theater workers in each historical period have sought the best forms possible to convey a definite ideological and political content. The ancient Greeks had their way of expressing the idea of "fate," and, when man's will came into conflict with fate, dramatists had to introduce the deus ex machina to solve life's contradictions, about which men at that time were incapable of finding solutions. The miracle and morality plays of the Middle Ages, with their angels and devils, demanded different methods of presentation, while Shakespeare had to resort to the "dynamic use of space" to give full expression to the outbursts of the men of the Renaissance period. The seventeenth-century Baroque school used a flamboyant and superficial style to put forward the reactionary ideas of absolute monarchy and pander to the tastes of the nobility. The Romantic theater of the late eighteenth century devoted itself so exclusively to the importance of the individual spirit that it became divorced from real life and declined into stereotyped formalism. Thus, each age has had its own dramatic techniques, and after a long process of evolution the best have been retained and have formed a part of the precious heritage handed down from generation to generation. When such a heritage grows into a system, a school of theater is born, and it is distinct and complete in itself.

For the sake of discussion I would like to take three divergent views on the theater, those of Mei Langfang, Stanislavsky, and Brecht, in order to discover their common features as well as their basic differences. I wish to explore the possibilities resulting from the influences one may exert on the other and see if anything new may or will emerge from the old.

Salient Features of Traditional Chinese Theater

Mei Langfang was the most representative and mature exponent of the traditional Chinese theater, a theater vastly different—indeed, fundamentally different—from that of the West. To my mind the traditional Chinese theater at its best has the following salient features:

1. Fluidity: there is no lowering and raising of the curtain or change of scenery as is usually the case on the modern Western stage; instead, the scenes follow straight on, one after another. It is an art that always has the appropriate tempo, rhythm, and montage.

2. Plasticity: the Chinese stage is highly flexible, with no limitations either of time or space.

3. Sculpturality: whereas the characters on the Western stage are two-dimensional beings enclosed, as it were, in a picture frame, those on the traditional Chinese stage stand out three-dimensionally.

4. Conventionality: the adherence to an elaborate system of commonly recognized conventions is a basic characteristic of the Chinese theater. We consider it impossible, if not distasteful, to present life, as it is, on the stage without any embellishments. A play is a play; it is frankly theatrical. For this we have created a set of conventions to break through the limitations of time and space so that life may appear more free and sublime on the stage.

The Most Basic Differences [between Mei, Stanislavsky, and Brecht]

What then are their differences? Put simply, the most basic difference is that Stanislavsky believed in the "fourth wall," Brecht wanted to demolish it, while for Mei Langfang such a wall did not exist and so there was never any need to pull it down, since the Chinese theater has always been so highly conventionalized that it has never set out to create an illusion of real life for the audience. In the theater the term *fourth wall* is fairly well-known, but probably few people inquire into its origin or comprehended fully its significance in dramatic theory and the far-reaching effect it has had on modern stagecraft.[1]

I would like to call attention to one question here. This mode of expression, this attempt to create a fourth wall, an illusion of real life onstage, is only one of many devices in the theater. In the twenty-five hundred years of theater history this method has a history of only ninety-three years, and even during this brief period not all playwrights have used it. Its influence has been so great, however, that some people seem to regard it as the only technique. This imposes limitations, restricting us by the framework of the stage and thereby seriously hampering creativity.

1. Next Huang launched into a succinct discussion of the history and ideas surrounding the "fourth wall" in modern Western theater.

Techniques of Chinese Traditional Acting

To Mei Langfang, that is, to the Chinese traditional school of acting, the ideal method is to combine the "inner technique" of introspection with the outgoing techniques of representation. Take Mei Lanfang's performance in *Beauty Defies Tyranny*,[2] in which he played the part of a young woman who feigned madness to tease her father, who wanted her to marry the emperor. In this part he impersonated insanity yet at the same time remained as sane as the impersonator himself.

Another example is an old play entitled *Writing a Letter to the Southern Tribe*,[3] or *Li Bai Composing a Poem while Drunk* in the *kunqu* opera. In this piece Li Bai, a great poet of the Tang Dynasty, is lying in bed intoxicated when an imperial mandate arrives summoning him to the court at once. An episode in the play depicts him riding a horse in great haste to carry out this order. To depict a drunkard the cliché would be to let the actor stagger about on the stage. But not with Chinese traditional acting, for, although the poet in the play is drunk, the actor must not forget that he is on horseback. So the two legs do not belong to the poet but to the horse, who is not at all drunk. Thereupon, when the great actor Wang Xiaonong (1858–1918) played the scene, at the turn of the century, the upper part of his body thoroughly and completely impersonated the drunken poet, but the lower part played the horse, sober and steady. So, may we not say that the upper part is Stanislavskian, while the lower part follows Brecht? The dialectical combination of opposites, sobriety and inebriation, sanity and insanity, is what makes the traditional Chinese theater so enchanting.

Inner Characteristics of Chinese Theater

To call the traditional Chinese theater "conventional" is looking at the matter from the viewpoint of form only; it is not the whole truth. If the keynote to Western art is realism, what then is the essence of traditional Chinese art? It is difficult to find an antonym. In Chinese we have a word for it, *xieyi*, but I have not been able to hit on its English equivalent. When I exchange views with foreign friends on this question, I have to resort to examples from painting. While Western painting is

---

2. This is a free translation of the play's title, which is *Yuzhou Feng*, literally *The Sword of Universe*.
3. The Chinese title for the play is *Xie Manshu*.

basically realistic, traditional Chinese painting is *"xieyi."* Take, for instance, the horses drawn by the Italian artist Giuseppe Castiglione[4] exhibited at the Palace Museum in Beijing. His horses are as good as real. But take a look at those horses painted by Xu Beihong (Peon Hsu);[5] they are over and above the real. Being well versed in anatomy, Xu, when he painted, did not go too far away, anatomically speaking, from the real horse, and yet, with those few bold touches of his brush, he made his horses not only appear physically true, but at the same time he made them seem spiritually alive.

Western critics contrast their own paintings with those of Chinese by saying that the Western artist takes "the utmost pains to be faithful to what his eye sees; the Chinese artist to what his mind knows." That is to say, the Chinese painter is preoccupied "with the essence rather than the appearance of things." Here I came across this very suggestive word *essence.* Being short of an apt translation, could we say that realism is the keynote of Western art and "essentialism" (*xie yi*) that of Chinese art? If we accept this contrast, the same may be applied to traditional Chinese theatrical art.

By way of summary, besides the four outer characteristics, the traditional Chinese theater has four inner characteristics:

1. the essentialism of life, that is, not life as it is but life as extracted, concentrated, and typified. Creative work should not only come out of life but should be sublimated, that is, refined from life;

2. the essentialism of movements, that is, human movements eurythmicized to a higher plane;

3. the essentialism of language, that is, not plain vernacularism but a language elevated to lyrical height;

4. the essentialism of decor, that is, not the real environment but one designed to achieve a high artistic level.

These four salient features, which I call the four inner features, plus the four outer features mentioned earlier are the sine qua non of the traditional Chinese theatrical style, and of this style Mei Lanfang was a great master.

---

4. Giuseppe Castiglione (1688–1766), an Italian Catholic priest, came to Beijing (Peking) in 1715 and was appointed by the Qing emperors as a court painter and artist [Huang's original note].

5. Xu Beihong (Peon Hsu, 1893–1953) was a distinguished Chinese painter [Huang's original note].

JIAO JUYIN

Spoken Drama: Learning from the Traditional Theater

Jiao Juyin (1905–75) was a leading director of Chinese spoken drama. Coming from a poor and troubled family, Jiao put himself through Beijing (Yanjing) University by doing private tutoring, writing for the newspaper, and doing translations. Among the translations he did were plays by Molière and Goldoni. It was while in the university that he read Marx's *Capital* and *The Communist Manifesto* and took part in the political theater on campus. After graduation Jiao Juyin got a job running a private school of traditional theater. For the next four years he was on the job learning about the traditional theater from the inside.

In 1935 Jiao left for Paris University and started working on his doctoral dissertation, "Chinese Theatre Today." Upon completion of his studies he returned in 1938 to a wartorn China. Aside from being a professor and directing an occasional play, Jiao was most involved in major translation projects. He translated the memoirs of Vladimir Nemirovich-Danchenko, the cofounder and artistic director of the Moscow Art Theater, and the plays by Anton Chekhov, among others. Jiao's career as a professional stage director did not begin until 1950 when he was invited to join the newly founded Beijing People's Art Theater. It was at the Beijing People's Art Theater that Jiao fully emerged as a great director, who was both a master of Western realistic traditions and an innovator dedicated to creating a modern spoken drama with distinctive native Chinese features. The plays he directed, such as Laoshe's *Longxu Canal* and *The Teahouse* and Guo Moruo's *Tiger Charm, Cai Wenji,* and *Wu Zetian* helped to establish the Beijing People's Art Theater as China's preeminent national theater of spoken drama. Jiao Juyin, however, was politically persecuted and physically and emotionally tortured during the notorious Cultural Revolution; he died of lung cancer in 1975.

The following essay is from a series of talks that Jiao Juyin gave in September 1963 at a forum for young directors of spoken drama held in Shengyang, China.[1]

I've been thinking about it a lot, that bringing spoken drama to the countryside poses many problems. Like the traditional theater, spoken

Translated from "Huaju xiang xiqu xuexi," from "He qingnian daoyande tanhua," *Jiao juyin xiju lunwenji* (Shanghai: Shanghai wenyi chubanshe, 1979), 210–16.
1. The speech is based on the shorthand notes taken by Wu Zhongrui. Chen Gang edited these notes into today's form in Jiao Juyin's book.

drama has its own conventions (*chengshi*). Starting with the creation of a script, spoken drama follows such conventions as dividing a play into a certain number of acts and scenes, packing lots of actions into a given time frame, not explaining crucial changes as they happen, or leaving many things in suspense intentionally for the audience's benefit until the last minute. This type of structural convention in spoken drama is baffling to the peasants, who are not used to it. The peasants have their own way of looking at things, their own aesthetic values. The traditional theater fares better with the peasants, because it states and demonstrates things clearly, having a definite beginning and end. According to the report by a work team that was sent from Beijing to the countryside, the peasants do like new plays, but they like the same play *Seizing the Seal* (*Duoyin*) in *pingju* opera form better than in spoken drama form. What they are not used to in spoken drama is that the costumes do not look attractive, that there is no singing, and that the story is told in separate acts. It seems to me that naturalizing spoken drama and making it more appealing to the masses is a big challenge. We should know that when we talk about the masses, it is not just the workers and students; we should think more of the peasants, who are the majority. A director should think more often of the peasants when he is given a play to direct, thinking about what better form to use, thinking about how to adopt native techniques that appeal to the masses, and learning from the traditional theater even though we are not doing traditional theater.

The spoken drama can learn a lot from our country's traditional theater art, which has a long history and rich tradition. As for how to do it, it is a very big subject that requires special research and theoretical analysis, and I'm not here to do any of that. In the past several years, while rehearsing some spoken dramas, I have experimented by learning from the traditional theater, but, not only is my practical experience in that area limited; I haven't really thought through systematically about what I have done. What I can do here today is to share with you some actual experiments I did in rehearsals and some of my own thoughts and feelings on the subject.

The Chinese traditional theater has its conventions and very pronounced conventions at that. The conventions are the traditional theater's means of expression; they are a part, maybe the most conspicuous part, of the traditional theater but not its entirety. The most important part of the traditional theater is its artistic principles and methods. Through the artistic methods we can approach the artistic principles. The artistic principles and methods are somewhat intangible, unlike the artistic conventions, which are tangible and can be easily perceived. Once this point is clearly understood, talking about what to learn from the traditional theater becomes a little easier.

The conventions of the spoken drama, generally speaking, are all transplanted from the West. To naturalize the spoken drama is to give it popular grassroots appeal. For this purpose it is very important for us to absorb the artistic methods from the traditional theater. Many people, including those from abroad, believe that the traditional Chinese theater is an art of symbolism. I feel personally, however, that the traditional theater, from its content to its expression, is all realistic.[2] The convention-alized gestures and movements of the traditional theater also have their basis in real life and are used to depict real life. It is through a process of artistic refinement of life that the conventions of the traditional theater came to be.

The traditional theater has many techniques for exaggeration or amplification, which can be used for the purpose of accentuating the characters' thoughts, emotions, actions, and attitudes—for instance, us-ing music and the sounding of gongs and drums to set off a character's thoughts and emotions. Zhou Xinfang[3] likes to use *lengchui* (cold ham-mer), which is sounding the gong just once. *Lengchui* usually comes right after a character says, "What do you mean by that?" Nothing more needs to be said after that because the character's thoughts and emotions are right there. Wouldn't soemthing like that be good for us to learn in the spoken drama?

I tried it with *Tiger Charm* (*Hufu*), though not all that successfully. [In the play,] after stealing the tiger charm, Ruji asked Xinling Jun to meet her at the graveyard. Just as she was about to hand the tiger charm over to him, King Wei showed up. The king had tailed Ruji there because he suspected that she was cheating on him with Xinling Jun, but these two thought he had discovered their stealing the tiger charm. The two sides had two different things on their minds. King Wei grabbed Xinling Jun with one hand, grabbed Ruji with the other, and then he said: "I know what you two are up to." The two turned ash white. Then he continued: "I know exactly what is going on between you two; you

---

2. It is important to note how the term *realism* is used sometimes in the post-1949 China. Realism is not only an artistic style but is also an issue of a particular ideology, a touchstone of whether an artist cares about and uses his art to engage in the real life of the people. This view of realism has the official sanction of the Party and government, while advocacy of any other *isms* is highly suspect, if not downright subversive.
3. Zhou Xinfang (1895–1975) wa a famous great Beijing opera actor, who specialized in playing old male roles.

have feelings for each other." That made the two feel ever so relieved. For this sequence of the play, first we played with gongs and drums, but it did not work. Then we tried some conventions of the traditional theater, that is, using *lengchui* for the first half and using *wujidou* (five beats) for the second half. "Dang!" the gong sounding once after King Wei, grabbing Xinling Jun's arm, said: "I know what you're up to." The very sound "dang!" sent cold shivers down Xinling Jun's back. Then the king turned to Ruji and said: "I know what you're up to, too." Another "dang!" gave her the shivers as well. Then he said: "I know you two have feelings for each other." "Cui, cui, cui, de cui"—[the five light-hearted beats of the gong] gave much needed relief to the two accused. When the two were completely relaxed we hit the gong two more times, one on a deep heavy-hearted note then on a high pitch. This way we might have, in an unobtrusive way, accentuated some characters' hidden thoughts and emotions. All these are techniques used in the traditional theater; how to adapt them to the spoken drama is something I'm still groping for.

The traditional theater has many techniques for creating prominence or spotlight, something similar to close-ups in films. For instance, bringing two people to the very front of the stage is kind of like a close-up or "zooming in." The traditional theater did not have stage lighting in the past, but years and years of artistic practice have produced a whole set of close-up techniques. It also has techniques of doing "fade in" or "fade out." In *Wujia Po* (*Wujia Hill*) there is a singing duet for two: when one person has finished his section, he turns his back to the audience, simulating a fade-out; when it is his turn again, he just [turns around and] fades in. These are the things that we can learn and put to use.

In the play *Cai Wenji* that I directed, in the second act Cai Wenji was about to leave King Danyu and return home: as she moved one step at a time toward the front of the stage accompanied by the chorus singing, "moving farther away step by step," the curtains were slowly closing; when she reached the front of the stage the curtains came to a complete close. The audience felt as if Cai Wenji were walking toward them, slowly, slowly toward the front, then came the curtains; they felt then that she had really left, going far away. I learned this from the traditional theater, from its techniques analogous to a camera's zooming in and pulling out.

Also in the second act [of *Cai Wenji*] I had the twenty-four super-numeraries (*longtao*) waving the flags, filing in and out, which really helped to create a powerful and dynamic scene. I learned this from the traditional theater. I also learned to use humans to create moving scenery. I adopted many techniques of scene design from the traditional theater for that scene. It is common in the traditional theater: one big tent, one table; first enter eight generals, next enter four generals, then enter the supernumeraries; someone announces: "The generals have arrived, the prime minister will soon open session, let the rest of us wait in the side wings." After the wind and percussion instruments do the fanfare, the prime minister enters. The big tent becomes the headquarter, which the audience accepts readily right away. I used the same technique in the second act of *Cai Wenji*. The guards of honor carrying red flags and white flags moved around the stage in all kinds of formations; when they came to a stop, the scenery was established as well as the locale. I learned that from the traditional theater, and there are many more techniques like that where it came from.

The physical movement in spoken drama should have a linguistic quality; this is also something that the traditional theater has made me realize. Many have said that stage conventions and *xuni dongzuo* (imaginary and stylized pantomime) are two important aspects of the traditional theater. I have very seldom used the term *xuni dongzuo,* I do not like using it because [the stylized movement in the traditional theater] came clearly from real movement in real life. Its stylization is the result of the process of artistic refinement. No matter what name it goes by—conventional, imaginary, or stylized—the movement itself speaks volumes.

Our actors in spoken drama are generally not good at using their eyes. They may make the eyes look bigger with eyeliners or dark eyeshadows, but the audience cannot see their eyes. The actors in traditional theater, on the other hand, are very particular about and very good at using their eyes. They can use their eyes to "lead" the audience. When an actor points and says, "You look," his eyes are following the tip of his pointing finger. The same applies to stage combat: the eyes are leading the audience as they follow the sharp edge of the weapon. When they are listening, their eyes often move left and right, caught in the rhythm of thought. The expression, or the spirit, of the eyes (*yanshen*) is a skill to which many actors pay great attention. Cheng Yanqiu,[4] for example, was very good at using his eyes. He was famous for his crossed eyes (*douyan*), especially in tragedies. In the *Injustice to Dou-e* (*Dou-e yuan*), when playing the scene in which Dou-e was about to die, the two black pupils of

4. Cheng Yanqiu (1904–58) was a famous Beijing opera actor whose great reputation as a female impersonator was comparable with Mei Lanfang.

his eyes just came together. When the crucial movement in a play called for strong and powerful expression of emotions, Yang Xiaolou,[5] whose small eyes usually seemed to be only half-open, would make his eyes look so big that he left very deep impressions on the audience. Eyes are truly important in holding the audience's attention.

The traditional theater has a very strong sense of tempo and rhythm, which is based on the character dynamics. I have also tried to learn some of that. In the first act of *Longxu Canal* madman Cheng was raving mad, and, no matter how hard Mrs. Cheng tried to calm him down, he not only would not listen, he just became worse and worse, and finally he ran out the door. Mrs. Cheng let out a shout at the top of her voice; the madman suddenly stopped cold. At that moment neither of the two could speak. After a pause Mrs. Cheng came out to check and found the madman staring blankly ahead. She hurried over and patiently comforted the madman as she quietly wiped the tears off her own face. The scene began fast and intense, followed by a pause, then she resumed her comforting. Here the basic dynamics between the characters were correctly established, and the pause helped to set off the sense of urgency and intensity. We continued to fine-tune and readjust the tempo and rhythm of the play even after the rehearsal was nearly complete.

When we try to establish tempo and rhythm, it is not a matter of simply speeding up a little here and slowing down a little there or putting a higher pitch here and putting a lower pitch there. We have to find the internal laws of tempo and rhythm in life itself. Take the example of the first act of *The Teahouse* (*Chaguan*). It was a public scene with lots going on and a very vocal crowd. How could I get the main characters to be noticed and heard in such an environment? I used that fortune teller, who was considered a nuisance, to help me out in several places. At one point Wang, the owner of the teahouse, said to him: "Cut it out, you big nuisance." When he insisted on telling Wang's fortune, the latter took him aside and offered him some free tea. As they two were talking, many in the teahouse moved closer to them to eavesdrop, and the buzzing quieted down momentarily. Then Wang burst out: "Don't try that on me. . . . You yourself, if you don't quit smoking opium, you would be unlucky all your miserable life. I can tell fortunes better than you"—at which the crowd started booing and hooting. The collective buzzing resumed until Er Dezi showed up. Being feared by all, as soon as his voice is heard, the crowd stopped talking; the buzzing faded out. Then

5. Yang Xiaolou (1878–1938) was a famous Beijing opera actor who specialized in playing male military roles.

somebody picked a fight with Chang Siye, sending everybody into a panic. After that bit of excitement there was another moment of quiet. Through this kind of up and down, noise and silence, the tempo and rhythm became established.

When rehearsing, if we put the actor in a clearly defined position, the character will emerge more easily. I did some experiments that were also inspired by the traditional theater. When rehearsing [*Cai Wenji* and *Wu Zetian*], very often I would ask Comrade Zhu Lin, who was cast to play the title roles, to just stand in the middle of the room, as I carefully rehearsed the other actors. When I was done with the others, I would ask her to communicate with and react to them. After I had fine-tuned and gotten right all the other characters' attitudes toward her, her sense of her character's presence also started to emerge, and I almost did not need to rehearse her anymore from that point on. Once I had defined the other actors' attitudes toward her so clearly and so precisely, she had no choice but communicate and react in a certain way. Once that communication and reaction got going, the personality and characterization became concrete. For the scenes between Wu Zetian and Pei Yan, once I had gotten Pei Yan right and once I had Wu Zetian communicate with and react to Pei Yan appropriately, she definitely knew how to act toward her minister; then we were practically all set with the main characters. To sum up, to help the actor to become her character we could try first creating the environment in which to put her then help her to adjust to that environment; when that adjustment is accomplished, the character will emerge. The traditional theater does this a lot. Before a character enters, it has already been made clear both to her and to the audience who she is and what she is, which makes it easier for the actor to step into her character.

In a word, for spoken drama to learn from the traditional theater it is most important for us to study the artistic methods of the traditional theater, getting to the heart of its artistic principles, or internal laws. The artistic principles of the traditional theater give expressions to Chinese people's aesthetic ideals and artistic taste, from which we can find ways and means to naturalize the spoken drama and make it appeal more to the masses. These are just some of my thoughts; if I have made any mistakes, I welcome criticism from you comrades.

JIANG QING

From "Revolutionizing Beijing Opera"

[Jiang Qing (1914–91) was the most influential and powerful woman in China until her downfall in 1976, when her husband Mao Zedong died. She and her three radical cohorts, the so-called Gang of Four, were arrested and charged with a series of crimes, including treason, committed during the Cultural Revolution (1966–76). Convicted, Jiang Qing drew a death sentence, which was, however, commuted to life imprisonment in 1983. The following year she was given permission to leave prison for medical treatment of cancer, and she committed suicide on 14 May 1991.

Born in Shandong Province, Jiang Qing began her career as an actress in Shanghai in the 1930s under the stage name Lan Ping. One of the roles she played was Nora in Ibsen's *A Doll's House*. In 1937 she went to the Communist base area in Yan'an, where she met Mao and became his third wife. After the 1949 Communist victory Jiang Qing became influential in cultural circles. During the 1960s she began to assert control in the theater, waging a campaign to "revolutionize Bejing opera," calling for the replacement of "ghost plays"— that is, plays in the traditional repertoire—with modern works on contemporary themes. In 1964 the Festival of Beijing Operas on Contemporary Themes was held in Beijing, and from then on practically no traditional operas were performed for the public until 1977. Jiang was a central figure during the radical Cultural Revolution, limiting people's theatergoing experience to a small number of so-called Model Revolutionary Operas, with modern themes, costumes, scenery, and characterization approved by Jiang Qing and her followers. The following excerpts are from a public speech Jiang Qing delivered on 28 November 1966 (six months into the Cultural Revolution) at a gathering of members of the cultural circle. Her rhetoric was typical of the radical Gang of Four.

Greetings, comrades in the field of literature and arts, friends, and the youthful Red Guards! I salute you in the name of the Revolution of the Proletariat!

This piece's original title is "Jiang qing tongzhi zai wenyijie dahuishang de jianghua," which can be found in *Selected Speeches of Comrade Jiang Qing* (*Jiang qing tongzhi jianghua xuanbian*), a thin volume internally published by the People's Publishing House in 1968. Some overly long paragraphs have been broken up to provide better focus on each point.

First, I'd like to talk to you about the process in which I came to understand the significance of the Great Proletarian Cultural Revolution.

The process began a few years ago: in order to help me improve hearing and vision weakened by illness, doctors suggested that I spend more time on my cultural life. As a result, I developed a relatively systematic perception of the state of our literature and arts. Initially, I wondered why there were again ghost plays on the stage of socialist China. Then I was very perplexed to find that some seriously counter-revolutionary plays like *Hairui Dismissed from Office* (*Hairui baguan*), *Li Huiniang,* and so on were being produced on the stage of the Beijing opera, an art form that had never been that responsive to social reality. There were also many plays centered around emperors, generals, and ministers, gifted scholars, and beautiful ladies (*diwang, jiangxiang, caizi, jiaren*), all in the legitimate name of "rediscovering tradition." The entire world of literature and arts was talking and producing the "famous" (*ming*), the "foreign" (*yang*), or the "ancient" (*gu*); it was an utterly repugnant atmosphere filled with sentiments favoring the past over the present, favoring the foreign over the native, and favoring the dead over the living. I began to realize that, if our literature and arts fail to adapt to the socialist economic base, then inevitably they will undermine that base. During that phase all I sought was the right to criticize, which turned out to be very difficult. . . .

It was during the next phase that some comrades and I started to think about making changes. In fact, over the years, in the constant struggle between the old and the new in social, political, and economic areas, the new literature and arts have emerged to oppose the old. Even in Beijing opera, which is supposedly a form most resistant to reform, there have been new works. Everybody knows that over thirty years ago Lu Xun was the leader of a cultural revolution. And it was over twenty years ago that Chairman Mao pointed out the direction for literature and arts to serve the workers, peasants, and soldiers and raised the issue of weeding through the old to bring forth the new (*tuichen chuxin*). Weeding through the old to bring forth the new is to put new contents and the masses of people in the native forms that the people love to see and hear.

As far as the contents [of traditional theater] go, it is very hard to weed through the old and bring forth the new. For instance, how can we accept, critically or otherwise, the ghosts, spirits, and religion? We cannot do that, because we are atheists; we are members of the Communist Party, and we absolutely do not believe there are ghosts, spirits, or God in the world. Also, how can we accept, critically or otherwise, the moral codes of the feudal landlord class or the capitalist class, for whom oppression and exploitation were perfectly justified? We cannot do that, because our country is under the proletarian dictatorship; we want to build socialism, our economic base is public ownership, and we resolutely oppose all those oppressive and exploitative systems of private ownership. One important aspect of the Great Proletarian Cultural Revolution is to wipe out all the residues of exploitative systems and to wipe out all the old beliefs, old cultures, old customs, and old habits of the exploitative class. We are still using some of the [old] terms, but the content is completely altered. For example, the word *loyalty* (*zhong*)—for the feudal landlord class it is loyalty to the emperor and to the feudal state, whereas for us it is loyalty to the Party, to the proletariat, and to the broad masses of working people. For another example, the word *integrity* (*jie*)—for the feudal class the so-called integrity is toward the emperor and the feudal state, whereas we are talking about the revolutionary integrity of the proletariat; that is, we believe unyieldingly in the proletarian and Communist cause, and we never give in to the enemies who oppress and exploit the people. So, you see, we are still using some of the same words, but the class content is completely the opposite.

As for the [traditional] forms, we can neither accept or reject them in a wholesale manner. Every nation has its own artistic forms and artistic characteristics. It is wrong if we, adopting an attitude of negativism,[1] do not accept in a critical manner the most valued artistic forms and artistic characteristics of our motherland. On the other hand, it is also wrong if we uncritically accept everything and do not weed through the old to bring forth the new.

As for the outstanding artistic forms from the other nations in the world, we should also do the work of weeding through the old to bring forth the new, in the spirit of Chairman Mao's directive: "Make foreign things serve China." Imperialism is capitalism in its death throes, parasitic and rotten—it cannot produce anything good. Capitalism has hundreds years of history, but the so-called classics are limited in numbers. They have some works that are imitations of the so-called classics, but, because they are so strained and unappealing, they no longer have a public. On the other hand, things that poison and paralyze the people are running rampant, such as the hooligan dance (*afei wu*),[2] jazz, striptease, impressionism, symbolism, abstract expressionism, animalism, modernism, and so

---

1. Here Jiang Qing used the term *nihilism* (*xuwu zhuyi*). The editor/translator believes *negativism* is the right concept in the context.
2. It is not clear if Jiang Qing is referring to a specific form of dance.

on—too many to mention. In short, they are decadent and obscene, poisoning and paralyzing the people.

Let me try and ask: [Since] the old literature and art cannot adapt to the socialist economic base and [since] the classical forms of art cannot completely adapt to the socialist ideological content, do we need a revolution? Do we need reform? I believe that the majority of comrades and friends will feel that the revolution and the reform are necessary, except that it is not only a very serious class struggle but also a very difficult task that requires great prudence and patience. Many people's fears and misgivings were compounded by the fact that the former Ministry of Propaganda and Ministry of Culture had opposed the Party and socialist leadership for a long time, making up all sorts of excuses to subvert the revolution and reform. There was a small group of people having an extra ax to grind; they tried to undermine the revolution and obstruct the reform. It was by overcoming all sorts of difficulties and obstacles that the reforms of Beijing opera, ballet theater, and symphonic music finally got under way.

SUN HUIZHU

From "Aesthetics of Stanislavsky, Brecht, and Mei Lanfang"

Sun Huizhu (1951–   ) is a playwright, critic, and theater professor. As one of the "educated young people" (*zhishi qingnian*) sent to be "reeducated" in the countryside, Sun spent ten years in the mountains of Jiangxi Province, working as a rice farmer, a porcelain worker, and a rural teacher, before returning to Shanghai to join the first postgraduate class in theater arts in China. Being passionate about both playwriting and critical theories, Sun was a noted theater artist and theorist in the 1980s, a watershed decade in the history of modern Chinese drama.

The following are the excerpts of part 1 of an article Sun Huizhu wrote in 1982, in which the author compares and contrasts the great theatrical systems of Stanislavsky, Brecht, and Mei Lanfang in term of their theatrical ideals—the triumvirate of the real, the good, and the beautiful.

The three great theatrical systems of Stanislavsky, Brecht, and Mei Langfang have had tremendous transnational impact on the theaters of the twentieth century and have won audiences both East and West. All this is closely related to the progressive nature of their aesthetic ideals, which the three systems have in common, and yet that they also have very disparate means of expression is related to the differences in their aesthetic ideals.

Generally speaking, all three systems are concerned with the truth and reality of social life, they all emphasize the positive educational function of theater, and they all strive to give audience enjoyment in the aesthetic beauty of their theater experience. That is to say, they share a basic common ideal, which is the unity of the real (*zhen*), the good (*shan*), and the beautiful (*mei*). Any good work of art is in essence the

This article's original title is "A New Study of the Three Great Theatrical Systems' Aesthetic Ideals" ("Sanda xijutixi shengmei lixiang xintan"). It was first published in the *Theatre Arts* (*Xiju yishu*) in 1982. It has since been anthologized in *The Anthology of Theoretical Writings on Chinese Traditional Theatre* (*Zhongguo xiqu lilun yanjiu wenxuan*) (Shanghai: Shanghai wenyi chubanshe, 1985); *The Anthology of Discourses on Conceptions of Theatre* (*Xijuguan zhengming ji*) (Beijing: Zhongguo xiju chubanshe, 1986); and two other anthologies.

union of the true, the good, and the beautiful. But, if we carefully compare and contrast individual artistic forms, we will discover the distinctions in their ways of expression.

According to Aristotle's *mimesis* theory, that distinctions exist between different arts is the result of each art having a different object for its mimesis as well as different means and ways of mimesis. The theater is distinguished by action: its object of mimesis is people in action, and its means of expression is to show people in action. That action unites both the object and means of expression makes theater, strictly speaking, the perfect art form of mimesis. . . . Unlike painting, sculpture, music, and literature, theater is the only form that can most faithfully and realistically represent humans and their actions in social life. Also because dramatic action onstage is either overtly or covertly driven by conflict, compared with other forms of art, theater encourages the spectators to take sides as they react to stage action. Since these reactions are propelled by moral values and world outlooks, theater has a particularly potent education function. And, in terms of creating the beautiful, theater, as a synthetic art, also has many superior advantages. The stage action not only can present fascinating stories, heart-throbbing passions, and thought-provoking ideas but also can satisfy many indispensable needs of the senses; in other words, theater has a vital aesthetic function.

Therefore, theater has great potential in all these three areas—the real, the good, and the beautiful. Can they, however, all be fulfilled equally well, thus surpassing all other forms of art? . . .

The three great theatrical systems, in fact, have distinctly different emphases on the shared basic aesthetic ideal of unity of the real, the good, and the beautiful. This essay will begin comparing and contrasting their individual differences by looking at action, the theater's most basic means of expression.

Different Emphasis on the Real, the Good, and the Beautiful

For action onstage the Stanislavsky system emphasizes the word real. Stanislavsky required his actors to get as close as possible to their characters and demanded the stage actions to replicate as closely as possible actions in real life in an extremely well-defined and specific given situation, so that the audience would feel as if they were peeping at people's life through the invisible fourth fall. Stanislavsky developed a complete set of psychophysical techniques to help actors to become one with their characters through the rehearsal process and to ensure that in actual performance they would act, both internally and externally, exactly like their characters in the given circumstance. The actors should forget, consciously or unconsciously, that they were acting, so that the audience would feel that they were witnessing something real happening for the first time. Stanislavsky insisted that each character's action should follow a through-line from beginning to the end, any interruption and deviation from which should not be allowed; as a consequence, the soliloquies and asides, which were common in theater but uncommon in real life, were eliminated.

Stanislavsky, of course, was also concerned with the good in his art, paying great attention to the theater's moral position, but he emphasized over and over that the good had to come naturally from the real. The same applies to the beautiful. The Stanislavsky system developed and matured, as a counter to the presentational[1] school of theater, in the struggle against the virtuoso acting prevalent at the time. Stanislavsky himself never denied that the presentational style of acting had its own beauty, but he was not fond of it, for those who practice it "believe that they can create on stage a beautiful life, which is not the kind of life we see in reality, but the kind of life revised for the stage" (*An Actor Prepares*).

The presentational school seems to have something in common with the Mei Lanfang system. What Mei was best at presenting onstage was precisely the kind of life so obviously embellished and perfected that it was beauty incarnate. Stanislavsky, on the contrary, believed that the beautiful should be what comes naturally from being real. He even went so far as to declare that the judgment of whether an actor's voice was beautiful should be based on how intimately he was living within his character. . . .

Due to the particular demand of the real in stage action, the Stanislavsky system calls for a particular kind of play. Stanislavsky himself had tried to stage plays in the styles of impressionism, expressionism, aestheticism, and other nonrealistic traditions, but he gave them up quickly. His system was developed in the course of staging plays by Chekhov, Gorky, Ibsen, Tolstoy, and other great masters of realism. Chekhov and Gorky had an especially great influence on the forming of the Stanislavsky system, because their plays, dramaturgically still different from the usual

---

1. In Chinese the term is *biaoxian pai,* which is a key concept in the ongoing debate about relative merits of realistic and nonrealistic styles of acting. The term can also be variously translated as "presentational" or "expressionistic."

Ibsenian realism, were concerned not with external conflicts or cleverly constructed "knots" but with life as it is, showing people coming and going, eating, chatting, and playing cards, thus creating onstage a life as complex and as simple as real life. Plays of this kind can benefit most when successfully staged with Stanislavsky's method, with his meticulous care to realistic details.

The union between this type of plays and this style of staging is a perfect one, which unites the dramatic structure with the characters' internal and external actions into a realistic whole. As far as creating the real in theater art is concerned, the Stanislavsky system has developed it to the maximum. When describing the production of *Seagull*, Vladimir Nemirovich-Danchenko recalled that the audience not only believed that they were witnessing real events unfolding; they were also "slightly embarrassed, as if they had intruded upon the private lives of those onstage." When the curtain came down after the first act, the silence in the theater lasted several minutes before applause burst out—the audience was completely captured by the performance. This is the enchantment of the real in the Stanislavsky system.

One of Brecht's famous lines goes: "I have feelings only when I'm having a headache, never when I'm writing; that's when I'm thinking."

Thinking is for the purpose of changing the society for the better. Brecht was basically a social activist who used theater as his tool. He became a Marxist very early in life, but his theater is very warmly received in the Western world. That may be precisely because he broke away from the traditional theater aesthetics and proposed an epoch-making new idea: stop the audience from believing that theater is real.

Brecht himself was a playwright. Many of his plays have no specific historical background, no precise locale, which is particularly true in plays from his mature period. Some plays do have place names, such as *The Good Person of Setzuan,* but it is not really about what happened in China; and the gods' visits to "Setzuan" (Sichuan) smack of Gulliver's travels. *The Caucasian Chalk Circle* relocates Judge Bao's story from China to the Soviet Union, a play-within-a-play, clearly showing the allegorical nature of the play. Other plays, like *Exceptions and Rules* and *Herr Puntila and His Servant Matti,* are also good examples of allegorical drama.

The Brechtian system usually does not aim at creating characters of flesh and blood, nor does it develop from one specific given circumstance; it aims more at expressing clearly and frankly a world outlook and teaching the audience a lesson in critical thinking. That is the reason it is not at all anxious about whether the characters, the events, and the time and place in a play are real or not. . . .

Even with his comparatively more realistic plays, Brecht would throw in something so inconsistent that a sense of unreality is created, pushing the audience to some critical realization with this "estrangement." For instance, both *Three-Penny Opera* and *Mother Courage and Her Children* have endings that are obviously intended to shake up the audience. Just when the audience is sure that Mack the Knife will be executed, Brecht, as John Gay did in his *Beggar's Opera,* introduces a highly inexplicable "reversal" to spare his life; just when the audience is sure that Mother Courage will have to come to her senses, the playwright shocks the audience by letting her carry on in her usual ways. The through-line of action and the realism and logic of characterization, which are so important to the Stanislavsky system, do not seem to be all that relevant to Brecht, for his characters only answer to his didactic needs. Brecht knew the audience psychology well, however. Unlike the usual playwrights who would do anything to cater to the audience or to make them emotional captives, this master of theatrical dialectics intentionally refused to go along with the audience, for he believed it to be the only way to keep the audience thinking critically, with their "eyes open." His *Galileo* is not at all like the Galileo in the common mass mythology, and it is purposely so. William Archer, in *Playwriting Techniques,* specifically warned against rehabilitating personalities of mythical statue, because the audience's emotional resistance would prevent them from being drawn completely into the play—but that is exactly what Brecht wanted. . . . It is not difficult to see that Brecht was primarily concerned with theater's educational function, that is, with the good the theater can do.

To achieve the principal goal of raising people's consciousness so that they would get up and change the world they live in and to accommodate Brechtian dramaturgy, the Brechtian system also has its own acting method, fundamentally different from that of the Stanislavsky system. The essence of this method is total rational control, the technique is critical narrative, and the effect is alienation, also called estrangement.

In Brechtian acting the external action is not as far removed from real life as in Chinese traditional theater, in which the external action is heavily conventionalized, but the internal action is very "unrealistic." Psychologically, the actor is asked to be as distanced as possible from the character in the given situation; just like the witness to a traffic accident, who critically narrates/reenacts the accident without becoming the characters involved. The purpose of the opinionated reenactment is just to help people reach a certain verdict critically. To realize this style of acting onstage Brecht also proposed three assisting measures: use third-person narrative, use past tense, and read stage directions out loud. The desired resulting stage action will be one that is only seemingly in compliance but actually at variance with real action in life.

[. . .]

Not particularly interested in taking advantage of theater's strength in capturing the real, Brecht focused on theater's ability to do good—its direct and immediate educational function—and developed it to the optimum in an audaciously inventive manner. . . .

Brecht believed that his theater was greatly inspired by the Chinese traditional theater. In fact, these two theaters do have two very similar characteristics: rather than representing life in all its realistic details, both present onstage a revision of that life, creating a distance between the stage action and real-life action; both use the free-roaming episodic structure, with its loosely connected scenes and not always continuous action. No wonder Brecht would be so excited when he saw Mei Lanfang's performance, believing he had finally discovered a special model he had been searching for, hence the essay "The Alienation Effect in Chinese Acting." Some Chinese critics also concede there is this perceived affinity.

Some Soviet experts, however, while promoting the Stanislavsky system in China, believed that the Chinese traditional theater operates on exactly the same principles as the Stanislavsky system. There are many Chinese critics who have found support for this assertion. Mei Lanfang himself also said: "What I have experienced my whole life onstage is compatible with the Stanislavsky system."

Neither assertions are groundless, but both are equally slanted. It is true that the Chinese traditional theater and Brechtian theater are similar in their insistence on "acting is acting" and in their efforts to create distance between stage action and real-life action. It is also true that the Chinese traditional theater and the theater of Stanislavsky have in common the demand for the actors to experience their characters in action and strive for believability. There are, however, many differences, too.

In the Brechtian system, while the external action is still relatively faithful to life, the internal action is removed from it, so that the actors cannot become the characters. The Mei Lanfang system, however, is just the reverse in this respect: while the external action is far removed from its natural appearance in real life—every little gesture, every utterance, is guided by convention and timed to music and rhythm—internally the actors are encouraged, however, to forget about "acting" and to move as close as possible to their characters; otherwise, the full meaning of the play will be lost on the audience. When talking about the conventionalized pantomime of smelling the flower in *Drunken Beauty* (*Guifei zuijiu*), Mei Lanfang said: "The important thing is for my heart and my eyes to see that flower (even though there is none in sight onstage), only that will give the audience a sense of reality."[2] Generally speaking, the Chinese traditional theater "relies on singing and dance-like movement to convey the emotions of the characters."[3] On the one hand, it is the emotions of the "characters" that are expressed in the internal action, not the kind of rational and critical attitudes the Brechtian actors demonstrate toward their characters. On the other hand, it is the conventionalized "singing and dance-like movement" that constitute the external action, not at all realistic and natural, as demanded by Stanislavsky.

In the Stanislavsky system the internal and external actions are unified, and here the emphasis is on being real, or realistic. In the Brechtian system the internal and external actions are intentionally divided so that the actors' rational acting may provoke a rational response from the audience, and here the emphasis is on being good, or useful. The Mei Lanfang system inadvertently also created a discrepancy between the internal and external actions, but its emphasis is mainly on being beautiful, or aesthetically pleasing.

The Chinese traditional theater also strives for the real, and it has always been the actors' desire to "be like a dragon when playing one and be like a tiger when playing one." Mei Lanfang clearly stated that for him the highest realm of acting is where "the actor and the character cannot be told apart."[4] The external action of that theater, however, is so dissimilar to real-life action that no wonder Brecht would reach the opposite conclusion after seeing Mei Lanfang perform. . . . Brecht correctly noted the need in the Chinese traditional theater for the actor to self-observe his own acting, but he misunderstood the purpose of that self-observation. In fact, the Mei Lanfang system definitely does not intend to create either distance or alienation. On the contrary, it aims to present believable characterization, and the seemingly "alienating" external action is out of aesthetic consideration only.

---

2. *Mei Lanfang on Theatre* (*Mei Lanfang xiju sanlun*) (Shanghai: Shanghai wenyi chubanshe, n.d.), 204.
3. Ibid., 36.
4. Ibid.

[The great Beijing opera actor] Gai Jiaotian once pointed out: "An actor on stage should consciously observe the standard, or he would lose the audience if he moves his eyes whichever way he feels like." The purpose of that self-observation is to ensure proper compliance to the aesthetic standard of stage conventions. The many unrealistic means of expression may seem to Brecht like means of alienation, but they are there to "create a sense of aesthetic beauty for the audience."

On the surface the structure of dramatic action in Chinese traditional theater seems to resemble that of the Brechtian theater, with frequent interruptions and various elements not directly related to the through-line of action. There are mainly three types of interruptions: characters' self-introductions; impromptu comic business and humorous remarks; and singing, dancing, acrobatics, and other displays of technical skills. They all seem to create alienation effects, but, again, they are intended to provide immediate aesthetic pleasure for the audience and are not neces-sarily meant to encourage critical thinking. Mei Lanfang put it very clearly: "The dramatists in those days only had two objectives, either to accentuate singing or to showcase acting, so that actors with or without a good voice all had opportunities to perform their skills."[5] In providing the audience with the aesthetic pleasure from a wide range display of skills, the distance is unavoidably created between the art of theater and the reality of life.

Furthermore, the stories or actions dramatized in the episodic struc-ture of the Chinese traditional theater are mostly quite removed from the reality of life; they have obviously gone through a beautification process. If Chekhov and Gorky excelled in depicting realistically "life's undesirable side" in a given society, if Brecht prevailed in using a con-spicuously make-believe form of allegory to raise people's consciousness and make them think, then the Chinese traditional theater prides itself on providing a temporary escape to an idealized realm from a defective real world. This is especially true with Mei Lanfang's Beijing opera. Mei Lanfang said: "The swaying power of the audience's likes and dislikes is overwhelming. . . . My audience often told me: 'We spent good money to come to the theatre to have some fun. . . . In the end we all want to have a happy-ending, so that we can give vent to all our pent-up sense of injustice and anger, so that we can go home and have a good night's

5. Mei Lanfang: *Forty Years on Stage* (*Wutai shenghuo sishinian*) (Beijing: Zhongguo xiju chubanshe, n.d.), 1:19.

sleep. . . . I'm afraid that the majority of the audience thought this way."[6] Zhang Geng,[7] when dealing with the dramatic content of the Chinese traditional theater, has come up with some of the following characteristics: there are more plays of an optimistic and comic nature; tragicomedies all have happy endings; and even tragedies give people hope. All this is a testimony to a special aesthetic demand by the Chinese populace, a people who have weathered life's trials and tribulations for thousands of years.

---

6. Ibid., 2:48.
7. Zhang Geng (1911–   ), theorist and historian, is a leading authority on the Chinese traditional theater.

LIN ZHAOHUA

The Director's Notes on
Wild Men

Lin Zhaohua (1936–) is one of the most innovative and sought-after stage directors in contemporary China. Having graduated from the Central Theatre Academy in 1961, Lin Zhaohua was an actor with the Beijing People's Art Theater until he turned to directing, in 1978. Between 1982 and 1985 Lin Zhaohua directed in succession three plays by China's leading avant-garde playwright Gao Xingjian, *Absolute Signal* (*Juedui xinhao*), *Bus Stop* (*Chezhan*), and *Wild Men* (*Yeren*), winning enormous recognition. Known for his great range of styles, Lin Zhaohua has directed many other highly acclaimed productions, such as Liu Jingyun's *Doggy Father's Nirvana* (*Gouerye niepan* [1985]), Shakespeare's *Hamlet* (1990), Friederich Durrenmatt's *Romulus the Great* (1992), Guo Shixing's *Bird Men* (*Niaoren* [1993]), and Goethe's *Faust* (1994).

I

After the opening of *Wild Men* some comrades asked, "Are there still rules in the theater?" What they are hinting at seems to be that there are certain rules (character, story, conflict, etc.) in theater that cannot be broken. It is really meaningless arguing about whether they can be broken or not; you can always follow your rules, and I can always make new ones. If one country can have two systems, why should the theaters in a country of one billion follow only one set of rules?! As far as I can tell, in the theater circle there are still too few innovators and too much uniformity. Only when the artists are exploring sincerely and honestly can worthwhile works of art be born.

I never direct my plays according to the dictates of some established theatrical concepts, systems, or styles. With each new play I wish to discover and explore something new, something never seen on the stage before. What has already been done on the stage is history; repeating others and repeating oneself are equally not worthy. . . . A director is the

Translated from "Yeren daoyan tigang," *Tansuo xiju ji* (Shanghai: Shanghai wenyi chubanshe, 1986), 355–63.

shaper, the creator, of a production; he should create his own stage language and discover new means of expression. A director should also be a creator of new theatrical concepts. Some people are worried that China will see an "antitheater" movement in the theater; these people just worry too much. Only really stupid people will dismiss all traditions. As I said when I was directing *Absolute Signal* (*Juedui xinhao*), one cannot develop something new without carrying forward the tradition, and one cannot successfully carry forward the tradition without developing something new. On China's stage today there are theaters of a multifarious variety for people to pick and choose; which is good, which is bad, let the people decide.

II

It is hard to say what kind of play *Wild Men* is; I have never seen or done anything like it before myself. Using the usual categories, is it realistic? xieyi? absurdist? symbolist? . . . *Wild Men* does not fit any category; it is something new. Time, it expands several thousands of years up and down; action, four parallel lines (ecological issues, search for the wild men, tragedy of modern man, and "The Story of Darkness"), or, in the author's own words, "several different motifs join together in a polyphony"; characters do not really have through-lines, and the story is far from complete; supposedly, there are three movements in the play, but there are actually over thirty scenes with huge jumps in between; and there are also songs, dances, and recitations. Faced with a play like that, I was excited and anxious all at the same time. Excited, because as a director I had a great big open space to explore freely; anxious, because I did not know what might happen if I did not handle it right. I had read the play many times over, and a month had gone by, but I was still not sure how to direct it. One day an idea suddenly came to me: this play should be shaped by the ecologist's stream of consciousness. With the absolute freedom of the human consciousness, the play could go anywhere and do anything without hindrance, be it going backward in time, be it jumping from one environment to another, be it opening up the sky at the dawn of the universe, be it floodwater overflowing, be it felling trees in the forest, be it staging the raindance ritual or anything else. This is how I came upon the shape of the production. My journal entry on 10 January 1985 reads: "Thinking and imagining about the play is the greatest pleasure. When you actually stumble onto something, you feel like the gold-digger who has found real gold." Once the imagination got going, I started picking up more and more things with my senses. First to appear were the images in the ecologist's head; I wanted to see the primeval forest shaped by human bodies. A huge piece of nylon covering the performers of every shape and size (ten men and ten women) resembled the vast earth. As the music played, the performers' hands started to reach up slowly; green-hued lights shone on the forty arms in various poses. Then human forms started to emerge, twenty different postures created by humans of all sorts of body build: tall, short, fat, thin, straight, bent, robust, underdeveloped, and so on—a sight of mysterious beauty provocative to the imagination.

III

Could I also use the human bodies and their posturing to set up the scenes for the felling, flooding, drought, urban pollution, or the dawn of the universe? Maybe an abstract style of presentation was what this play needed.

A director must have the conviction that nothing is impossible on the stage.

I would like the performers in this production to be able to embody not only their characters but also the flowing human consciousness, the state of human emotions and moods, and to live not only in the present reality but also in memory, in imagination, and in remote antiquity, and to step in as animals, vegetation, floods, noise, and even scenery and stage props. This was an exploration of the total theater; there was speaking, singing, dancing, pantomime, and vocal mimicry, and so on. Some comrades ask: Is this still spoken drama? I say this is theater.

Once I had made up my mind on this, I felt the overall conception of this production began to enter a realm of relative freedom. In the second movement there was a scene in which the old choirmaster sang the song of the beginning of the world, "The Story of Darkness." It took me a long time to come up with a way to present it. Who really knows what it was like way back then? Since the legends, writings by Laozi, Zhuangzi, and *The Book of Change* (*Yi jing*), all say it was dark and murky, so, as the old choirmaster intones "The Story of Darkness" on the hill, I tried to conjure a nonrealistic feel of the beginning of time against a dim, misty, and shadowy background, with drums making thunderous explosions in the middle of the sky and a huge ball of fire rising and rolling between heaven and earth. The twenty human forms under the nylon sheet playfully make the fireball rise and fall as if the hills and valleys were alive. Suddenly the hills and valleys all disappeared without a trace, leaving a huge parachute heaving up and down holding the fireball. . . . Is this the universe? A ball of fire? The sun? The earth? The energies of yin and yang? The audience may think whatever it likes. Some have asked how I came up with this approach. I rally cannot tell; it was my gut feelings that helped me. Directing is an art of instinct, thinking plays a regulating function.

IV

Why shouldn't a scene design be appreciated on its own? As long as it is needed by the play, I feel it should be. I never worry that music, scenery, or set might distract the audience from the play. What is wrong with giving the audience more aesthetic stimuli? The problem here is how to bring them all into a unified vision. It is up to the director to have an overall plan about when to let the audience look at the scenery and when to hear some music. . . . *Wild Men* didn't use one single piece of real scenery or stage prop. The empty stage was an extremely free space, and the backdrop was done in the spirit of splashing ink of the Chinese traditional painting. It was the human forms, lighting, and acting together that created stage scenery and prop, moving and still, expressed characters' changing emotions and moods, and produced a sense of the universe in perpetual motion amid emptiness and void.

V

Was I trying to say too much in this production? I think not, not nearly enough!

Today's theatergoers come into the theater bringing with them not only their own lives but also the information given to them by the mass media, such as film, television, and newspapers. Maybe we have already arrived at a time when it is necessary to pack more information into a short time frame, into a few evening hours, in order to meet the audience's new aesthetic need! What is scary is that we have not sensed this strongly or even not at all.

VI

Traditionally, a play develops around one story or situation, and the director usually uses one focus and one soundtrack to approach the stage space and character action. *The Bus Stop* was the first to experiment with a multilayered soundtrack. In that production different characters formed different parts of the soundtrack, and several action lines developed simultaneously. In real life it is hard to find a space inhabited by one sound only—your home, the bus stop, the forest, the meeting room, the beach, the factory's workshop, the park. . . . *Wild Men's* multilayered soundtrack consists of more than just words from different voices; it is a coming together of words, songs, music, and body movements, and it is expressing in one space the multiple spaces of the present physical reality, the internal psychological state, and the remote antiquity . . . The emancipation of the performers' body and mind is especially crucial to this production. First, I encouraged the performer to get completely relaxed, just playing around, dancing to different types of music, doing improvisation, feeling less and less self-conscious. The performers were really feeling with their bodies and souls, and many physical movements, postures, and formations they came up with naturally on their own were better than any genius director or choreographer could show them! . . . During the process of directing this production, I seldom talked about what I thought; instead, I laid the stress on the performers' own instincts, discoveries, and abilities to adjust, allowing them the freedom to choose the best means of expression and not asking them to abandon their own individuality. Even during actual performances I permitted a certain freedom of improvisation, which, however, had to abide certain restrictions of the director's final score.

    Wild Men is indigenous, but it is also contemporary, and this is what I am searching for.

HU WEIMIN AND YE CHANGHAI

East Meets West Onstage:
A Dialogue on "Chinese Traditional
Theater Doing Shakespeare"

In 1985 China held its First Shakespeare Festival. The fact that many productions of Shakespeare were presented in Chinese traditional theater forms gave
rise to a great deal of critical deliberation. The following is a dialogue published
in the leading academic theater journal, *Theatre Arts*, between Hu Weimin
(1932–89), director of *Twelfth Night*, and Ye Changhai (1944–), the journal's
deputy editor-in-chief.

   Hu Weimin was a pathbreaking modern spoken drama director in the
1980s, the most innovative and experimental decade in the history of Chinese
modern theater. Ye Changhai is an established scholar of Chinese classical
theater whose long list of publications includes such major books as *History of
Chinese Theatre Studies* (*Zhongguo xijuxue shigao* [1986]) and *Annotated Writings on
Theatre in Chinese History* (*Zhongguo lidai julun xuanzhu*, with Chen Duo [1987]).

Ye Changhai: Presenting Shakespeare's plays in the forms of Chinese
traditional theater is a prominent characteristic of China's First Shakespeare Festival. There has been a lot of discussion about that in the
papers. I feel that performing Shakespeare in Chinese traditional theater
forms is an extraordinary cultural encounter on the Chinese stage between the East and the West. In today's China, with the opening up to
the outside world in our reform efforts and against the backdrop of
cultures from the East and West coming into contact, clashing as well as
merging, it seems only historically inevitable and realistically logical that
there should be such enthusiasm in presenting foreign drama on the stage
of Chinese traditional theater. The significance of such happenings will
only become more and more apparent. As many have already pointed
out, Chinese traditional theater doing Shakespeare facilitates a two-way

Translated from "Zhongxi wenhua zai xiju wutaishangde yuhe—guanyu 'zhongguo
xiqu yu shashibiya' de duihua," in Hu Weimin, *Daoyande ziwo chaoyue* (Beijing:
Zhongguo xiju chubanshe, 1988), 85–93. The piece originally appeared in *Theatre Arts*
(*Xiju yishu*) in 1986.

movement: the Chinese traditional theater absorbs elements of foreign theatrical culture, and the Chinese theater goes out to the world. In fact, the "Chinese traditional theater doing Shakespeare" has already become a tangible artistic entity, which can be examined and analyzed from many different perspectives, including issues in basic critical theory, applied methodology, and matters of technical nature. All these issues deserve serious study and careful summarization. The subject of Chinese traditional theater doing Shakespeare naturally includes two areas of comparative study—modern [or spoken] drama (*huaju*) and the traditional theater, Chinese theater and foreign theater.

Chinese Traditional Theater Embraces Shakespeare

Hu Weimin: During China's First Shakespeare Festival, in Shanghai alone four of the Bard's plays—the comedies *Twelfth Night* and *Much Ado about Nothing,* the tragedy *Macbeth,* and the romance *Winter's Tale*—were presented in three regional forms of Chinese traditional theater (*kunqu, yueju,* and *huangmeixi*).[1] The dialogue between the ancient Chinese traditional theater and Shakespeare became a theatrical phenomena that drew a great deal of attention. That which once had been considered "inconceivable" suddenly became not only a reality but did so with such commanding presence that it truly astonished many people. Furthermore, because of the variety of styles in the "dialogue," great interests were aroused not only among people in the theater circle but also among all those concerned with cultural trends and developments. Now, in the wake of the initial excitement, let's calm down, seriously think about and analyze the productions mentioned here, from the surface to the essence. What does the emergence of those productions of Shakespeare in Chinese traditional theater forms signify?

I believe we should first look at this theatrical phenomenon from a broader perspective. With the advancement of reform and an open-door policy, we have finally awakened from a nightmare of isolation, coming face to face with a diverse and complex world with which we have no other choice but to get acquainted. To open up new political and economic horizons requires a cultural climate of relative stability and

---

1. *Yueju,* also called *shaoxingxi,* is a major regional operatic theater form that originated in Zhejiang Province. *Huangmeixi* is another major regional operatic theater form that originated in Anhui Province.

peaceful accord. It was against this broad background that the Shakespeare festival was held. The painful lessons of the past thirty years have taught us that the human civilization must be respected and that absorbing valuable cultural achievements from all over the world is an important premise to building a new socialist culture. As far as the attitude toward foreign culture goes, moving from rejection to acceptance and from prejudice to embracing signifies this important change.

When the Chinese traditional theater warmly embraces Shakespeare, it uses its unique artistic vocabulary to express Shakespeare. This means that we do not carelessly lose ourselves when accepting the other. The productions mentioned earlier all carry with them an aesthetic quality and theatrical charm uniquely Eastern and Chinese. The strong consciousness of native culture and that of the Western culture mutually absorb, penetrate, and fuse, merging into a new cultural stream. This tendency clearly shows that, while we are against Sinocentric narrow-mindedness, we are also against blind worship of the West and wholesale Westernization.

We cannot say that these four productions are perfect, but we are certain that they, born in this new historic age, are true harbingers of contemporary culture.

Looking for Harmony through "Conflict"

Ye Changhai: I feel the four productions are actually quite different from one another. First, in terms of the extent of adaptation, the *kunqu Story of Bloody Hands (Xueshou ji)* is based on segments of *Macbeth,* while the other three are based on entire plays. Second, in terms of stage design, especially costumes, *yueju Twelfth Night* is in a foreign period style, while the other three are thoroughly Chinese, with the *huangmeixi Much Ado about Nothing* opting for a "newer" modern look and the other two for an "older" traditional look. The production done in "foreign" costumes has a very big impact on the traditional theater, affecting the performance as a whole. To this the audience responses are divided: the younger audience members are very pleased, but the older theater fans are dissatisfied. The productions in "Chinese" costumes have departed quite a lot from the conventional "Shakespearean" style, which astonishes those who are familiar with Shakespeare plays. Here, again, opinions are divided: supporters hail the innovation as "delightfully refreshing," but the detractors call it "far-fetched" and "incongruous." . . .

Third, in terms of the age of each traditional theater form, *kunqu* is an old and ancient form, *yueju* is a new and young form, and *huangmeixi* is somewhere in between. *Kunqu* doing Shakespeare is the meeting today between the two old classical forms of theater, a late-bloomer in a sense. *Yueju* doing Shakespeare is the rebirth of an old tradition in a contemporary theater form. There are still many other distinctive characteristics with each production worth noting and comparing, all of which demonstrate the richness of these productions and show the great creativity of the Chinese artists.

Hu Weimin: The process of rehearsing *Twelfth Night* was like conducting a dialogue between the East and West theatrical traditions in search for harmony. Maybe *dialogue* is too mild a word; more precisely, the whole creative process was full of "conflict" or "collision," which was not at all harmonious. In fact, what happened very often in the entire creative process was tempestuous and painful conflict.

Was it really that serious? Don't we often say that Shakespeare and Chinese traditional theater have a great deal in common? That belief is not wrong, because in dramatic structure and performance style Shakespeare and the Chinese traditional theater do share many similarities. For instance, they both use episodic structure, completely unrestrained by the "three unities," temporal and spatial changes are flexible and free, brevity and elaboration are handled accordingly; as the saying goes, "a hundred years passes with one snap of the fingers, the ends of the world exit within a foot." Shakespeare's plays are called poetic dramas, in which he uses poetic language to delineate his characters' personalities, psychology, and emotions. The traditional Chinese theater is similar in this emphasis on poetry. They both pay a great deal of attention to creating a sense of poetry, striving to unify the poetic language with dramatic action. It is noted by many that, in performing Shakespeare, the shift in time and place is often indicated by characters' lines, which is quite like the practice in Chinese traditional theater, in which a scene change is dictated by a character's emotion and action. Both Shakespeare and the Chinese traditional theater pay more attention to expressing subtle internal feelings than to creating detailed realistic external settings, utilizing to the full extent the stage's ability of make-believe to advance a play's narrative action.

From these examples we can say that theater aesthetics and production techniques [Shakespeare's theater and the Chinese traditional theater] share a surprisingly great affinity.

If this is the case, where does the conflict come from?

The Chinese traditional theater and Shakespeare, after all, belong to two different cultural traditions. They have quite a few similar artistic characteristics, but, in terms of philosophical content, they have a great many differences, which we must fully recognize.

As a great man of the Renaissance era, Shakespeare was challenging the authority of the church, the hierarchy of the feudal system, and oppressive asceticism. In his works Shakespeare celebrated friendship and love, lauded the rising of humanism, and called for the awakening of human-centric consciousness. "What a piece of work is a man, [how noble in reason, how infinite in faculties, in form and moving, how express and admirable in action, how like an angel in apprehension, how like a god:] the beauty of the world, the paragon of animals." In his poetry Shakespeare enthusiastically affirmed the conviction that humanity determines its own fate. This is the central motif of Shakespeare's works.

Human spirit also resides in Chinese classical drama through the rebellious characters like Cui Yingying [in the *West Chamber Story*] and Du Liniang [in the *Peony Pavilion*]. In comparison, however, we will discover that Shakespeare's characters are more daring, unyielding, and fervent in their pursuit of personal happiness, possessing almost an irrepressible force of nature. In *Twelfth Night* Viola, determined to marry the duke, is one of those new human beings who are spirited and indomitable. The famous "unveiling" scene is, in fact, a manifesto against feudalism. In [late] medieval Europe, in order to end the long rule of feudalism, it was of great urgent need to create new images of human beings who were ardently against religious authority, espousing humanism and natural instincts. Even when these [new artistic creations] met with setbacks or failures in their struggle, the works [by the Renaissance artists] still managed to impart something stirring and uplifting to inspire continued courage and conviction. In our classical drama, when up against the oppression of feudalism, the characters would also behave with heroic dignity, rather break than bend (rather be a shattered piece of jade than an unbroken piece of tile). In terms of resolve and conviction, however, because of the differences in the entire cultural milieu, the [Chinese] characters' action and struggle to better their fate often pale in comparison to Shakespeare's. They often lack self-affirmation or confidence, trusting their prospect for victory in some enlightened rulers, righteous officials, or deities. Two different historical milieux, two different cultural soils, naturally produced different products. China, long shackled by feudalism, never experienced the immersion in the Renaissance and the great liberation of the mind. It is thus not surprising that [in our traditional theater] the humanistic consciousness of self-recognition and self-affirmation is greatly wanting.

I believe it is of vital importance that we understand the differences between Shakespeare and the Chinese traditional theater when we attempt to adapt his work for production. Shakespeare's plays have a universal and eternal appeal that transcends time and national boundary because they deal with the true essence of life, encompassing human nature and human emotions in all dimensions. Shakespeare's plays provide great visual spectacle, and his plot development is just as exciting and full of surprises. All this allows Shakespeare's plays to be presented and interpreted in many different ways, classical or modern, Eastern or Western, or in any number of combinations. It does more harm than good to cast Shakespeare in one single mold. The most important thing to remember is that, no matter what form, one should pay particular attention to retaining the work's rich essence and universal meaning and should never just keep an eye on the external form and plot line. If treated as usual melodrama about talented gentlemen and beautiful maidens, you then diminish the work's complexity and richness. It requires great care if one decides that the production is to be costumed in our native tradition. Costumes are symbols carrying with them certain connotations. If Shakespeare's [female] characters were to appear in the costumes from China's feudal period and proceeded to proclaim their love and passion in public without the least hesitation, it would strike the audience as being completely implausible. The designers for [the *huangmeixi* version of] *Much Ado about Nothing* used good sense when they made certain changes to the traditional costumes from the past. The production was set in a remote border area, where the male leads had pheasant feathers sticking out of their headdresses, clearly identifying for the audience the characters as part of a minority nationality. Generally speaking, among all the nationalities in China, the majority Han Chinese have suffered much more deeply from the burden of feudalism and all its unnatural restrictions on human conduct than the minority nationalities, who, in fact, have lived a more natural, carefree, and spontaneous existence. Therefore, the spirited verbal exchanges in the *huangmeixi Much Ado about Nothing* seemed quite credible. The greatest distinction of this production is that it has kept alive the humanist spirit of Shakespeare, brimming over with enthusiasm, vigor, humor, and joy of life. It has also quite adequately reconciled the contradictions between the Chinese traditional cultural psychology and the Western cultural psychology. The use of unspecific time and locale [in this production] has helped to create a more truthful reality.

In short, when we stage Shakespeare in Chinese traditional theater forms, we should not allow the appearance to hurt the spirit. We should never apply in a wholesale fashion the conventions of Chinese traditional theater to the creations and images that could only be born of the Renaissance. We should prevent the form from being separated from the content. While our attitude should be one of humility, enthusiasm, and respect as we embrace Shakespeare, we had better be discrete, discriminating, and original when we stage his plays.

When I was directing *Twelfth Night* I used the phrase, literally, "China Shanghai *yueju* Shakespeare" as the central creative guideline. Shakespeare is the subject; the rest are attributes. In other words, while the production should definitely possess the distinctive cultural and artistic characteristics unique to this regional theater form in Shanghai, China, the central focus should be on Shakespeare, on making every effort to convey the essence of his work faithfully.

Stepping Out but Staying Close to Home

Ye Changhai: If the traditional theater represents in artistic substance the spirit of Chinese Traditional Culture, then Shakespearean drama represents the literature and art of European humanism. Today, they both face the issue of "modernization" as well as the issue of further self-assessment and exploration in terms of their historical identities. Many European and American theater artists have experimented with modernizing Shakespeare, just as many Chinese theater artists have tried various ways to make the traditional theater more contemporary. These four productions and some others that I have seen recently all embody that spirit of search and quest, which has generated a great number of issues for deliberation and analysis. . . . I feel, however, in order not to reduce the living spirit of search and quest to some dry theoretical musing, we should really listen more to what the practitioners actively engaged in that search and quest have to tell us.

Hu Weimin: It is a well-known fact that it benefits the innovation of the traditional theater to absorb creative nourishments from various sources. This also applies to staging Shakespeare.

We will certainly encounter this question when staging Shakespeare: How do we make the traditional techniques and conventions serve the creation of Shakespeare's characters?

There are usually three situations: (1) when we need to learn those specific details of Western life such as certain gestures, postures, customs, and rituals that are so different from our own and have no equivalents in our theatrical conventions; (2) when we can almost directly apply our traditional techniques and conventions; and (3) when we can use some of our traditional techniques and conventions only if we attempt new combinations, rearrangements, and transformations.

The first two situations are easy to deal with. It is the last situation that happens most often and requires a lot of hard work.

In his performance as Malvolio in [*yueju*] *Twelfth Night*, Shi Jihua incorporated many diverse elements, ancient and modern, Chinese and foreign. His feet movements ranged from ballet to English folk dance, from conventionalized steps for a young civilian male in Sichuan opera to those for a military male in a Beijing opera. His hand movements ran the gamut from certain gestures in *kunqu* to those in Western dance. In his singing, which was well grounded in the *Fan* [*Ruijuan*] style of *yueju*, Shi Jihua ingeniously assimilated some vocal techniques from other regional forms and even Western opera. All these worked together very effectively in the two key scenes for Malvolio—the letter-reading scene in the garden and the marriage proposal scene to the countess. Shi Jihua's innovative performance has proved to us that we can neither thoughtlessly cast out nor apply as usual the conventions and techniques of traditional theater. We must be selective and creative. The optimal state of creativity is when we are immersed in an artistic fusion, open and flexible, being oneself and more. In other words, everything is done to serve the creation of characters; every specific method, convention, or technique exists for this expressed purpose alone, not for showcasing individual virtuosity. We may also call this process "stepping out but staying close to home."

WEI MINGLUN

I Am Dreaming a Very Absurd
Dream: Thoughts on *Pan Jinlian*

Wei Minglun (1941–   ) is an established essayist and a leading playwright of Sichuan opera (*chuanju*) who is known for his experimental innovations in modernizing the traditional theater. Trained as a Sichuan opera actor since age nine, Wei is today a resident playwright of Zigong Sichuan Opera Company. His best-known and most controversial play is his 1985 Sichuan opera *Pan Jinlian: The Story of One Woman and Four Men,* a postmodern reappraisal of probably the most infamous female villain in the history of Chinese literature. As an adulteress who murders her own husband, Pan Jinlian first appeared in Shi Naian's fourteenth-century novel *The Water Margin* (*Shui hu*) and had a repeat performance in Xiao Xiaosheng's sixteenth-century novel *The Golden Lotus* (*Jinpin mei*). "Pan Jinlian, the plaguing slut (*yinfu huoshui*)" was a verdict practically carved in stone. Wei Minglun, in his version of *Pan Jinlian,* is attempting more than a simple reversal of the verdict, as some others have tried before. In the following piece, written in 1986, he engages his readers in an "absurd dream" about his play, its conception, execution, reception, and many other important related issues.

Busy season. The sounds of the rehearsal hall pound my eardrums as I wearily attempt another rewrite at the desk. . . .

Auspicious snow is falling. Letters arrive with the snowflakes at my little house. A few more letters from *Theatre Circle* (*Xijujie*) in Anhui have come, urging me to talk about my clumsy new play, the absurd Sichuan opera *Pan Jinlian.* I have such warm feelings toward Anhui, a propitious place full of talented people, that no matter how busy I am I owe it to Anhui to write something. I'll stay up all night, but how do I begin? This play is so wild and unruly both in content and form, even though I wrote it, being no theorist, I have a hard time theorizing about it. At this particular moment how I envy Kafka, the author of *On the Building Site of China's Great Wall,* who was able to "communicate what cannot be communicated and explain what cannot be explained." Should I try something new, choosing a form of writing that helps to

Translated from "Wo zuozhe feichang huangdande meng—*Pan Jinlian* xiaxiang," in Wei Minglun, *Wei Minglun wenxuan* (Chendu: Sichuan wenyi chubanshe, 1996).

convey my complex thoughts in a lively way? I light a cigarette, get up from the desk, and lean my head on the pillow. Wind of the night is blowing outside the window, luring one to the land of dreams. . . .

(Suddenly, the celebrated author Shi Naian dashes in right in the front of my eyes, accompanied by 105 valiant outlaws. I mutter to myself: Why are the three valiant females missing?)

SHI *(Stroking his beard)*: Tonight it is a debate between men of letters. I need these men here for moral support, and women really shouldn't show their faces on occasions like this.

I: I see. In your eyes, Mr. Shi, those three valiant females don't really count. You put them in your book *The Water Margin* simply because *Xuanhe Yishi,* Yuan drama, and folklore had long included them in the Liang Mountain Hall of Fames. No wonder, since you only put them grudgingly into your book, they come across weak and lacking substance, really pale in comparison to the heroic females such as Tang Saier and Chen Suzhen whom you personally knew well. That's truly regrettable.

SHI: Young lad, so you're not a casual reader of my masterpiece.

I: I devoured it as a youngster, and really studied it later on. I truly admire you for speaking up for the peasants' uprising and for making true heroes household names. But it's a pity that only men could be your heroes! Excuse my frankness, Mr. Shi, but you treated women with such contempt, prejudice, and hostility. Your women characters were mostly base, vulgar, immoral, and wicked, [many of whom were killed off by your Liang Mountain heroes]. Wu Song killed Pan Jinlian, Shi Xiu killed Pan Qiaoyun, Song Jiang killed Yan Xijiao, Lu Junyi killed Jiashi, Shi Jin killed Li Shuilan, Lei Heng beat Bai Xiuying to death. From Liu Zhizhai's wife to Li Gui's wife, from the female singer in Xunyang to the maid Yinger . . . your female characters seem to vividly illustrate Confucius' famous line—"The females are as much trouble as the wicked."

LIN CHONG[1] *(Interrupting)*: My wife was an exception. She was a good person!

I: Don't forget her name was "Zhenniang" (the "chaste woman"). Because she stayed chaste and faithful to one man, Mr. Shi made her a good person, an exception. The majority of women, represented by Pan Jinlian, however, violated the *sancong side* (the three obedi-

---

1. Lin Chong is one of the "one hundred and eight" famed Liang Mountain outlaws in the novel *The Water Margin.*

ences and four virtues) and other traditional moralities, and brought destruction to themselves and others. Many law-abiding men were forced to resort to violent acts, including hollowing the insides out of the wicked women and joining the other outlaws on the Liang Mountain . . .

WU YONG[2] (*Defending*): Sure, Mr. Shi's pen was not too kind to the female sex, but, as some authorities on the matter pointed out, "it was a historical limitation for all men of letters in ancient times."

I: The "limitation" theory can hardly excuse Mr. Shi's misogynist bias. Take a look at the history of literature, both Chinese and foreign; there have been thousands of writers who were not only sympathetic to women but also held them in high esteem. Right off the top of my head: Bai Juyi and Li Shangyin before Mr. Shi's time; Guan Hanqing and Wang Shifu, Mr. Shi's fellow Yuan Dynasty writers; Pu Songling and Cao Xueqin after Mr. Shi's time; also Tang Xianzu, Kong Shangren, Hong Fangsi, Li Ruzhen, and many more. All these writers understood and respected women. Why did the historical limitation not afflict them but Mr. Shi? If Pan Jinlian and others had been portrayed by writers like Guan, Wang, Pu, or Cao, they certainly would have been quite different.

WU SONG[3] (*Roaring*): You audacious fellow, how dare you try to reverse the verdict on that notorious slut Pan Jinlian!

I: No! I'm not simply trying to "reverse the verdict." I'm trying to reexamine Pan Jinlian from today's perspective. . . .

SHI (*Attempting dissuasion*): The verdict on this woman is irreversible— the coffin is closed and sealed tight. Don't imagine the impossible, or do you wish to repeat what happened to Ouyang Yuqian?[4]

(In the direction that Shi's sword is pointing, the venerable Mr. Ouyang appears solemnly. Patting me gently on the shoulders, he speaks to me like a caring elder.)

OUYANG: You young people are fearless, just as newborn calves are not afraid of tigers. Your youthful boldness reminds me of myself in the

---

2. Wu Yong is another one of the Liang Mountain outlaws.
3. Wu Song is the younger brother of Wu Dalang, who is married to Pan Jinlian. After he killed Pan Jinlian for murdering his brother, Wu Song joined the Liang Mountain outlaws.
4. Ouyang Yuqian (1889–1962), a leading figure in establishing modern drama in China, wrote his play *Pan Jinlian* in the mid-1920s. In the play Pan Jinlian is portrayed as a rebel who is defiant about traditional feudal morality in her pursuit of love and sexual freedom.

1920s when I wrote a play to redress the injustice done to Pan Jinlian. Because of that I became the target of controversy for a long time, haunted by remorse in my old age . . .

I: The venerable one, I do see things differently from the others. Let me first salute you, for I admire your courage in your youth, as for your remorse later in life . . .

OUYANG: Don't mention that play of mine anymore. Several versions of *History of Modern Chinese Literature* have already had their say, and even I myself have "negated" it.

I: The great man of letters Kuo Moluo's "self-negation" was far more "thorough" than yours. In his old age Kuo even claimed that he would set all his early writings on flame! But those words were uttered against his own true convictions, merely twisted expressions of a tortured mind. Now time has changed, and we are no longer children of blind faith but a new generation of independent thinkers. If the theater can reassess a play like *Sai Jinhua,* which was once repudiated by [the towering] Lu Xun, why can't we reopen the case of your play *Pan Jinlian* just because a few versions of *History of Modern Chinese Literature* condemned it?

OUYANG (*Smiles wryly*): I'll leave it to later generations to judge my work.

I: The May Fourth Movement put the issue of women's liberation on top of its agenda, quickly winning widespread support for attacking the three obediences and four virtues and demanding freedom in choosing one's own marriage partners. Your play *Pan Jinlian* was a product of that moment in history, very much in tune with the ethos of the time. When looking back on women's fate in past history, you didn't linger on Zhu Yingtai[5] and other characters like her, who were adored by all through the ages in surprising unanimity. Why were antifeudalism women characters like Zhu Yingtai approved of even by the most staunch defenders of feudalism in all those dynasties? At least it tells us that the type of rebellion Zhu Yingtai waged did not strike at the roots of the feudal marriage practice, not deemed "great scourges." Within the tolerance of a feudal society people could feel sympathetic toward this type of innocent and perfect tragic figures, turning them in their fantasy into beautiful butterflies and spirits. Very few people, however, have looked at another bloody picture, in which the society turned

---

5. Zhu Yingtai is the heroine of the romantic tragedy *Liang Shanbo and Zhu Yingtai,* also translated as *Butterfly Lovers,* in which a pair of star-crossed lovers only become united in death.

people into ghosts. The fate of women like Pan Jinlian is much more complex, tragic, and thought-provoking. They were victims of feudal marriages, abused, corrupted, twisted, and left to sink or float on their own. . . . Should we place the blame on the "immoral femmes fatales" or a ruthless human-eating society? You, the venerable Ouyang, boldly raised this question. It was a very timely good question!

OUYANG: Now, you are really sailing against the current, talking so glowingly about the significance of my *Pan Jinlian!*

I: Yes, positively. Because the question you were asking was not merely about the appraisal of a fictional character in a classical novel; it was a social issue concerning the fate of women like Pan Jinlian in real life. What you did was stunning, rare, and commendable. My venerable one, the only pity was that the answers you came up with were not entirely correct, something did not go quite right in your inquiry. Given the historical circumstances, you did not and could not re-examine Pan Jinlian from the perspective of historical materialism and dialectical materialism. Suffering from the same weakness common in works of literature of the time, your play fought feudalism from the standpoint of bourgeois individualism and tried to reverse the verdict on Pan Jinlian by relying on the Freudian supremacy of sexual desire. You exalted Pan Jinlian's unrequited love for Wu Song to excess, making her out to be a Salome of the East and even kind of a "forerunner of women's liberation!"

OUYANG: When I was writing my *Pan Jinlian,* I did begin with sympathy and end on exaltation.

I: Today when I wrote *Pan Jinlian,* I began also with sympathy but ended on a pensive sense of loss. Let me try this analogy. Faced with the same Pan Jinlian of the same hard lot, Shi Naian chose to cast the lens downward, condemning the wickedness of her immoral ways; you chose to aim the lens upward, glorifying the beauty of her rebellious acts. I set my angle somewhere in between you two. I put my character in the grotesque social environment, following the different stages of her character development, allowing the lens angles to go in an upward or downward fashion as appropriate and expressing emotions of sympathy, admiration, regret, and contempt accordingly. Thinking in retrospect about the way in which this daughter of a poor family of the old days turned into an adulterous murderer has given me cause for a series of associations. . . .

OUYANG: What associations?

I: Marital and family problems in our own contemporary society!

[In the next section Wei Minglun carries on an imaginary dialogue with Liu Xiaoqing, a real-life movie star from Wei's native Sichuan province, whose personal life has long been a source of public gossip.]

I: . . . If strong women like yourself still have to put up with so much pressure of public opinion, then what about the average womenfolk, what about the peasant women in the villages, in the mountains, in all the forgotten corners? There, bizarre things, things clearly in direct opposition to the Marriage Laws, happen all the time. Arranged marriages and marriages in which women are sold or bought as merchandise have paired up many a mismatched couples like Wu Dalang and Pan Jinlian. How many young girls are abused? How many of the weak sex have turned hard and twisted? The issue of women's liberation should still be on the agenda of the 1980s. Because of all this, my absurdist Sichuan opera *Pan Jinlian* came to be. . . .

(A peal of laughter cuts me off in the middle of my monologue. I turn to look; it's no longer the lady from my native Sichuan but a fellow playwright from another country with a script of Bald Soprano *in hand, Oh, it's him, Eugène Ionesco, the French absurdist playwright.)*

IONESCO: Ha, an absurdist Sichuan opera, how interesting! My dear Chinese friend, tell me, how "absurd" is your play?

I: Sir, the unusual nature of my play demands an unusual or absurd form; otherwise, it would be impossible to delineate my central character. Pan Jinlian is a well-known fictional character who has been a convicted villain figure throughout history and who remains controversial today. In my play, however, she undergoes enormous transformations, from simple naïveté to complicated worldliness, from trying to fight against the odds to sinking into total depravity, from an innocent victim to a criminal. When, where, and whether shall we sympathize with her, admire her, pity her, or condemn her? Audience members all feel differently from different perspectives. Since a majority of the audience members have such deep-seated prejudice against Pan Jinlian, it would be difficult to change their bias and make them open to a more just verdict by giving them a play written in a conventional manner, in which characters are defined by what they do and say alone. For this "exceptional" play we need assistance of offstage voices, disinterested outsiders, who can help not only facilitate the onstage action but also serve as a channel through which the audience's different private views are expressed in a public forum. As a result, I have various characters, ancient and modern, Chinese and foreign, assembled on one stage, quite absurd but spectacular, nonetheless!

IONESCO: Fascinating, who are those ladies and gentlemen you have gathered?

I: [Empress] Wu Zetian[6] comes, crossing dynasties and generations; Anna Karenina[7] comes, crossing countries and continents; Jia Baoyu comes, dashing out of *Dream of the Red Chamber;* young Hongniang comes, flying from *The West Chamber Story;* the author of *The Water Margin* interprets his own work; the woman reporter Shasha from [the contemporary novel] *No. 5 Garden Street (Huayuan jie wuhao)* voices women's grievances; some contemporary punks off the street come booing and hooting to create more disturbance; the minor official of the seventh rank *(qipin zhimaguan)* is at his wit's end; the woman chief justice of the People's Court comments on the ancient case. . . . All these people are not just there fulfilling narrative and lyrical functions; they often jump right into action, communicating emotions with the characters, comparing with one another the cards that life has dealt them or engaging in direct confrontations. For instance, the punks of today are in cahoots with Ximen Qing, Hongniang carries on a dialogue with the Tiger of Jingyang Mountain, Shasha follows Pan Jinlian on a stroll across town, Shi Naian gives Wu Song orders to kill his sister-in-law, Pan Jinlian begs Wu Zetian for mercy, and Anna urges Pan Jinlian to join her in suicide by throwing themselves on the railroad tracks . . . Has there ever been a play as absurd as this in the history of Chinese traditional theater? Because it exceeds what is reasonable and normal, I have labeled it an absurdist Sichuan opera.

IONESCO: Now I see, my Chinese friend, this "absurdist Sichuan opera" of yours is coming from a quite different place as our "Theater of the Absurd" in the West.

I: Your Theater of the Absurd, an expression of existential philosophy, uses an absurdist form to express an absurdist content—the absurdity of human existence. Your take on the absurd is that human beings are alienated from the objective world, that they cannot communicate with one another or understand the world they live in, and that there is nothing they can do about the past, the present, or the future. In short, "Long live the Absurd!" I'm afraid the word *absurd* works differently in my play than yours. Relying on the dialectic potential of

---

6. Wu Zetian was a Tang Dynasty empress who reigned from 690 to 705.
7. Anna Karenina is the heroine in Leo Tolstoy's novel of the same title.

an absurd form to expose the inequities in life, I have disregarded temporal and spacial boundaries in order to reveal the close relationship between the individual and society and the intrinsic connection between the past, the present, and the future. My conclusion is that the tragedy of the past should not repeat itself, because women will be liberated, mankind will make progress, and society will move forward! My respected friend from abroad, you have your absurd philosophy, I have my absurd intent. Since the word *absurd* is not copyrighted exclusively for use in the West, let's each use it the way we see fit.

IONESCO: But does this absurdist Sichuan opera of yours really have no relation at all to our Theater of the Absurd or other postmodern literature?

I: Yes, of course, there are certain connections. Despite philosophical differences, you have certain artistic techniques that will serve our purpose very well. Being a believer in Lu Xun's idea of "taking whatever is useful" (*nalai zhuyi*), I have in my play not only used many Brechtian techniques of alienation effect but also certain modernist techniques. For instance, using "free association" to go in and out of Pan Jinlian's subconscious freely, using a multilayered structure and multiple points of view to develop a narrative that is comparative and associative, and using the wild "stream of consciousness" to express the aberrant psychology of Pan Jinlian, the antihero. While trying to develop credible characterization, I have also added to the play a critical dimension, using numerous "voices" to express the author's own views and thought process, thus creating a balance between artistic images and critical ideas. In *The Waste Land* T. S. Eliot weaved the legend of the Holy Grail with the images of contemporary life. If you would take a closer look at my clumsy play and then compare it to Eliot's long poem, you might say that my Sichuan opera's way of transposing past and present is not unlike that of Eliot's *The Waste Land*. If you would care to analyze *Pan Jinlian*'s central artistic design, might you not even see some trace of magical realism?

IONESCO: Oh, magical realism, my artistic neighbor. The mystifying *One Hundred Years of Solitude* [by Gabriel García Márquez]! The absurd *Pedro Paramo* [by Juan Rulfo]!

I: You're right, but magical realism is not only a neighbor to absurdism; it doesn't live far from realism, either; in fact, it is comparatively more engaged to real life than other schools of modernism. I'm sure you are much more knowledgeable on this than me—would you care to check some of my study notes? Magic realism, deeply rooted in the folk literature of Latin America and nourished as well by the literary tradition of Europe, combines the tradition of realism and the innovations of modernism. It employs a fantastic or absurd style to depict major social problems and expose acute social conflicts. Magical realism breaks down completely the boundaries of life, death, time, space, reality, dream, and fantasy, but what makes it truly magical is its ability to "remain real even though reality has turned dreamlike." I have taken some techniques from magical realism and applied them to the central design of *Pan Jinlian,* creating a "rhapsody" that knows no boundaries of time and space, life and death, or past and present. If one may say that magical realism is a bridge between modernism and realism, I hope I have placed a small springboard between magical realism and the Chinese traditional theater.

IONESCO: Bravo! The "Silk Road" of theater will need hundreds of camels. May there be more camel teams traveling back and forth, may camel bells keep on ringing. . . .

I: Then we may finally realize what Meyerhold envisioned—the great union between theaters East and West!

IONESCO: I look forward to seeing more Chinese style absurdist drama!

I: Each of my plays is different in style. Now that I've written an absurdist play, maybe my next one will be very sensible, and I certainly don't have the least inclination to incite others to write plays in the style of crisscrossing dynasties and countries. My clumsy play is just an experiment. If my colleagues find the spirit behind this experimental piece worthy, I would urge them to keep it alive. Chinese traditional theater is in a worrisome slump. How do we revitalize it? In theoretical exploration we have yet to let a hundred schools of thought contend, and in practical experiment we have yet to let a hundred flowers blossom.

IONESCO: What do the audiences of your majestic country say about this wildflower of yours?

I: Mr. Ionesco, please go and see for yourself at the theater . . .

IONESCO: Wow, full house every performance, very involved audiences, young people are particularly receptive . . . but who are those people frowning? Oh, the critics.

VOICES: What kind of play is this? In content it justifies adultery and entices women to go home and kill their husbands! In form it doesn't quite meet the standard of the Theater of the Absurd; of course, it would be even worse if it met the standard—that would be anti-Marxist! Mindless pursuit of new fashions, cheap commercial tricks— this is no "art." What we want are masterpieces, refined, something to last forever in the repertory! If everybody is to do something as absurd as *Pan Jinlian,* it would not help revitalizing the traditional theater; it would only hasten its decline! . . .

How horrible! I am shocked out of my mind hearing that I would be held responsible for the decline of the traditional theater. When I wake from the dream, there is some light in the eastern sky.

January 1986

Selected Bibliography

Bonner, Joey. *Wang Kuo-wei: An Intellectual Biography*. Cambridge: Harvard University Press, 1986.

Chinese Theater: From Its Origins to the Present Day. Edited by Colin Mackerras. Honolulu: University of Hawaii Press, 1983. Paperback ed. 1988.

Hu, Weimin. *Daoyande ziwo zhaoyue (A Directors' Self-Transcendence)*. Beijing: Zhongguo xiju chubanshe, 1988.

Jiao Juyin xiju lunwenji (Collection of Jiao Juyin's Writing on Theatre). Edited by Chen Gang. Shanghai: Shanghai wenyi chubanshe, 1979.

Jiang Qing tongzhi jianghua xuanbian (Selected Talks by Comrade Jiang Qing). Beijing: Renmin chubanshe, 1968.

Jingju jumu cidian (Beijing Opera Repertoire Dictionary). Edited by Zeng Bairong. Beijing: Zhongguo xiju chubanshe, 1989.

Li, Yu. *Xianjing ouji (Casual Expression of Idle Feelings)*. Edited by Shan Jinhang. Hangzhou: Zhejiang guji chubanshe, 1985.

Mao, Nathan, and Liu Ts'un-yan. *Li Yu*. Boston: Twayne Publishers, 1977.

Mao, Zedong. *Mao zedong xuanji (Selected Works of Mao Zedong)*. Vol. 3. Beijing: Renmin chubanshe, 1960. New ed., 1966.

Mei Lanfang wenji (Collection of Mei Lanfang's Writings). Edited by Zhongguo xijujia xiehui. Beijing: Zhongguo xiju chubanshe, 1962.

Tansuo xiju ji (Collection of Experimental Plays). Shanghai: Shanghai wenyi chubanshe, 1986.

Wang, Guowei. *Wang Guowei xiqu lunwenji (Wang Guowei's Writings on Theatre)*. Beijing: Zhongguo xiju chubanshe. New ed., 1983.

Wei, Minglun. *Wei Minglun wenxuan (Selected Writings of Wei Minglun)*. Chengdu: Sichuan wenyi chubanshe, 1996.

Wu, Zuguang, Huang Zuolin, and Mei Shaowu. *Peking Opera and Mei Lanfang*. Beijing: New World Press, 1981.

Xijuguan zhengming ji (Discussions on Conceptions of Theatre). Vol. 1. Beijing: Zhongguo xiju chubanshe, 1986.

Ye, Changhai. *Zhongguo xijuxue shigao (History of Chinese Theatre Studies)*. Shanghai: Shanghai wenyi chubanshe, 1986.

Ye, Dabing. *Zhongguo baixi shihua (History of Chineses Baixi)*. Hangzhou: Zhejiang renmin chubanshe, 1985.

Zhongguo gudian xiqu lunzhu jicheng (Collection of Chinese Classical Writings on Theatre). Edited by Zhongguo xiqu yanjiuyuan. 10 vols. Beijing: Zhongguo xiju chubanshe, 1959.

Zhongguo lidai julun xuanzhu (*Annotated Writings on Theater in Chinese History*). Edited by Chen Duo and Ye Changhai. Changsha: Hunan wenyi chubanshe, 1987.

Zhongguo meixueshi ziliao xuanbian (*Selected Writings of Chinese Aesthetic History*). Edited by Beijing daxue zhexuexi meixue jiaoyanshi. 3 vols. Beijing: Zhonghua shuju, 1980.

Zhongguo shida gudian beiju ji (*Ten Great Chinese Classical Tragedies*). Edited by Wang Jisi. 3 vols. Shanghai: Shanghai wenyi chubanshe, 1982.

Zhongguo xiandai xiju shigao (*History of Chinese Modern Drama*). Edited by Chen Baichen and Dong Jian. Beijing: Zhongguo xiju chubanshe, 1989.

Zhongguo xiqu lilun yanjiu wenxuan (*Selected Theoretical Writings on Chinese Traditional Theatre*). Edited by Zhongguo yishu yanjiuyuan xiqu yanjiusuo. 2 vols. Shanghai: Shanghai wenyi chubanshe, 1985.

Zhongguo xiqu tongshi (*History of Chinese Traditional Theatre*). Edited by Zhang Geng and Guo Hancheng. Beijing: Zhongguo xiju chubanshe, 1992.

Chinese Glossary

A Jia, 阿甲

afei wu, 阿飛舞

bagu wen, 八股文

Bai Renfu, 白仁甫

Baiyue ting, 拜月亭

bense, 本色

biaoyu kouhao shi, 標語口號式

Bimuyu, 比目魚

Bishang liangshan, 逼上梁山

Cai Wenji, 蔡文姬

caizi, 才子

Chaguan, 茶館

Chang hong xue, 萇弘血

chang, zuo, nian, da, 唱、做、念、打

Changban po, 長板坡

Changsheng dian, 長生殿

Chen Chun, 陳淳

Chen Duo, 陳多

Chen Duxiu, 陳獨秀

Chen Shimei, 陳世美

chen zi, 襯字

chengshi, 程式

Chezhan, 車站

Chi renrou, 吃人肉

chou, 丑

Chu ci, 楚辭

chuanju, 川劇

chuanqi, 傳奇

Chuanshen ji, 傳神記

Ci xue, 詞謔

Ci yue, 詞樂

cifu, 辭賦

cong neixin dao waixing, 從內心到外形

Cui Lingqin, 崔令欽

Cui Yingying, 崔鶯鶯

Da xue, 大學

Damian, 大面

dan, 旦

Danghu chuan, 蕩湖船

dao, tao, 道

daomadan, 刀馬旦

Daoyande ziwo chaoyue, 導演的自我超越

Dawu, 大武

dazhong hua, 大眾化

Ding Yaokang, 丁耀亢

diwang, 帝王

Dou-e yuan, 竇娥冤

douyan, 斗眼

Du Fu, 杜甫

Du Liniang, 杜麗娘

Du Renjie, 杜仁杰

du, 度

Duoyin, 奪印

Ehu cun, 惡虎村

erhuang, 二簧

ershi shiji dawutai, 二十世紀大舞台

Fachang huanzi, 法場換子

Fang Xiaoru, 方孝孺

Fei Tangchen, 費唐臣

Fei yue, 非樂

fenchang, 分場

Feng dong shan, 風洞山

Feng long tu, 封龍圖

Feng, 風

fengqu, 風趣

fengshen, 風神

Fenxiang ji, 焚香記

Fu Yi, 傅毅

Gai Jiaotian, 蓋叫天

Gao Ming, 高明

Gao Xingjian, 高行健

Ge dai xiao, 歌代嘯

Gong Dayong, 宮大用

Gouerye niepan, 狗兒爺涅槃

gu yu, 古語

Guan Hanqing, 關漢卿

guan, yue, 莞、籥

Guang ju, 廣舉

Guanyu biaoyan yishude jianghua,
  關于表演藝术的講話

Guifei zuijiu, 貴妃醉酒

guimendan, 閨門旦

Gujin qunying yuefu geshi,
  古今群英樂府格勢

Guju jiaose kao, 古劇角色考

Guo Moruo, 郭沫若

Guofeng, 國風

Guqu chentan, 顧曲塵談

Handan ji, 邯鄲記

Hanggong qiu, 漢宮秋

Hong fu, 紅拂

Hong luan xi, 紅鸞禧

Honglou meng, 紅樓夢

Hongmei ge, 紅梅閣

Hongzong liema, 紅鬃烈馬

Hu Weimin, 胡偉民

Hu Zhiyu, 胡祗遹

Huabu nongtan, 花部農譚

huadan, 花旦

huagong, 化工，畫工

Huainanzi, 淮南子

Huaji liezhuan, 滑稽列傳

huaju, 話劇

hualin xi, 華林戲

Huan sha, 浣沙

Huang Daozhou, 黃道周

Huang Fanchuo, 黃幡綽

Huang Zuolin, 黃佐臨

Huanghe lou, 黃鶴樓

huangmeixi, 黃梅戲

Huangshi shijuan, 黃氏詩卷

Hufu, 虎符

Hui long ge, 回龍閣

huiqu, 蟪蛄

Huoshao jie zi tui, 火燒介子推

Ji chu, 激楚

Ji Yun, 紀昀

Jiang Qing, 江青

jiangxiang, 將相

Jiao Juyin, 焦菊隱

Jiao Xun, 焦循

jiaobai, 教白

jiaodi, 角抵

Jiaofang ji, 教坊記

jiaren, 佳人

Jie feng, 結風

jie fufa, 戒浮乏

Jie xue, 借靴

jie, 節

jieming quyi, 解明曲意

Jin shu: liu yu zhuan, 晉書：劉毅傳

jing, 淨

Jing Ke, 荊軻

jing, 境

jingju, 京劇

Jiuge, 九歌

Juding guanhua, 舉鼎觀畫

Juedui xinhao, 絕對信號

kang qu xi, 康衢戲

kugan, 苦干

kunju, 昆劇

Kunlun nu, 昆侖奴

206

xipi, 西皮
Xiqingzhai biji, 惜青齋筆記
xiqu, 戲曲
Xishu meng, 西蜀夢
Xixiang ji, 西廂記
Xu Wei, 徐渭
xu, 虛
Xueshou ji, 血手記
Xun Kuang, 荀况
xun, chi, 塤、篪
xun, jin, ci, ti, 熏、浸、刺、提
xuni dongzuo, 虛擬動作
Ya, 雅
Yang a, 陽阿
Yangzhou huafang lu, 揚州畫舫錄
yanshen, 眼神
Yanxi bu, 演習部
Yao Fu, 堯夫
Yao Hua, 姚華
Ye Changhai, 葉長海
Yeren daoyan tigang, 野人導演提綱
Yeren, 野人
Yi, Yijin, 易, 易經
Yihuangxian xishen qingyuanshimiao ji,
    宜黃縣戲神清源師廟記
yijing, 意境
Yinbian yanyu, 吟邊燕語
Yipeng xue, 一捧雪
Yisuling xueshe, 易俗伶學社
You Meng, 優孟
yu qiu xiaosi, 語求肖似
yu, sheng, 竽、笙
Yuan Chonghuan, 袁崇煥
Yuan Yuling, 袁于令
yuan, 源
Yuanju yanjiu, 元劇研究
Yuanjuzhi wenzhang, 元劇之文章
Yue Fei, 岳飛
yue, 樂

Yue lun, 樂論
Yueben pian, 樂本篇
Yuehua huan, 月華緣
yueju, 越劇
Yuewei caotang biji, 閱微草堂筆記
Yujue ji, 玉玦記
Yunmeng, 云門
yunshou, 云手
Yuzhou feng, 宇宙鋒
Zai yan'an wenyi zuotanhui shangde jianghua,
    在延安文藝座談會上的講話
Zaju shier ke, 雜劇十二科
Zaju, 雜劇
Zhang Dai, 張岱
Zhang Geng, 張庚
Zhang Heng, 張衡
Zhang Liang, 張良
Zhang qian ti sha qi, 張千替殺妻
Zhao Zhen, 趙真
Zhao Ziang, 趙子昂
zhaojun, 朝菌
Zhaoshi guer, 趙氏孤兒
zhen, 真
Zheng Dehui, 鄭德輝
zhong jiqu, 重機趣
Zhong Sicheng, 鐘嗣成
zhong, 忠
Zhongguo gudian xiqu lunzhu jicheng,
    中國古典戲曲論著集成
Zhongguo lidai julun xuanzhu,
    中國歷代劇論選注
Zhongguo meixueshi ziliao xuanbian,
    中國美學史資料選編
Zhongguo xiqu gailun, 中國戲曲概論
Zhongguo xiqu lilun yanjiu wenxuan,
    中國戲曲理論研究文選
Zhongguo xiqu tongshi, 中國戲曲通史
Zhongyong, 中庸
Zhou Quan, 周全

Zhou Xinfang, 周信芳
Zhu Chusheng, 朱楚生
Zhu Quan, 朱權
Zhu Yingtai, 祝英台
Zhuangzi, 庄子
Zhuo Renyue, 卓人月

Zhuo Yan, 卓炎(?)
Zichai ji, 紫釵記
Zixia, 子夏
Zixiao ji, 紫簫記
zonghe xing, 綜合性

Index